Praise For Golf For Dummies

"Even if you've already read *Golf For Dummies,* you've got to get Gary McCord's latest book, *Golf For Dummies,* 2nd Edition. You'll still get the vintage McCord wit and wisdom — plus simple tips and techniques on improving your swing, your short game, and everything in between."
— Jim Nantz, CBS Sports Anchor and 1998 National Sportscaster of the Year

"With his signature wit and irreverent style, Gary McCord once again proves that he's not just a good golf analyst, but a great one!"
— Peter Kostis, CBS Sports/USA Network Golf Analyst

"I can't think of a more insightful or entertaining introduction to the game of golf. I wish I had had a book like this and a teacher like Gary when I was getting started."
— Peter Jacobsen, PGA Tour Player

"Once again, leave it to Gary to tell it like it is!"
— Chi Chi Rodriguez, Senior PGA Tour Player

"Gary is one of golf's most charismatic commentators. His book proves no exception . . . a perfect blend of instruction and frequently hilarious anecdotes that will have you doubled over with laughter even as you perfect the follow-through on your swing."
— David Feherty, CBS Golf Analyst

"A must-read for anyone who cares about the game. Gary tells it like it is and then some. Filled with great tips, instructional photographs, and Gary's famous sense of humor, *Golf For Dummies* is not to be missed. Stick it in your golf bag so you don't venture out onto the green without it!"
— Roger Maltbie, PGA Tour Player and NBC Sports Golf Analyst

"If you play golf, you must keep your sense of humor. Gary helps with both of the above."
— Judy Rankin, ABC Golf Commentator and Captain of the 1998 U.S. Solheim Cup Team

"Like your favorite golf story, Gary just keeps getting better. This second edition continues to share the knowledge and insight, which makes Gary a masterful teacher as well as a winner on the Senior PGA Tour."
— Paul Hospenthal, PT, ATC, CSCS

". . . should immediately be added to every golfer's library . . . . It's a fun reference for players of all levels, but especially beginners."
— John Marvel, *The Valley Times*

"Everything you need to know from driving to putting. This is a new way to learn this old game. Very in-depth instruction. I use many of these techniques in our golf programs. Also in our golf clinics. Our members who have read this book loved it!"
— Mike McLellan, South Florida PGA Golf Professional of the Year 1995 and Director of Golf, Boca Lago Country Club, Boca Raton, FL

"As a left-handed novice who hates to fail at anything, I can now view golf as something other than a four-letter word!"
— Judith Orloff, President and CEO, Educational Discoveries

"Helpful, concise, and very funny. *Golf For Dummies* is a must-read for serious golfers and for those who are not so serious."
— Wm. Neal McCain, PGA Teaching Professional, Chicago, IL

"At last, a golf book for everyone — or, at least, those of us happy hackers who fancy ourselves as a cross between Arnold Palmer and Bill Murray in *Caddy Shack.*"
— Bill Stedman, Sports Editor, Walpole, MA

"A breath of fresh air compared to the usual self-important, overly technical golf instructional book. Charming, irreverent, goofy, informative and practical . . . uniquely McCord."
— Michael Dougherty, President of Gymboree Play Program

"Gary McCord is to be highly commended for putting together a very helpful, easy to read, and instructional guide to golf without getting into the technical "mumbo jumbo" often found in traditional texts. I look forward to improving my team's game (and my own game) with *Golf For Dummies.*"
— Julio C. Diaz, Jr., Associate Athletic Director/ Varsity Golf Coach, Fordham University

"I found *Golf For Dummies* to be an easy read with great instructions. I only wish it had been written over 50 years ago. Kudos to IDG Books for making my retirement real fun again!"
— Jack Berkowitz, Retired, Boca Raton, FL

"Everything that one would expect in a first rate golf book: intrepid, relaxed, rhythmic, straightforward, high reaching, and . . . deadly accurate."
— Michael Featherston, President, I.C.B. International, Berkeley Heights, NJ

"*Golf For Dummies* will help anyone become a master of the game. Among his other tips, you'll learn that the top ten excuses for a bad shot do not include calling yourself a 'dummy.'"
— Allan H. Weitzman, Attorney, Boca Raton, FL

"I learned more about the game of golf after reading *Golf For Dummies* than I ever did from any instructional video or club pro. I have a greater understanding of how to approach the game, have more fun with it, and improve my score as well. I have a number of your books and I love them. *Golf For Dummies* offers the same terrific advice that your other books do."
— Timothy Burke, Mortgage Banking/Assistant Vice President, Brookfield, CT

"This book is a hole-in-one! Gary and John's sense of humor make this an informative, fun read that is sure to create an epidemic of golf fever. After reading just half of it, I went out and broke 80 for the first time!"
— Joe Stephens, Controller, Summit, NJ

"From the hacker who still hasn't found a tree he doesn't miss, this book is a must. If not for this book, I would have given up the first 18 holes and spent all my time at the 19th hole reading *Beer For Dummies*. My advice to prospective *Golf For Dummies* readers, read this book and hit 'em hard and long!"
— Matt Kilcullen Jr., Men's Basketball Coach, Manhattan College

"Gary McCord scores a hole-in-one in *Golf For Dummies,* superb instruction with a sense of humor."
— Faye Bildman, former Chairperson of Woodmont Country Club Golf Group, Rockville, MD

TM

References for the Rest of Us! TM

BESTSELLING BOOK SERIES

Do you find that traditional reference books are overloaded with technical details and advice you'll never use? Do you postpone important life decisions because you just don't want to deal with them? Then our *...For Dummies*® business and general reference book series is for you.

...For Dummies business and general reference books are written for those frustrated and hard-working souls who know they aren't dumb, but find that the myriad of personal and business issues and the accompanying horror stories make them feel helpless. *...For Dummies* books use a lighthearted approach, a down-to-earth style, and even cartoons and humorous icons to dispel fears and build confidence. Lighthearted but not lightweight, these books are perfect survival guides to solve your everyday personal and business problems.

> *"More than a publishing phenomenon, 'Dummies' is a sign of the times."*
>
> — The New York Times

> *"A world of detailed and authoritative information is packed into them..."*
>
> — U.S. News and World Report

> *"...you won't go wrong buying them."*
>
> — Walter Mossberg, Wall Street Journal, on IDG Books' ...For Dummies books

Already, millions of satisfied readers agree. They have made *...For Dummies* the #1 introductory level computer book series and a best-selling business book series. They have written asking for more. So, if you're looking for the best and easiest way to learn about business and other general reference topics, look to *...For Dummies* to give you a helping hand.

1/99

GOLF FOR DUMMIES®
2ND EDITION

by Gary McCord

Foreword by Alice Cooper

IDG BOOKS
WORLDWIDE

IDG Books Worldwide, Inc.
An International Data Group Company

Foster City, CA ♦ Chicago, IL ♦ Indianapolis, IN ♦ New York, NY

Golf For Dummies,® 2nd Edition

Published by
IDG Books Worldwide, Inc.
An International Data Group Company
919 E. Hillsdale Blvd.
Suite 400
Foster City, CA 94404
www.idgbooks.com (IDG Books Worldwide Web site)
www.dummies.com (Dummies Press Web site)

Library of Congress Catalog Card No.: 99-62290

ISBN: 0-7645-5146-9

Printed in the United States of America

10 9 8 7 6 5 4

2B/RX/QY/ZZ/IN

Distributed in the United States by IDG Books Worldwide, Inc.

Distributed by CDG Books Canada Inc. for Canada; by Transworld Publishers Limited in the United Kingdom; by IDG Norge Books for Norway; by IDG Sweden Books for Sweden; by IDG Books Australia Publishing Corporation Pty. Ltd. for Australia and New Zealand; by TransQuest Publishers Pte Ltd. for Singapore, Malaysia, Thailand, Indonesia, and Hong Kong; by Gotop Information Inc. for Taiwan; by ICG Muse, Inc. for Japan; by Norma Comunicaciones S.A. for Colombia; by Intersoft for South Africa; by Eyrolles for France; by International Thomson Publishing for Germany, Austria and Switzerland; by Distribuidora Cuspide for Argentina; by LR International for Brazil; by Galileo Libros for Chile; by Ediciones ZETA S.C.R. Ltda. for Peru; by WS Computer Publishing Corporation, Inc., for the Philippines; by Contemporanea de Ediciones for Venezuela; by Express Computer Distributors for the Caribbean and West Indies; by Micronesia Media Distributor, Inc. for Micronesia; by Grupo Editorial Norma S.A. for Guatemala; by Chips Computadoras S.A. de C.V. for Mexico; by Editorial Norma de Panama S.A. for Panama; by American Bookshops for Finland. Authorized Sales Agent: Anthony Rudkin Associates for the Middle East and North Africa.

For general information on IDG Books Worldwide's books in the U.S., please call our Consumer Customer Service department at 800-762-2974. For reseller information, including discounts and premium sales, please call our Reseller Customer Service department at 800-434-3422.

For information on where to purchase IDG Books Worldwide's books outside the U.S., please contact our International Sales department at 317-596-5530 or fax 317-596-5692.

For consumer information on foreign language translations, please contact our Customer Service department at 1-800-434-3422, fax 317-596-5692, or e-mail rights@idgbooks.com.

For information on licensing foreign or domestic rights, please phone +1-650-655-3109.

For sales inquiries and special prices for bulk quantities, please contact our Sales department at 650-655-3200 or write to the address above.

For information on using IDG Books Worldwide's books in the classroom or for ordering examination copies, please contact our Educational Sales department at 800-434-2086 or fax 317-596-5499.

For press review copies, author interviews, or other publicity information, please contact our Public Relations department at 650-655-3000 or fax 650-655-3299.

For authorization to photocopy items for corporate, personal, or educational use, please contact Copyright Clearance Center, 222 Rosewood Drive, Danvers, MA 01923, or fax 978-750-4470.

 is a registered trademark or trademark under exclusive license to IDG Books Worldwide, Inc. from International Data Group, Inc. in the United States and/or other countries.

About the Author

A calm sea does not make a good sailor.

This ancient proverb describes Gary McCord's approach to his job as golf commentator for CBS Sports. Over the years, he's been referred to as irreverent, witty, approachable, colorful, and delightfully different, and he's one of the few players to successfully make the transition from the golf course to the microphone.

McCord, a 25-year Tour veteran, stumbled into broadcasting when a CBS executive asked him to do color commentary by tossing him a headset with 15 minutes to prepare. CBS liked Gary's style under pressure, and he was on his way to a career in broadcasting. He teams up with the very polished Jim Nantz and shares duties with such names as Ken Venturi, Peter Kostis, David Feherty, and others to bring a fresh and professional approach to what's going on in the world of golf.

Occasionally, McCord has the opportunity to view the game from the other side of the camera, as a player on the Senior PGA Tour. Despite being under intense pressure, Gary maintains a lighthearted philosophy. "You just try to get your ball around the course and not hurt anybody. That's my goal," he says.

When Gary isn't broadcasting or playing golf, he keeps busy with myriad other projects. He portrayed himself and served as a technical director in the golf movie *Tin Cup,* starring Kevin Costner and Don Johnson. He has also teamed up with *Tin Cup* producers Ron Shelton and Gary Foster to write and produce an upcoming film based on the life and times of "Titanic Thompson," a notorious golf gambler.

Gary is also an accomplished author, writing the best-selling instructional book *Golf For Dummies* as well as a collection of essays and stories from his life on the Tour, *Just a Range Ball in a Box of Titleists.*

Gary possesses tremendous teaching ability and instructs and consults with more than 20 Tour players. With his friend and fellow CBS commentator Peter Kostis, he cofounded the Kostis/McCord Learning Center at Grayhawk Golf Club in Scottsdale, Arizona.

In all his activities, Gary brings a sense of fun, never taking himself too seriously. He says, "I want to be known as a broadcaster who was a little different, started a new trend, made people look at golf a little differently. I'm not going to compromise myself. I'll continue to push the envelope."

ABOUT IDG BOOKS WORLDWIDE

Welcome to the world of IDG Books Worldwide.

IDG Books Worldwide, Inc., is a subsidiary of International Data Group, the world's largest publisher of computer-related information and the leading global provider of information services on information technology. IDG was founded more than 30 years ago by Patrick J. McGovern and now employs more than 9,000 people worldwide. IDG publishes more than 290 computer publications in over 75 countries. More than 90 million people read one or more IDG publications each month.

Launched in 1990, IDG Books Worldwide is today the #1 publisher of best-selling computer books in the United States. We are proud to have received eight awards from the Computer Press Association in recognition of editorial excellence and three from Computer Currents' First Annual Readers' Choice Awards. Our best-selling ...For Dummies® series has more than 50 million copies in print with translations in 31 languages. IDG Books Worldwide, through a joint venture with IDG's Hi-Tech Beijing, became the first U.S. publisher to publish a computer book in the People's Republic of China. In record time, IDG Books Worldwide has become the first choice for millions of readers around the world who want to learn how to better manage their businesses.

Our mission is simple: Every one of our books is designed to bring extra value and skill-building instructions to the reader. Our books are written by experts who understand and care about our readers. The knowledge base of our editorial staff comes from years of experience in publishing, education, and journalism — experience we use to produce books to carry us into the new millennium. In short, we care about books, so we attract the best people. We devote special attention to details such as audience, interior design, use of icons, and illustrations. And because we use an efficient process of authoring, editing, and desktop publishing our books electronically, we can spend more time ensuring superior content and less time on the technicalities of making books.

You can count on our commitment to deliver high-quality books at competitive prices on topics you want to read about. At IDG Books Worldwide, we continue in the IDG tradition of delivering quality for more than 30 years. You'll find no better book on a subject than one from IDG Books Worldwide.

John Kilcullen
John Kilcullen
Chairman and CEO
IDG Books Worldwide, Inc.

Steven Berkowitz
Steven Berkowitz
President and Publisher
IDG Books Worldwide, Inc.

WINNER

Eighth Annual
Computer Press
Awards ≥1992

WINNER

Ninth Annual
Computer Press
Awards ≥1993

WINNER

Tenth Annual
Computer Press
Awards ≥1994

WINNER

Eleventh Annual
Computer Press
Awards ≥1995

IDG is the world's leading IT media, research and exposition company. Founded in 1964, IDG had 1997 revenues of $2.05 billion and has more than 9,000 employees worldwide. IDG offers the widest range of media options that reach IT buyers in 75 countries representing 95% of worldwide IT spending. IDG's diverse product and services portfolio spans six key areas including print publishing, online publishing, expositions and conferences, market research, education and training, and global marketing services. More than 90 million people read one or more of IDG's 290 magazines and newspapers, including IDG's leading global brands — Computerworld, PC World, Network World, Macworld and the Channel World family of publications. IDG Books Worldwide is one of the fastest-growing computer book publishers in the world, with more than 700 titles in 36 languages. The "...For Dummies®" series alone has more than 50 million copies in print. IDG offers online users the largest network of technology-specific Web sites around the world through IDG.net (http://www.idg.net), which comprises more than 225 targeted Web sites in 55 countries worldwide. International Data Corporation (IDC) is the world's largest provider of information technology data, analysis and consulting, with research centers in over 41 countries and more than 400 research analysts worldwide. IDG World Expo is a leading producer of more than 168 globally branded conferences and expositions in 35 countries including E3 (Electronic Entertainment Expo), Macworld Expo, ComNet, Windows World Expo, ICE (Internet Commerce Expo), Agenda, DEMO, and Spotlight. IDG's training subsidiary, ExecuTrain, is the world's largest computer training company, with more than 230 locations worldwide and 785 training courses. IDG Marketing Services helps industry-leading IT companies build international brand recognition by developing global integrated marketing programs via IDG's print, online and exposition products worldwide. Further information about the company can be found at www.idg.com.   1/24/99

Dedication

This is dedicated to all those golfers who read the first edition of *Golf For Dummies* and have lived to tell about it. You are now a better person and should be able relate to your pets at a higher level. The perception of the world should be amazingly simple for you to contemplate, and when you talk to traffic lights, they will, indeed, change.

The second edition of *Golf For Dummies* was written to walk those who read the first edition slowly out of "Dummiedom" and to become a consummate player of worldly proportions. When you speak, they will now listen. For those of you reading *Golf For Dummies* for the very first time, your journey is just beginning!

Author's Acknowledgments

I had some valuable assistance along this ink-highway and called upon a few well placed friends to enrich this epistle. **Dr. Craig Farnsworth,** author of the book *See It and Sink It* and the performance specialist for the Jim McClean Golf School at PGA West and at Sports Eye Enhancements in Denver, for his unique look into the eyes and how they guide the golfer to his or her goals. **Tim Rosaforte,** a true journalist who needs to read both editions of *Golf For Dummies* before we play again! **Donna Orendar,** who was my teacher and inspiration to get into this business of televised golf. She runs PGA Tour Productions and has a hand in every televised golf event you see on the air, so blame her. **Paul Calloway,** who has helped my broken and bent body to stand upright through bogies and birdies for the last 15 years. He was a valuable asset in this latest endeavor. Listen to his advice and enjoy your golf more. **Dave Shedloski,** for his solid writing and wonderful demeanor. Dave is a guy I can call in a moment's notice for 3,000 words and get it back with no excuse. Come to think of it, if he is that good a writer, why does he have all that spare time? **Jon Winokur,** who is the King of the Lists, thanks for simplifying my life. Keep writing those books, Jon; the royalties will allow you to join a better country club!

My wife, Diane, is simply the best. My life takes on the appearance of a traveling salesman with a bad sense of direction. Her patience with my work and understanding with my schedule I am unable to comprehend. She is my life's caddie, and a better one I could not have. To my parents, Don and Ruth, my daughter, Krista, and my four granddaughters, Breanne, Kayla, Jenae, and Terra: You will all get free books. Thanks for thinking about me when I've been away my whole life.

Alan "Mad Dog" Skuba, you got paid this time for editing so I'm not to going say anything nice about you this time. Stay literate.

Many thanks to Stacy Collins for chasing me all over the map and keeping my nose in the book. It must have been quite a burden traveling to Scottsdale, Arizona, during the winter.

I'd also like to thank the Indianapolis team: Pam Mourouzis, Stacey Mickelbart, Tom Missler, Maridee Ennis, Tyler Connor, Linda Boyer, Shelley Lea, Angie Hunckler, Brent Savage, Michael Sullivan, Janet Withers, and Melissa Buddendeck. Thanks for making and unmaking and remaking the changes to get this book just right!

I take great pride is declaring this book to be Y2K compliant, so enjoy it into the next millennium.

Publisher's Acknowledgments

We're proud of this book; please register your comments through our IDG Books Worldwide Online Registration Form located at http://my2cents.dummies.com.

Some of the people who helped bring this book to market include the following:

Acquisitions and Editorial

Senior Project Editor: Pamela Mourouzis
  (Previous Edition: Colleen Totz Rainsberger)

Acquisitions Editor: Stacy S. Collins

Copy Editor: Stacey Mickelbart
  (Previous Edition: Kelly Ewing)

Technical Reviewers: Doug Cooper, David J. Clarke IV, Wm. Neal McCain

General Reviewers: Harriett Gamble, Mark Psensky, David Steele

Editorial Manager: Rev Mengle

Editorial Coordinator: Maureen F. Kelly

Production

Project Coordinators: Tom Missler, Maridee Ennis

Layout and Graphics: Linda M. Boyer, J. Tyler Connor, Angela F. Hunckler, Brent Savage, Janet Seib, Rashell Smith, Michael A. Sullivan

Special Art: Pam Tanzey

Photography: Paul Lester, Scott Baxter Photography

Proofreaders: Kelli Botta, Melissa Buddendeck, Christine Berman, Brian Massey, Nancy Reinhardt, Rebecca Senninger, Toni Settle, Ethel M. Winslow, Janet M. Withers

Indexer: Anne Leach

Special Help: Jonathan Malysiak, Lisa Roule, Allison Solomon, Kevin Thornton

---

General and Administrative

IDG Books Worldwide, Inc.: John Kilcullen, CEO; Steven Berkowitz, President and Publisher

IDG Books Technology Publishing Group: Richard Swadley, Senior Vice President and Publisher; Walter Bruce III, Vice President and Associate Publisher; Steven Sayre, Associate Publisher; Joseph Wikert, Associate Publisher; Mary Bednarek, Branded Product Development Director; Mary Corder, Editorial Director

IDG Books Consumer Publishing Group: Roland Elgey, Senior Vice President and Publisher; Kathleen A. Welton, Vice President and Publisher; Kevin Thornton, Acquisitions Manager; Kristin A. Cocks, Editorial Director

IDG Books Internet Publishing Group: Brenda McLaughlin, Senior Vice President and Group Publisher; Diane Graves Steele, Vice President and Associate Publisher; Sofia Marchant, Online Marketing Manager

IDG Books Production for Dummies Press: Michael R. Britton, Vice President of Production; Debbie Stailey, Associate Director of Production; Cindy L. Phipps, Manager of Project Coordination, Production Proofreading, and Indexing; Shelley Lea, Supervisor of Graphics and Design; Debbie J. Gates, Production Systems Specialist; Robert Springer, Supervisor of Proofreading; Laura Carpenter, Production Control Manager; Tony Augsburger, Supervisor of Reprints and Bluelines

Dummies Packaging and Book Design: Patty Page, Manager, Promotions Marketing

◆

The publisher would like to give special thanks to Patrick J. McGovern, without whom this book would not have been possible.

◆

Contents at a Glance

Cartoons at a Glance

By Rich Tennant

page 365

page 293

page 91

page 7

page 239

page 329

page 195

Fax: 978-546-7747 • **E-mail:** the5wave@tiac.net

Table of Contents

Foreword

*W*hen Gary asked me to write the foreword for his upcoming bestseller, I, of course, asked the title. When he said *"Golf For Dummies,* 2nd Edition," I immediately had to ponder the question: Does this mean that this book is for "advanced dummies" or for those people who weren't smart enough to pick up the first edition of *Golf For Dummies?* Either way, it's a dumb idea whose time has finally come.

Golf is not a dumb game, but it can bring out the stupidity in the best of us. Just the fact that the end of *Tin Cup* has Kevin Costner knocking 12 successive balls in the water couldn't really happen . . . right? Wrong! That ending was based on a true life story starring none other than Gary McCord himself.

So don't ever let Mr. McCord refer to any of you as dumb. He has had some legendary moments of idiocy himself, and his were on TV.

Now the reality of this whole foreword. Gary is one of the most knowledgeable teachers to grace this game. Not only is he one of the best putters ever, he's also one of the great strikers of the ball and actually one of the smartest. Behind that mustache, there's something going on. We just are never certain what.

Your Pal and His Unworthy Student,

Alice Cooper

P.S. I don't suppose we will ever hear the end of the great American saga — McCord's first win on the Senior Tour. Every time he tells it, the winning putt gets longer and longer and longer.

Introduction

· ·

Welcome to *Golf For Dummies,* 2nd Edition. If this is the first golf book you've ever read, don't worry. I've read more of them than I can count. Plus, I've had a chance to go back over everything I wrote in the first *Golf For Dummies* and make it even clearer and funnier.

My first thoughts about writing this book were no doubt similar to your present feelings about golf. I knew that I wanted to do it, but I also knew that it wouldn't be easy and would take a lot of my time and attention. Did I want to devote most of my spare time to an endeavor of this magnitude? Why not? I haven't given anything back to society in a while!

Besides, the whole thing sounded like fun. So is golf.

About This Book

I want this book to appeal to players at every level. Although my buddies on the PGA Tour will probably read it just to see if I can construct a sentence, I like to think that I have something to offer even the best golfers. The guys I grew up with at San Luis Rey golf course in southern California will check out *Golf For Dummies* to see whether I've used any of their funniest lines. And I hope that the title will pique the interest of many people who have never played the game.

In any case, you have in your hands a sometimes-funny, instruction-packed, wide-eyed look at a game full of fascination that will serve you for the rest of your days on the links.

This, then, is no ordinary golf instruction book. Most of the volumes you can find in your local bookstore are written by professional players or teachers. As such, these books focus solely on the golf swing. *Golf For Dummies* covers a lot more than the swing. This book ought to be the only book you need before you develop a golf dependency. (Please contact a reliable physician when you feel the first symptoms coming on — frustration, talking to yourself after missing a shot, that kind of thing. These are the warning signs. ***Remember:*** From a medical standpoint, this book is cheaper than a house call.)

Having said all that, I'm assuming that you have dabbled with golf, have found that you like it, and would like to get better. In my experience, most people give golf a try before they pick up the instructions. It must be an ego thing, kind of like those people who don't like to ask for directions when they get lost because they feel that it's an admission of failure. Most people want to see what they can achieve on their own before they call in the cavalry. Then, if they still can't find their way, they'll admit defeat or become frustrated.

My aim is to get you beyond whatever stage your golf game is at without your having to resort to other texts. *Golf For Dummies* will build for you the solid foundation needed to become not just someone who can hit a golf ball, but a real golfer. There's a big difference between the two, as you'll soon discover.

Why You Need This Book

If you don't get help with the basics of the golf swing, you'll be like the old me. When I started on the Tour in 1974, I was full of fight and enthusiasm but lacked a basic knowledge of golf swing mechanics. That was understandable to an extent. At the time, there wasn't a lot of golf instruction around. Now most pros on the Tour have their own swing gurus travel with them. With all the money available in professional golf, you don't want to stay in the middle of a slump for too long!

Anyway, before I learned how to really play the game, I recall warming up for play and trying to find a swing that would work that day. A warm panic would start to rise in me about ten minutes before I was due to tee off. Doubt and dread would surface and accompany me to the first tee. My brain would be racing, trying to figure out what *swing thought* (that one aspect of the swing that you meditate on to keep focused) I'd been working on so desperately. I rarely remembered. Most of the time, I'd be left with a thought like, "Keep the left elbow toward magnetic north on the downswing." Usually, that action resulted in a silly-looking slice into a small tractor parked 40 yards right of the fairway.

I swung the club that way for most of my gutterlike career. So I know what it's like to play without knowledge or a solid foundation. Believe me, I'm a lot happier — and have a lot more fun — now that I know what I'm doing.

Don't make the mistake I made. Here's what will happen: You'll be up at the end of the practice range swinging away. Sometimes you'll hit the ball, and sometimes you won't. If you have a fleck of athletic talent and good eye/hand coordination, you'll start to improve. Those *whiffs* (swings where you miss the ball) will become less frequent, and you'll begin to hit the ball higher and farther. Then, however, you'll "hit a wall." Your improvement will slow to a trickle and then dry up altogether. You'll be stuck at whatever level your inborn talent has taken you to. And you'll be that golfer for the rest of your life.

Why? Because your technique — or rather, lack of it — won't let you get any better. You'll either be good in spite of your technique, or bad because of it. It doesn't matter. You'll be swimming at the deep end of a pool filled with Jell-O.

The reason I'm qualified to help you now is that I have made a serious effort to become a student of the game. When I started working on television for CBS, I didn't know much about the inner workings of the golf swing. But my new job encouraged me to learn. My odyssey led me to seek advice from some of the world's greatest teachers. If I was to be an authority on the game in front of millions of viewers, I had to know a little more about how to put the club on the ball.

My search led me to someone I grew up with in southern California. He has developed a knowledge of the golf swing that, in my opinion, is unequaled. His name is Mac O'Grady. He has researched his method since 1983 with a passion that is admirable. The result is a swing model that has been tested and not been found wanting, neither by himself nor by the many tour players who follow his preachings. As such, O'Grady is sought by the masses. I have been lucky to study under him. I can't thank him enough for his patience and friendship while guiding me through this maze of wisdom. I do not cover any of Mac's model in this book; his knowledge is for a more advanced golfer. No one has ever called me advanced, so I'm gonna get down to basics.

How to Use This Book

As far as reading the book goes, pick your spots. It isn't designed to be read like a novel from cover to cover. If you're a complete novice, read the glossary first. Learn the language. If you're a little more advanced and need help with some specific aspect of your game or swing, you can find that information in Chapters 7 through 13. The rest of the book will help you make that jump from "golf novice" to "real golfer."

As my former boss at CBS, Frank Chirkinian, said, "Golf is not a game; it's a way of life. If it was a game, someone would have figured it out by now."

I hope this book helps you "figure it out."

How This Book Is Organized

This book is organized so that you can walk through the learning process of becoming a golfer. Beginners need many questions answered as they take on the game. I have organized this book so that you take those steps one at a time and can return anytime for a quick reference. May this walk be a pleasant one!

Part I: Getting Started — No, You Can't Hit the Ball Yet

Where do I play, and what's the course record? Wait a minute! You need to know what this game is about. You need clubs. You need to know how to swing the clubs. You may even want to take a lesson to see whether you like the game and then find golf clubs that fit you. In this part, I show you where to shop for clubs and give you some tips on the questions to ask when you make your purchase. Then I give you some ideas about what kind of golf courses you ought to play. Picking up golf is a never-ending learning process, and you can start right here.

Part II: You Ain't Got a Thing If You Ain't Got That Swing

This part gets right to the point. I give you a close look at the workings of the golf swing and help with your mental preparation. You also get a good look at the short game, where most scoring takes place. I show you how to make those 4-footers and blast your way out of bunkers.

Part III: Special Shots, Conditions, and Considerations

In this part, I tackle the tough shots and help you deal with the weather when it gets ugly. You will develop many faults during your golfing life, and this part addresses a majority of them. (You bought this book, so I won't fault you for that.)

Part IV: Taking Your Game Public

In this part, you get the final touches of your education as a golfer. You see how the rules were established, how to conduct yourself on the golf course, and the fine art of betting. You even get the do's and don'ts of golf course etiquette. After you read this part, you'll be able to walk onto any golf course and look like you know what you're doing.

Part V: Other Golf Stuff

A sad fact of life is that you can't always be out on the course. In this part, I show you golf-obsessed folks how to tap into the best of golf on television and online. Turn on the TV to see tournaments to fantasize about and, of course, my smiling face. Boot up your PC, and I'll introduce you to a world of information, golf forums, and more.

Part VI: The Part of Tens

The best of, the worst of — things that don't mean anything to anybody except me. I just felt that you might enjoy knowing these things.

Part VII: Appendixes

Golfers have a language all their own. Appendix A lists all the terms you'll need to add to your vocabulary. Appendix B lists some of the more popular golf organizations, products, and resources, along with a select list of schools around the country.

Icons Used in This Book

I'll guide you through this maze of golf wit and wisdom with some handy road signs. Look for these friendly icons; they point you toward valuable advice and hazards to watch out for.

Duck! This is an awareness alert. Pay attention.

This icon marks golf hazards to avoid. Be careful!

This icon flags information that shows you really easy ways to improve your golf game.

Do this or I will never speak to you again.

Talk like this, and those golfers in plaid pants will understand you.

This information will make your head spin; take two aspirin and get plenty of rest.

This icon flags information that's important enough to repeat.

Part I
Getting Started — No, You Can't Hit the Ball Yet

"I like this course – I just wish the fairways weren't so long."

In this part . . .

This part explores the Zenlike qualities of golf: Why is golf here? Who in the world would think of something this hard to do for fun? This game must have been invented by someone who guards the netherworld!

In this part of the book, I describe a typical golf course. I also show you how to buy clubs and accessories that will make you look spiffy.

I show you how to learn this game. I discuss where to take lessons and how best to survive the lesson tee. In this part, you get a whirlwind tour, starting on the driving range and working your way up to a full 18-hole course — including the penthouse of golf, the private country club. Get ready; it's time to play golf!

Chapter 1

What Is Golf?

Golf is a simple game. You've got a bunch of clubs and a ball. You have to hit the ball with a club into a series of holes laid out in the middle of a large, grassy field. After you reach the 18th hole, you may want to go to a bar and tell lies to anyone you didn't play with that day about your on-course feats. If you're like most people, you play golf for relaxation and a chance to see the great outdoors. If you're like Arnold Palmer, Jack Nicklaus, and Greg Norman, you do this and make a bazillion dollars on top of seeing the great outdoors.

Of course, there are some obstacles. To paraphrase Winston Churchill, who called golf "a silly game played with implements ill-suited for the purpose," the game isn't always so straightforward.

Why Golf Is the Hardest Game in the World

As I see it, golf is the hardest game in the world for two reasons:

✔ The ball doesn't move on its own.

✔ You have, on average, about three minutes between shots.

In other words, you don't react to the ball as you do in most sports. A baseball is thrown, hit, and spit on. A football is passed, tossed, kicked, and run up and down the field. A basketball is shot, rebounded, and dribbled all over the place. A golf ball just sits there and defies you not to lose it.

In most sports, you have but an instant to react to the ball. Your natural athleticism takes over, and you play to the whim of the ball. In golf, you get to think about what you're doing for much too long. Thinking strangles the soul and suffocates the mind.

Golf would be much easier if the ball moved a little and you were on skates.

Goals of the Game

Simply stated, the goal of golf is to get the ball into each of 18 holes in succession with the fewest number of shots possible by hitting the ball with one of 14 clubs. After you hit the ball into all the holes, you add up your score from each hole to figure out your total score, which usually comes out to some number IBM's Big Blue couldn't calculate. The lower your score, the better your game. That is golf. That is the goal.

The game lies in the journey. As you play, you (to the best of your ability) devise a plan to get the ball into the hole in as few strokes as possible. Many outside stimuli — and many more inside — make this endeavor very interesting.

The best advice that I can give you is to take the game slowly, make prudent decisions, and never hit a shot while contemplating other matters. Golf is a game to be played with total concentration and a complete disregard for your ego. Try a monastic existence, at least for the duration of the round. Golf challenges you with shots of derring-do. You are the sole judge of your talents and abilities. You alone make the decision for success or failure: Should you try to make it over the water or go for the green that's 240 yards away?

Figure 1-1 shows how to plan your own course of action. You start at the teeing ground and move to position A. If the ball goes 240 yards and a watery grave is lurking to the left, don't try the improbable and go for it. Lay up to position B, and from there, to the green via C. Management of your game is your best weapon. Take the talents that you have and explore this ever-fascinating game of maneuvering a ball through the hazards of your mind. Welcome to my nightmare.

Score is everything. As you see in Chapters 9, 10, and 11, most scoring occurs within 100 yards of the hole. If you can save strokes here, your score will be lower than that of the player whose sole purpose in life is to hit the ball as far as possible. So practice your putting, sand play, and short shots twice as much as your driving. Your hard work will pay off at the end of the round, and your friends will be the ones dipping into their wallets.

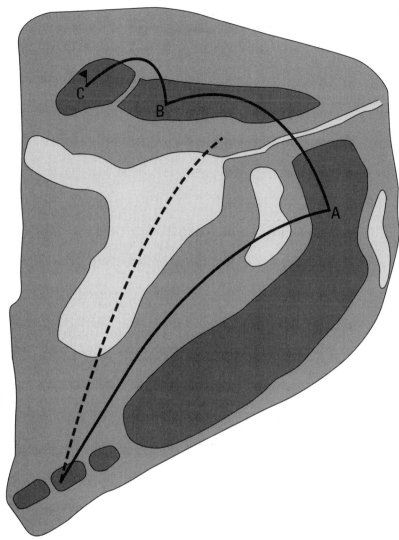

Figure 1-1:
Don't
get too
ambitious —
play the
game one
step at a
time.

A Typical Golf Course

Most golf courses have 18 holes, although some courses, usually because of a lack of money or land, have only 9. The *19th hole* is golfspeak for the clubhouse bar — the place where you can reflect on your game over a refreshing beverage of your choice. (See Appendix A for the lowdown on golf jargon.)

How long is a typical golf course? Most are between 5,500 and 7,000 yards. A few monsters are even longer, but leave those courses to the folks you see on TV. Start at the low end of that scale and work your way up.

The holes are a mixture of par-3s, par-4s, and par-5s. *Par* is the number of strokes a reasonably competent player should take to play a particular hole. For example, on a par-5 hole, a regulation par might consist of a drive, two more full swings, and two putts. Two putts is the standard on every green.

Three putts isn't good. One putt is a bonus. The bottom line is that in a perfect round of par golf, half the allocated strokes should be taken on the greens. That premise makes putting important. I talk about how to putt in Chapter 9.

Obviously, a par-5 is longer than a par-4 (two full swings, two putts), which in turn is longer than a par-3 (one full swing, two putts). The rules of golf say that par-3s are anything up to 250 yards in length; par-4s are between 251 and 475 yards long, barring severe topography; and par-5s are anything over that.

Many courses in the United States have a total par of 72, consisting of ten par-4s (40), four par-3s (12), and four par-5s (20). But you can, of course, find golf courses with total pars of anywhere from 62 to 74. Anything goes. Table 1-1 lists the yardages that determine par on a hole, for men and women.

Table 1-1	Regulation Yardages	
	Women	*Men*
Par-3	Up to 210 yards	Up to 250 yards
Par-4	211 to 400 yards	251 to 470 yards
Par-5	401 to 590 yards	471 to 690 yards
Par-6	More than 590 yards	More than 690 yards

Source: *U.S.G.A.*

That's the big picture. You often find several different teeing areas on each hole so that you can play the hole from different lengths. The vast majority of holes have more than one teeing area — usually four. I've seen courses that have had as many as six different tees on one hole. Deciding which tee area to use can make you silly. So the tee areas are marked with color-coded tees that indicate ability. The gold tees are invariably the back tees and are for blessed strikers only. The blue tees are usually slightly ahead of the gold and make the holes shorter, but still plenty hard. Club competitions are played from these tees. The white tees are for everyday, casual play, and are the early homes of beginning golfers. Stray from the white tees at your peril. Finally, the red tees are traditionally used by women, although many women I play with use the same tees I play.

I'm getting a little ahead of myself for right now; I get into where to play later in Chapter 6. First, because our past helps dictate our future, let's explore the dusty book of golf's infancy and widen our eyes for the future of this game in Chapter 2.

Chapter 2

The Fore! Fathers of Golf

Golf, an insidious game invented by men of lesser intellect to infect all those who are consumed by its lure.

—Gary McCord, circa 1998

*N*o sport's chronicled past has been explored with as much virtuosity and dusty recollection as golf. The game has roots in the beginning of civilized behavior, and it has reduced those who play it to uncivilized madness. No other game has been played with wild passion for decades upon decades yet can still give, day to day, a burning desire to solve its mystery. Welcome to the chaos that a round ball will produce: golf. This chapter tells you about golf's glorious history and where the game may be headed.

Where and How the Game Began

The exact origins of golf remain a subject of continual debate, although Scotland is generally regarded as the birthplace of the game as it is played today. This is due in large part to a host of specific historical references dating back as far as the mid-1400s.

The most commonly cited of these references is a written record that a game called *goff, gowf,* or *gawd, this is a hard game* (take your pick — spelling wasn't a hangable offense in those days) was being played during the reign of James II of Scotland, an offensive little man who was prone to moments of mental discomfort in trying to organize a formidable fighting machine from shepherds. In 1457, King James proclaimed by royal decree that the playing of "futeball" and "gowf" were forbidden so that the men of Scotland could concentrate on their archery practice, the slinging of arrows being the primary means by which they defended themselves against enemy England. (Little did they know that just showing them what was under their kilts would have stopped the English cold in their tracks.)

The pursuit of golf remained outlawed until the signing of the Treaty of Glasgow in 1501, which brought peace between the warring parties, giving Scotland's James IV the occasion to take up golf himself. A long association between royalty and golf ensued — although both commoners and gentry alike frowned upon Mary Queen of Scots when, in 1567, she was found to be playing golf just days after the death of her husband, Darnley, who died of a bad first name. (Unfortunately, that was the last time a woman had a preferred tee time.)

In an alternate theory on golf's beginning, a Dutch historian, Steven von Hengel, argued that golf originated in Holland around 1297. A form of the game, called *spel metten kolve* and also called *colf* (which means *club*), was popular in the late 13th century. Colf, it is believed, was played primarily on ice; the greens committee at the Masters took this to heart and prepared their greens accordingly. Nevertheless, golf may have grown out of this game and another game that was popular in Holland, called *Jeu De Mail*. This letter-carrying game was played in wooden shoes with soft spikes.

Without question, golf's major growth occurred in Great Britain, primarily in Scotland. Golf became an accepted part of the culture as early as 1604, when William Mayne was appointed Royal Clubmaker, although the game was still reserved for the elite and the insane, who had the wealth and the leisure time to pursue it. And wealth was indeed necessary. Early golf was played with a feathery golf ball — a stitched leather ball stuffed with boiled goose feathers — that was expensive because they had to wait for the geese to land. A feather ball cost three times as much as a club, and because feathery balls were delicate, players had to carry three to six balls at a time. In addition, the balls flew poorly in wet weather (a problem in this fine country), a fact that further dissuaded the working class, who, unlike the gentry, did not possess the flexibility to pick which days to play.

The ball, as it has throughout history, dictated other matters pertaining to the development of the game. (See the section "The balls" later in this chapter for more on the development of the golf ball.) Because the feathery performed so inadequately when damp, early golf was played predominantly on the relatively more arid eastern side of Scotland. Furthermore, the eastern seaside location was popular because the underlying sandy soil drained more rapidly and the grass was naturally shorter — no small consideration when the invention of the lawn mower was centuries away. This short-grassed, seaside golfing location came to be referred to as *links*.

If the Scots didn't invent golf, they certainly had a hand in creating the golf club — the kind that you join. Leith is considered the birthplace of organized golf, and the golf club called the Honourable Company of Gentlemen Golfers was founded by William St. Clair in Leith in 1744 and later became the Company of Edinburgh Golfers. Ten years later, the Royal and Ancient Golf Club was founded under its original name, the Society of St. Andrews Golfers. The Royal and Ancient Golf Club runs the British Open and British Amateur, duties it assumed in 1919, and since 1951 has administered the rules of golf in cooperation with the United States Golf Association. The R&A also established 18 holes as the standard golf course. In 1764, the Old Course at St. Andrews consisted of 22 holes, with golfers playing 11 holes out and 11 back. Eventually, the last 4 holes on each side, all short, converted into 2 holes, leaving 18 to be played.

Searching for Better Equipment

Without a doubt, certain developments contributed to the increased popularity of the game. Perhaps my witty banter has intrigued many, but enough about me. Although I'll tell you about the early history of golfing equipment, I believe that no period rivals the first ten years of the 20th century for ingenuity. Several important innovations in equipment occurred that can be identified as the forerunners of modern equipment forms and standards.

The balls

Although the handmade feathery, a stitched leather ball stuffed with boiled goose feathers (this goes well with a light-bodied Fume Blanc), was a vast improvement over stones or wooden balls and served golfers faithfully for more than 200 years, the gutta percha was an extraordinary breakthrough. In 1848, the Reverend Adam Paterson of St. Andrews introduced the gutta percha ball, or *gutty,* which was made from the sap of the gutta tree found in the tropics. When heated, the rubberlike sap could easily be fashioned into a golf ball. This invention, not to mention the spread of the railways, is thought to have contributed to the expansion of golf. The gutty was considerably more durable than the feathery and much more affordable because it could be mass produced. After golfers discovered that bramble patterns and other markings on the gutty enhanced its aerodynamics, this ball swiftly achieved dominance in the marketplace.

In 1900, the arrival of the Haskell rubber-cored ball quickly replaced the gutta percha as the ball of choice among players of all skill levels. Invented two years earlier by Cleveland resident Coburn Haskell and manufactured by the B.F. Goodrich Rubber Company of Akron, Ohio, the Haskell ball, featuring a gutty cover and a wound rubber core, traveled a greater distance (up to 20 yards more on average) and delivered greater durability. For more information on the Haskell ball, check out "Oh, Say, Can You Tee . . ." later in this chapter.

It didn't take much time for the Haskell ball to gain acceptance, especially after Alexander "Sandy" Herd defeated renowned Harry Vardon and James Braid in the 1902 British Open at Hoylake, England, using the same Haskell ball for 72 holes. Most golfers today, on the other hand, use as many as six to eight golf balls during a single round of a tour event.

The rest of the 20th century has been spent refining the Haskell. In 1905, William Taylor invented the first dimpled ball, improving flight because the dimple pattern maximized lift and minimized drag. Around the time Taylor was playing with his dimples, Elazer Kempshall of the U.S. and Frank Mingay of Scotland were independently experimenting with liquid-core balls. In 1920, gutta percha began to fade entirely from use, replaced by balata as a more effective ball cover. It was another 50 years before a popular alternative to the Haskell was developed. In 1972, Spalding introduced the first two-piece ball, the Executive.

The weapons

Since the earliest days of golf, players have sought to make better equipment. Players initially carved their own clubs and balls from wood until skilled craftsmen assumed the task. Long-nosed wooden clubs are the oldest known designed clubs — and the most enduring equipment ever conceived, remaining in use from the 15th century until the late 19th century. Long-noses were made from pear, apple, beech, or holly trees and were used to help achieve maximum distance with the feathery golf ball, which began coming into use in 1618.

Later, other parts of the golf set developed: *play clubs,* which included a range of spoons at varying lofts; *niblicks,* a kin of the modern 9-iron or wedge that was ideal for short shots; and a *putting cleek* — a club that has undergone (and is still undergoing) perhaps the most rigorous experimentation. I know that my putters have undergone certain tests of stamina and stress. You're probably familiar with the "I'm going to throw this thing into orbit and let Zeus see if he can putt with it" test, as well as the ever-popular "break it over my knee so that it won't harm anyone again" test. These short-term tests should be conducted only by professionals.

The development of the new gutta percha ball, much harder than a feathery, was also responsible for forcing club-makers to become truly revolutionary. Long-noses became obsolete because they couldn't withstand the stress of the sturdier gutty.

Some club-makers tried using leather, among other materials, in their clubs in an attempt to increase compression and, therefore, distance (obviously, a recurring theme throughout the ages). Others implanted metal and bone fragments into the clubface. In 1826, Scottish club-maker Robert Forgan began to use hickory imported from America to manufacture shafts, and hickory was quickly adopted as the wood of choice.

Bulgers, which were shaved-down versions of long-noses with bulbous heads resembling the shape of today's woods, became popular implements that golfers could use with gutties. By the turn of the century, bulgers were made almost exclusively of persimmon imported from America.

Metal heads were around as early as 1750, but they took a significant turn for the better when a man named E. Burr applied grooves to the irons, which contributed to even greater control of the golf ball through increased backspin. In 1910, Arthur Knight introduced steel-shafted clubs, which perhaps precipitated the first clash concerning technology.

Most players preferred hickory shafts for more than 20 years after the advent of steel, and golf's ruling bodies may have contributed to this attitude. The U.S. Golf Association didn't legalize the use of steel shafts until 1924. The Royal and Ancient Golf Club of St. Andrews, Scotland, procrastinated until 1929, finally relenting after the Prince of Wales used steel-shafted clubs on the Old Course at St. Andrews. Billy Burke was the first golfer to win a major championship with steel-shafted clubs when he captured the 1931 U.S. Open at Inverness Club in Toledo, Ohio.

These ball and club innovations, combined with the mass-production applications of the emerging American Industrial Revolution, provided golfers with relatively inexpensive equipment that was superior to anything they had known a few years before. The result: accelerated growth in the game.

Putting for Dough: The Early British Tournaments and Champions

In 1860, eight professionals competed in a golf tournament at Prestwick in Scotland, playing three 12-hole rounds for a red leather belt. The idea for the prize was derived from medieval knights' tournaments, and any player who could win this tournament three years running would gain permanent possession of the belt. The event, won by Willie Park, was the forerunner of the British Open Championship.

The early years of the championship were dominated by Old Tom Morris and his son, Young Tom Morris. (The English were not imaginative when it came to nicknames.) Tom Morris, Sr., was one of the most prominent figures in the early development of golf. He was, among other things, a ball- and club-maker at Prestwick and St. Andrews, and he later became influential in golf course architecture. He was also an expert player, winning the Open championship in 1861, 1862, and 1864.

Young Tom, however, was even more skilled, winning four Opens, including three in a row from 1868 to 1870, and thereby claiming possession of the coveted belt. Three years later, the Claret Jug was introduced as the Open prize, and it remains so today.

The Morris duo dominated early, but the Open championship and British golf had never seen anything like the Great Triumvirate of Harry Vardon, John Henry Taylor, and James Braid. Together, the trio won 16 titles from 1894 to 1914 and placed second a combined total of 12 times.

Of the three, Vardon had the most significant impact on the game, as he had the ability to influence the game beyond his competitive lust. His exhibition tours, both at home and abroad, introduced golf to millions of people. In 1899, Vardon endorsed his own line of gutty ball, the Vardon Flyer, thus becoming the first professional athlete to endorse commercial products. (No wonder Michael Jordan likes golf.)

Vardon conducted an extended tour in the U.S. in 1900 to promote the new ball and used the occasion of his visit to enter the U.S. Open, which he won at Wheaton (Illinois) Golf Club, finishing two strokes clear of Taylor. The presence of Vardon and Taylor provided the infant championship welcome credibility. Vardon was also the creator of the Vardon grip — an overlapping grip — still the most widely practiced by golfers.

Cool historical things to know about golf

✔ The first instruction book, written by Thomas Kincaid, appeared in 1687. Among his tips: "Maintain the same posture of the body throughout (the swing) . . . and the ball must be straight before your breast, a little towards the left foot." How did he know?

✔ In 1890, the term *bogey* was invented by Hugh Rotherham — only back then it referred to playing a hole in the perfect number of strokes, or a *ground score,* which we today call *par.* Shortly after the invention of the Haskell ball, which made reaching a hole in fewer strokes possible, bogey came to represent a score of one over par for a hole.

✔ The term *birdie* wasn't coined until 1898, emanating from Atlantic Country Club out of the phrase "a bird of a hole." This gap in terminology is no doubt attributed to the difficulty in attaining a bird, a fact that endures to this day.

✔ A match-play exhibition was held in 1926, pitting Professional Golfers' Association members from Britain and America. Played in England, the home team dominated 13½ to 1½. The next year, at Worcester Country Club, the teams met again, only this time possession of a solid gold trophy was at stake, donated by a wealthy British seed merchant named Samuel A. Ryder. Thus were born the Ryder Cup Matches.

✔ The Hershey Chocolate Company, in sponsoring the 1933 Hershey Open, becomes the first corporate title sponsor of a professional tournament. So blame the cocoa guys.

✔ A local telecast of the 1947 U.S. Open in St. Louis marks the advent of televised golf, a red-letter day in golf history if ever there was one. Now I could finally have a job.

"Oh, Say, Can You Tee . . ."

The birth of golf in America is far less shrouded in mystery than the game's birth. In 1743, one year before the formation of the Company of Gentlemen Golfers, there is a record of a shipment of 96 clubs and 432 balls delivered from Leith to a David Deas in Charleston, South Carolina. The size of the order suggests that it was intended for a group of golfers. It is believed that another club or society of golfers may have been organized in Savannah, Georgia, in 1796 but was disbanded when they sensed impending problems with the Y1.8K computer bug.

Not until 1888, in Yonkers, New York, did the first permanent club appear on the United States golfing map. The St. Andrews Golf Club was formed by John Reid and a group of associates who came to be known as the Apple Tree Gang. Reid and his friends were dogged devotees of golf, and in the beginning enjoyed their pursuit on a makeshift three-hole layout that began and ended near a large apple tree. They hung their coats on the tree prior to the start of play, and after completing their game they found their coats heisted by a rival gang known for their disdain of fruit. All this is part of New York's legend, but I doubt its truth.

In the eyes of many, Reid is considered the father of American golf, although others argue that Charles Blair Macdonald, a player, writer, and course architect, deserves the distinction.

Macdonald, whom *Golf Journal* called "a true pioneer of golf in America," was the driving force behind the creation of the Chicago Golf Club, the first 18-hole golf course in the U.S. In 1892, Macdonald convinced 30 Chicago business associates to pitch in $10 apiece so that a nine-hole golf course could be constructed on what is now the site of the Downers Grove Golf Course. An additional nine holes, like the first nine designed by Macdonald, were built the following year.

Macdonald, who studied in Scotland at St. Andrews University, is also credited with the development of golf course architecture in America (his signature creation is the National Golf Links on Long Island) and with assisting in — or perhaps insisting on — the formation of the United States Golf Association (USGA).

The USGA emerged from the wake of a dispute between the St. Andrews Golf Club and the Newport (Rhode Island) Golf Club, each of which in the summer of 1894 hosted an invitational tournament and declared the winner the national amateur champion. The cantankerous Macdonald, a loser in both events, actually precipitated the debate and then suggested that an official tournament be staged by an official organization that would also administer the rules of the game. What followed was a meeting of delegates from Newport Golf Club, St. Andrews, Chicago Golf Club, Shinnecock Hills

Country Club, and The Country Club in Brookline, Massachusetts. These delegates founded the Amateur Golf Association of the United States — that later became the USGA — on December 22, 1894. (That meeting is still going on.) Theodore A. Havemeyer, whose name appears on the U.S. Amateur trophy, was the first president.

The following October, on successive days, the USGA conducted the first U.S. Amateur Championship and the first U.S. Open at Newport Golf Club. Among a field of 11 players, Englishman Horace Rawlins shot a 173 over 36 holes to defeat Willie Dunn by 2 shots in the inaugural Open. The day before, 32 players teed it up in the Amateur, and none other than Macdonald captured the title, dispatching Charles E. Sands, 12 and 11 (meaning that he was up 12 strokes with 11 holes left), in the final.

Three years later, in 1898, the first unofficial professional tournament was played on January 1 at Ocean Hunt and Country Club in Lakewood, New Jersey. The purse was $150, and ten pros crazy enough to compete in 20-degree weather with light snow entered, showing their collective lack of intelligence. Val Fitzjohn defeated his brother, Ed, in a playoff for the $75 first prize. The following summer, the Western Open was staged at Glenview Golf Club, the first event in what would eventually evolve into the PGA Tour.

The small but growing legion of enthusiastic golfers in America at the turn of the century was comprised mainly of transplanted Scots and Englishmen. But those legions grew dramatically with the invention in 1900 of the Haskell ball, which replaced the gutta percha. The brainchild of Cleveland resident Coburn Haskell, and created in concert with his friend Bertram Work of the B.F. Goodrich Rubber Company of Akron, Ohio, the Haskell ball, with its wound rubber core, was a revolutionary development because of its superior distance and truer flight. The Haskell was the forerunner of the modern ball, although its evolution was not without a hitch along the way.

In 1906, Goodrich introduced a rubber-cored ball filled with compressed air, called the Pneu-matic. It was livelier than the Haskell but became an example of going for too much of a good thing. In warm weather, the ball was prone to exploding. Because players often carried balls in their pockets in this period, you can guess the inevitable conclusion to a painful surprise. At this time, the Haskell achieved dominance in the marketplace, and the game attracted a dramatically growing number of participants who, from then on, carried their golf balls in their bags.

Noted American golf writer Herbert Warren Wind called the invention of the Haskell ball and the appearance of steel shafts in the 1930s the most significant changes in the game in the 20th century. Nevertheless, the game did not truly find its place in America until it had a face to go with it. Francis Ouimet conjured up what sportswriter Will Grimsley called "the great awakening of golf in America" when, at age 20, he stunned the sporting world by defeating British greats Harry Vardon and Edward (Ted) Ray in a playoff to win the 1913 U.S. Open at The Country Club. Ouimet, a self-taught 20-year-old local caddie, shot a 2-under-par 72 in the playoff while Vardon, the premiere player in England, shot 77 and Ray 78.

After closing out the heavily favored Brits, Ouimet was carried to the clubhouse by some of the 7,500 in attendance — the first recorded phenomenon of what is now called *crowd surfing*. News of Ouimet's victory made the front page of many of the nation's newspapers. The triumph had a profound impact on Americans' interest in the game. Within a decade, the number of players in the U.S. tripled, and public courses began to take hold in places where access to private clubs was limited.

Bobby Jones, Gene Sarazen, and Walter Hagen

As fate would have it, in the gallery at The Country Club on the September day that Ouimet won the U.S. Open was a young and talented player of Georgia heritage, Robert Tyre Jones, Jr. No discussion of golf history would be close to legitimate without mentioning the contributions of Bobby Jones, who is regarded as among the greatest players — and greatest sportsmen — of all time.

Jones, who remained an amateur throughout his competitive career, won 13 major titles, the first in the 1923 U.S. Open after several disappointing setbacks. Jones's consistency of excellence was most evident in his string of performances in the U.S. Amateur. From 1923 to 1930, he won five Havemeyer trophies, was once runner-up, and was qualifying medalist (which means that he had the lowest round of the tournament) five times. Jones capped his incredible reign in 1930 when he claimed the Amateur and Open titles of the U.S. and Britain. That grand slam was his crowning achievement; Jones retired from competitive golf at the age of 28.

He was far from through contributing to golf, however. In 1933, the Augusta National Golf Club, a collaborative creation of Jones and the architect Dr. Alister Mackenzie, opened. The following year, Jones hosted his peers for an informal spring invitational tournament, which grew in prominence quickly thanks to Gene Sarazen. Sarazen, who with Jones and Walter Hagen made up the first American golf triumvirate, struck perhaps the most famous shot in golf lore when he knocked a 4-wood into the hole at the par-5 15th from 220 yards away for a double eagle in the 1935 invitational tournament. The shot propelled Sarazen "The Squire" to a playoff victory over Craig Wood in the championship that became known as the Masters.

That same year, Glenna Collett Vare passed Jones in national amateur crowns as she won her sixth U.S. Women's Amateur at Interlachen Country Club in Minneapolis, the place where Jones had won the 1930 U.S. Open for the third leg of his grand slam.

Jones dominated his era but often shared the spotlight with Sarazen and the indefatigable Hagen. Sarazen became the first of four men (the others are Ben Hogan, Jack Nicklaus, and Gary Player) to win all four of the modern major championships — the Masters, the U.S. Open, the British Open, and the PGA Championship (which began in 1916 with the founding of the Professional Golfers' Association of America) — and invented the sand wedge.

The enigmatic and charismatic Hagen possessed an unquenchable thirst for fun and was renowned as much for his gamesmanship and game pursuit of the night life as he was for his golf skills. The "Haig" won the first of his 11 major championships in the 1914 U.S. Open, but it was his triumph in the 1922 British Open that in the eyes of many golf historians signaled the onset of American dominance that Jones soon thereafter manifested.

The Other Legends of Golf

The lineage of American champions descending from Jones consists of many fine players. Five stand out above the rest: Sam Snead, Byron Nelson, Ben Hogan, Arnold Palmer, and Jack Nicklaus. Each of their careers was magnificent, and significant to golf's overall growth. Contemporaries Snead, Nelson, and Hogan, born seven months apart in 1912, ruled golf from 1936, the year of Snead's first victory, to 1958, when Palmer took over as the driving force in the game. Together, the trio combined for 195 victories and 21 major championships. They had some of the best nicknames, too.

Snead, or "Slammin' Sammy," possessed a gorgeous, languid, and powerful swing and used it to win 81 times (84, according to Sam), the all-time PGA Tour record, including 7 majors. He was 24 when he won the 1936 West Virginia Close Pro tournament, and 53 when he won his eighth Greater Greensboro Open in 1965, his final conquest.

One of the game's most consistent ball-strikers, Nelson collected 52 wins and 5 majors, but his claim to fame is the astounding 11 wins in a row he strung together in 1945, a record that isn't likely to be eclipsed. In 30 starts, "Iron Byron" posted 18 victories in all, never finished out of the top ten (another record), and averaged 68.33 strokes per round.

Hogan was so good that he had three nicknames: "Bantam Ben," "The Hawk," and "Wee Ice Mon." The recalcitrant Texan, who spoke nary a word on the golf course, was arguably the most diligent practice player of all time and honed a swing that was as close to perfect as any golfer could get. His daily regimen included hitting a bag of balls for each club in his bag. Hogan's 63 victories included 9 majors. Remarkably, five of those major titles — three in the U.S. Open — were achieved after Hogan was nearly killed in an automobile accident in February 1949. Hogan and his wife, Valerie, were en route from El Paso, Texas, to Phoenix when a Greyhound bus pulled out in front of Hogan's car on a fog-laden two-lane highway. Hogan reflexively threw his body across his wife as the bus hit them head-on, an instinctive move that probably saved his life. Nonetheless, the damage to his body was extensive, and it was thought that he would never play golf again. But he produced one of the most stirring human interest tales in all of sports when he returned to the U.S. Open championship in 1950 at Merion Golf Club just 16 months after the accident. Miraculously, Hogan survived the grueling 36-hole Saturday round, plus a playoff against Lloyd Mangrum and George Fazio, to win the second of his four national championships.

Hogan's remarkable comeback was not the only story in golf in 1950. Led by Babe Zaharias, Louise Suggs, and Patty Berg (its first president and the first winner of the U.S. Women's Open in 1946), the Ladies Professional Golf Association was founded to replace the ailing Women's Professional Golf Association started in 1944. Its first tournament, the Tampa Open, was held January 19 to 22 at Palma Ceia Country Club and was won by amateur Polly Riley, but the season was dominated by Zaharias, who won 6 of the 11 events, while Berg captured 3 titles. Though prize money lagged behind the men's tour, the LPGA had expanded to 24 events within a decade and was a legitimate product in the sports marketplace.

In contrast to Hogan's stoicism was Arnold Palmer's charisma, which attracted the common folk to what heretofore had been perceived as an elite pursuit. Palmer, the son of a greenskeeper from Latrobe, Pennsylvania, galvanized a generation of sporting fans with the slashing, go-for-broke style of a penniless pirate. His legion of fanatical followers became known as Arnie's Army. What's more, Palmer's approach to the game, his emotional reaction to his successes and failures, and his congenial personality were all well-suited to a new medium, television, spurring his and golf's popularity. He became the post-World War II version of Francis Ouimet.

Of course, none of that would have been possible had he been an average player, but Palmer, who turned professional in 1954, was an exceptional talent who chalked up 60 victories in his illustrious career, including 4 Masters titles among his 7 major conquests. Palmer not only ignited growth of the game in America, but also worldwide. Most tellingly, after winning the Masters and rallying to claim his only U.S. Open crown at Cherry Hills in Denver in 1960, Palmer went in search of the modern grand slam and traveled to St. Andrews for the British Open. He fell a stroke shy, finishing second to Kel Nagle, but in the process Palmer single-handedly restored the prestige of the Open championship. It's no wonder that they call him the King.

It's also no mystery why Jack Nicklaus was voted Golfer of the Century. The Golden Bear arrived on the scene from Columbus, Ohio, in 1962, at the height of Palmer's popularity, and while Arnie collected accolades, Nicklaus hoarded hardware. A telling denouement for the golf world occurred at the 1962 U.S. Open, when Nicklaus defeated Palmer in a playoff at Oakmont (Pennsylvania) Country Club — dead in the heart of enemy territory. As the years rolled by, Nicklaus routinely routed his adversaries and exhausted all the adjectives the media could find. His 70 PGA Tour titles is second only to the number Snead has, and his 18 professional major championships is second to none. Perhaps the greatest compliment to Nicklaus's abilities came from his idol, Jones, who upon watching the young phenom uttered the now-famous remark, "He plays a game with which I am not familiar." Jones or anyone else.

Stepping Right Up

We are now on the verge of the Millennium Players, new professionals with skills that belie their age. These youngsters have been brought up playing golf from a very young age. Some have had audio tapes about golf played to them while still in the womb. They are serious.

Examples of new players who are Y2K-proof are David Duval, the retrospective birdie-indulger who won the money title at the age of 26, and Phil Mickelson, a fine young golf ball director who has won 13 tournaments (and he's not out of his twenties yet!).

Golf has become cool, and parents are pushing their offspring into this gilded cage at an early age. The scenic confines and safe-house environment of golf courses has eased minds of many parents when they wonder what influences are directing their children.

The new millennium of golf is rich with talent and long with reach. We are blessed with a game that can last as long as you wish to pursue it. It's an odyssey of memories and stories yet to be told. Enjoy the association.

Tiger Woods

Tigermania was Tigermania because Tiger Woods produced the type of golf that was utterly dominating. He slayed courses with his length, made every putt he needed to make, trademarked a fist pump, and for the first couple of years could do no wrong. His first three wins came against Davis Love III, Payne Stewart, and Tom Lehman — and he ran through those men as if they were players in the U.S. Amateur. He turned Augusta National into the proverbial pitch-and-putt course, reaching the par-5s with wedges. He was golf's highlight tape. *Newsweek* put him on the cover. *Sports Illustrated* made him its Athlete of the Year. Jack Nicklaus predicted that Tiger would win as many Masters titles as he and Arnold Palmer combined had won.

Because he is of mixed heritage — his father is black and his mother is Thai — Tiger is more than just a golfer with the skills to excel. He is also a golfer of the people, a young man who represents the breaking down of ethnic barriers. People said that he transcends the game, that he is a crossover personality who brought people to golf who had never considered golf a sport. Kids started to turn up at golf tournaments — in droves. They were white and black, Asian and Hispanic, boys and girls. Golf had a new crowd, and it was hungry for this kid from Cypress, California, who turned golf into a video game. When Tiger smiles, it seems that the whole golf world smiles with him. It is a powerful thing.

What we relearned in 1998 was that golf is not like basketball. One player cannot dominate it the way Michael Jordan did the NBA. Golf is a game of cycles, and as Tiger continues to improve his game, he will have his runs like he did from the Greater Milwaukee Open in September 1996 until the Western Open in July 1997. That was the most exciting time in golf since the early 1960s, when Arnold Palmer burst on the scene and "invented" the game. For a while, it looked like Tiger was going to reinvent it, but Tiger has more great players to beat than Palmer did. He also has to deal with more than Palmer did, and those pressures can turn a young man old in a hurry. Tiger plays almost every tournament under a death threat, surrounded by a phalanx of security personnel. He cannot go to dinner or a movie without being mobbed.

Potentially, he still could be the greatest golfer who ever lived. Time is on his side, and he certainly has all the tools. But there's more to golf than warp clubhead speed and a burning competitive edge. Tiger must refine those tools and learn to live with the highest set of expectations placed on any golfer who has put a peg in the ground.

Chapter 3

The Gear of Golf

*I*n the last 100 years, golf has changed enormously, but perhaps the most noticeable difference is in the area of equipment. The game may be inherently the same, but the implements used to get from tee to green and into the hole are unrecognizable compared to the rather primitive implements used by Young Tom Morris (one of the great, early pioneers of golf whom I tell you about in Chapter 2) and his Scottish buddies in the late 19th century. Okay, so early golf equipment had more romantic names: Niblick, brassie, spoon, driving-iron, mashie, and mashie-niblick are more fun than 9-iron, 2-wood, 3-wood, 1-iron, 5-iron, and 7-iron. But golf equipment today is much better and more reliable.

The old Scottish "worthies" (a great name for players) used clubs whose shafts were wooden — hickory, to be exact. Individually, these clubs may have been fine, but what were the chances of finding a dozen or so identical pieces of wood? Slim to none.

In fact, the great Bobby Jones, who also played with hickory-shafted clubs (steel shafts were legalized by the United States Golf Association in 1924) ran into that very problem — finding identical shafts. Years after he retired, his old clubs were run through a sophisticated battery of tests to see how they matched. And, as you'd expect, his clubs were all pretty close, Jones having built up the set over a period of many years. But one club, the 8-iron, was markedly different, especially the shaft. That difference came as no surprise to the great man: "I always had trouble with that club," Jones said.

Nowadays, you have no excuse for playing with equipment ill-suited to your swing, body, and game. There's too much information out there to help you. And that's the purpose of this chapter — to help you find a path through what can be a confusing maze of statistics and terminology.

Golf Balls — What to Choose?

A number of technological advances have occurred in the game of golf over the years, but perhaps nothing has changed more than the golf ball. It's no coincidence that the USGA (United States Golf Association) and R&A (Royal & Ancient Golf Club) keep a tight rein on just how far a ball can go nowadays. If the associations didn't provide regulations, almost every golf course on the planet would be reduced to a pitch and putt. We'd all be putting through windmills just to keep the scores up in the 50s.

For the record, here are the specifications the USGA imposes on Titleist, Maxfli, and the rest of the ball manufacturers:

- **Size:** A golf ball may not be smaller than 1.68 inches in diameter. The ball can be as big as you want, however. Just don't expect a bigger ball to go farther. I've never seen anyone use a ball bigger than 1.68 inches in diameter. In fact, I've never even seen a golf ball that size.

- **Weight:** The golf ball may not be heavier than 1.62 ounces.

- **Velocity:** The USGA has a machine for measuring velocity. No ball may exceed 250 feet per second at a temperature of 75 degrees. A tolerance of no more than 2 percent is allowed. This rule ensures that golf balls don't go too far.

- **Distance:** Distance is the most important factor. No ball, when hit by the USGA's "Iron Byron" machine (named after Byron Nelson), can go farther than 280 yards. A tolerance of 6 percent is allowed here, making 296.8 yards the absolute farthest the ball can go. Yeah, right. Iron Byron, meet John Daly! He regularly blasts drives way past 300 yards!

- **Shape:** A golf ball must be round. An antislice ball on the market a few years ago was weighted on one side and failed this test. Nice try, though!

Even with these regulations, take a look around any golf professional's shop, and you'll see a lot of golf balls and a lot of different brands. And upon closer inspection, you'll find that every type of ball falls into one of two categories: Either the manufacturer is claiming that this ball goes farther and straighter than any other ball in the cosmos, or it's telling you that this ball gives you more control than your other brand.

Try not to get overwhelmed. Keep in mind that golf balls come in only three basic types: one-piece, two-piece, and three-piece. And you can forget one-piece balls. They tend to be cheap and nasty and found only on driving ranges. So that leaves two-piece and three-piece balls.

Don't worry; deciding on a type of ball is still easy. You don't even have to know what a two-piece or three-piece ball contains or why it has that many "pieces." Leave all that to the scientists.

Go with a two-piece ball. I wouldn't recommend a three-piece, balata-covered ball to a beginning golfer. *Balata* is a relatively soft, rubber-type material designed to give advanced players better feel and therefore more control. Control isn't what a beginning golfer needs. Besides, balata, being softer, is more susceptible to cutting and scraping, especially if you aren't hitting every shot right off the middle of the clubface. Going through as many as ten balls per round can get expensive in a hurry.

Unless you have very deep pockets and more cash than Greg Norman, go the surlyn, two-piece route. (*Surlyn* is a type of plastic first developed by the Dupont Corporation.) Most amateurs with double-digit handicaps use this type of ball. Balls covered in surlyn are more durable. Their harder cover and lower spin rate give you less feel — which is why better players tend not to use them — but, assuming that you don't whack them off the premises, they last longer. Surlyn-covered balls also go a little farther than balata balls.

Golf balls also come in three compressions: 80, 90, or 100 compression. The 80-compression ball is the softest, and the 100 is the hardest. When I was growing up, I thought that the harder the ball (100 compression), the farther it would go. Not the case. All balls go the same distance, but each one feels a little different. How hard or soft you want the ball to feel has to do with your personal preference.

I use a 90-compression Titleist Professional golf ball. It gives me a slightly softer feel than the 100-compression ball when I'm chipping and putting. Those 80-compression golf balls feel much too soft to me. This is a personal feeling; you have to experiment in order to form your own opinion.

Take all the commercial hype with a pinch of salt. Make that a handful. Again, the most important things you need to know when buying golf balls are your own game, your own tendencies, and your own needs. All that information will help you choose the golf ball best suited to you.

How to Choose the Clubs in Your Bag

Deciding on a type or brand of clubs to use can be as simple or as complicated as you want to make it. You can go to any store that doesn't have a golf pro, pick a set of clubs off the shelf, and then take them to the tee. You can go to garage sales. You can check with the pro at your local municipal course as a source of information and advice. Any or all of these methods can work. But the chances of choosing a set with the correct loft, lie, size of grip, and all the other stuff involved in club-fitting is unlikely at best.

Having said that, it wasn't so long ago that *unsophisticated* was a fair description of every golf club buyer. Yeah, the better player might waggle the club a few times and "know" that it's not for him — hardly the most scientific approach!

If you're just beginning to play golf, keep in mind that you may discover that this game is not for you. So you should start out with rental clubs at a driving range. Most driving ranges around the country have rental clubs. Go out and hit balls with these clubs. If you still want to play golf after hitting a few balls, then buy your own clubs.

Find an interim set of clubs

If you're just starting out (and you've played with the rental clubs for a while), find cheap clubs to use as an interim set during your adjustment period. You are learning the game, so you don't want to make big decisions on what type of clubs to buy yet. If you keep your ears open around the golf course or driving range, you may hear of someone who has a set that he or she is willing to sell. You can also ask whether he or she has any information on clubs that could be sold cheaply. Go take a look at garage sales that have golf clubs for sale, or try the classified ads of your weekend newspaper. If you are computer friendly, check the Internet and find somebody in your area who is selling clubs. (In Chapter 21, I describe some of my favorite golf sites on the Internet.) You can become your own private investigator and hunt down the best buy you can find. Buy cheap for now — you've got plenty of time for the big purchase.

Try all sorts of golf clubs — ones with steel shafts, graphite shafts (which are lighter and therefore easier to swing), big-headed clubs, forged clubs, cavity-backed clubs. You have more choices than your neighborhood Baskin Robbins. Remember: You're in your experimental stage.

Don't be afraid to ask your friends to try their clubs on the range. I do this all the time on the tour when a new product has been introduced. Try out these clubs, and you can judge for yourself whether they feel good. But if you don't like the club that you just tried, don't tell the person who loaned it to you that the club stinks — that's not good golf etiquette. Simply handing the club to the person and saying that it has a different feel usually works.

Try this club on for size

Today, club-fitting is big business. Tour pros and average amateur golfers have access to the same club-fitting technology and information. It's important for all golfers, male and female, to use the appropriate equipment for their body types and physical conditions. Many manufacturers of golf clubs specialize in creating clubs for women that have softer shafts, which are lighter and more flexible.

Here are some factors to consider:

- **The grip:** Determine how thick the grip on your clubs should be. The grip is very important. Grips that are too thin encourage too much hand action in your swing; grips that are too thick restrict your hands too much. Generally, the proper-sized grip should allow the middle and ring fingers on your left hand to barely touch the pad of your thumb when you take hold of the club. If your fingers don't touch your thumb, the grip is too big; if your fingers dig into the pad, the grip is too thin.

- **The shaft:** Consider your height, build, and strength when you choose a club. If you're really tall, you need longer (and probably stiffer) shafts.

  What does your swing sound like? If your swing makes a loud swish noise and the shaft is bending like a long cast from a fly-fishing rod at the top of your swing, you need a very strong shaft. If your swing makes no noise and you could hang laundry on your shaft at the top of your swing, you need a regular shaft. Anybody in-between needs a medium-stiff to stiff shaft.

- **Loft:** Then there's your typical ball-flight. If you slice, for example, you can get clubs with less loft — or perhaps offset heads — to help alleviate that problem. For more information about slicing, see Chapter 13.

- **The clubhead:** Consider the size of the clubhead. Today, you can get standard, midsize, and oversize heads on your clubs. I recommend that you get bigger clubheads for your early days of golfing. Bigger clubheads are more forgiving and can help psychologically, too.

- **The iron:** Advanced players choose irons that are best suited to their swing. Forged, muscle-backed irons are for good players who hit the ball on the clubface precisely. Cavity-backed irons (hollowed out in the back of the iron) are for those players who hit the ball all over the clubface.

  The bigger the clubface, the more room for error — hence the bigger-headed metal woods that are popular today for all you wild swingers out there.

Ten questions to ask when you buy clubs

1. Do you have a club-fitting program?

Check with the local PGA (Professional Golfers' Association) golf professional and see whether he has a club-fitting program. If he doesn't have one, he will be able to direct you to someone in the area who does. Once you have started this game and like it enough to continue playing, choosing the right equipment is the biggest decision you will have to make. So involve a PGA golf professional.

2. What's the price of club-fitting?

Don't be too shy to ask this question. Club-fitting can be very expensive and not in your budget. You should be the judge of how much you can afford.

3. What shaft length do I need for my clubs?

People come in different heights and builds. Some people are very tall with short arms, and some are short with long arms. People have different postures when they bend over to address the golf ball, and they need different shaft lengths to match that posture. This is where PGA golf professionals can really help; they have been trained to answer questions like these and can make club-fitting very easy.

4. What lie-angle do I need on my clubs?

Here's the general rule: The closer you stand to the ball, the more upright your club needs to be. As you get farther away from the ball, your club should be flatter.

5. What grip size do I need?

The bigger your hands are, the bigger-sized grip you need. If you have a tendency to slice the ball, you can get smaller grips put on your clubs that help your hands to work faster. If you have a tendency to hook the ball, you can put bigger grips on your clubs that will slow your hands down and help slow down that hook.

6. What material — leather, cord, all-rubber, half-rubber — do you recommend for my grips?

Many different materials can make up a golf grip. Leather is the most expensive and the hardest to maintain. This material is for accomplished players; I wouldn't recommend leather for beginners. Stick to an all-rubber grip — and change them every year if you play at least once a week.

I use a combination of rubber and cord in my grip. This allows me to hold on to the club much better in hot weather. My hands are callused, though, so they don't hurt from the rubbing of the cord.

7. What kind of irons should I buy — investment cast, forged, oversized, or cavity back?

The best advice I can give is to look for an investment cast, cavity backed, oversized golf club. For beginners, this is the best choice. Just take my word for it — I haven't got enough paper to explain all the reasons.

8. Should I use space-age materials like boron, titanium, or graphite in my shafts? Or should I go with steel?

Steel shafts are the cheapest; all the others are quite a bit more expensive, so keep your budget in mind. See if you can test some of these other shafts to see how they compare with steel, which is still very good and used by most of the players on tour.

9. What type of putter should I use: center-shafted, end-shafted, or a long putter?

You can easily test putters at the golf course where you play. Just ask the pro if you can test one of the putters on the rack. If you have a friend or playing partner who has a putter you think you might like, ask to try it.

10. If you are going to buy new clubs, ask the pro if you can test them for a day.

Most of the time, if someone is trying to make a sale, they will afford you every opportunity to try the clubs. Golf pros are just like car dealers; they'll let you test-drive before you buy.

Because of all the technology that is available, purchasing golf clubs nowadays is like buying a computer: Whatever you buy is outdated in six months. The influx of ideas is ever-changing. So be frugal and shop for your best buy. When you get a set that fits you and you're hitting the ball with consistency, stick with that set. Finding a whole set of clubs that matches the temperament of your golf swing is hard. Find the ones that have your fingerprints on them and stick with 'em.

Build your own clubs

You can get quite sophisticated when choosing a club, if you want. Club component companies specialize in selling clubs piece by piece. You can literally build your own set of clubs to your own specifications; you just have to do some research first. A lot of people are building their own clubs, judging by the success of firms like Golfsmith. For one thing, these clubs are cheaper than the clubs you can buy off the shelf.

Although building your clubs does require time and effort, the end result is the same. Component companies can sell you everything you need. You can get catalogs or call their 800 numbers (see Appendix B). Component companies have grip tape, solvents, clamps, epoxy, shaft-cutting tools, shaft extensions, grip knives, and every kind of shaft, head, and grip imaginable. You name it, they've got it. You just have to know what you're ordering. If you're not sure, order a club-making video or book. You never know — you may end up an expert in the field.

When You Know Your Game

Before 1938, the rules of golf allowed players to carry as many clubs as they wanted to. Since then, however, golfers have been restricted to a maximum of 14 clubs in their bags at any one time. But no rule tells you what 14 clubs you should be using, so you have leeway. You can match the composition of your set to your strengths and weaknesses.

I'm assuming that you are going to carry a driver, a 3-wood, a putter, and a 4-iron to 9-iron. Nearly everyone does. So you have five clubs left to select. The first thing you need to know, of course, is how far you are likely to hit each club. (That's golfspeak for hitting the ball with the club. Don't go smashing your equipment!) After you know that distance, you can look into plugging the gaps. Those gaps are more important at the short end of your set.

I recommend that you carry three wedges/sand wedges, each with a different loft. I do. I use 48 degrees for my pitching wedge, 54 degrees for my sand wedge, and 59 degrees for my lob wedge. I look to hit each of them 125 (pitching wedge), 105 (sand wedge), and 85 (lob wedge) yards. That way, the yardage gap between them is not significant. If I carried only the 125-yard wedge and the 85-yard wedge, that would leave a gap of 40 yards. Too much. If I leave myself with a shot of about 105 yards, right in the middle of my gap, I've got problems. Carrying the 105-yard wedge plugs that gap. If I didn't have it, I'd be forced to manufacture a shot with a less-than-full swing. And that's too hard, especially under pressure. Full swings, please!

Okay, that's 12 clubs taken care of. You have two left. I recommend that you carry at least one lofted wood. Make that two. Low-numbered irons are too unforgiving. Give yourself a break. Carry a 5-wood and even a 7-wood. These clubs are designed to make it easy for you to get the ball up in the air. They certainly achieve that more quickly than a 2-iron, so take advantage of them.

When to Use Each Club

Table 3-1 lists how far the average golfer generally hits with each club. When you first start to play this game, you probably won't attain these yardages. As you practice, you'll get closer to these numbers. You should know your average. The best way to find out is to hit, oh, 50 balls with each club. Eliminate the longest five and the shortest five and then pace off to the middle of the remaining group. That's your average yardage. Use your average yardage to help you gauge which club to use on each shot. Figure 3-1 shows the clubs that I have in my bag.

Table 3-1	Which Club Should You Use?	
Club	*Men's Average Distance (In Yards)*	*Women's Average Distance (In Yards)*
Driver	230	200
3-wood	210	180
2-iron	190	Not recommended; 4-wood = 170
3-iron	180	Not recommended; 5-wood = 160
4-iron	170	150

Club	Men's Average Distance (In Yards)	Women's Average Distance (In Yards)
5-iron	160	140
6-iron	150	130
7-iron	140	120
8-iron	130	110
9-iron	120	100
Pitching wedge	110	90
Sand wedge	90	80
Lob wedge	65	6

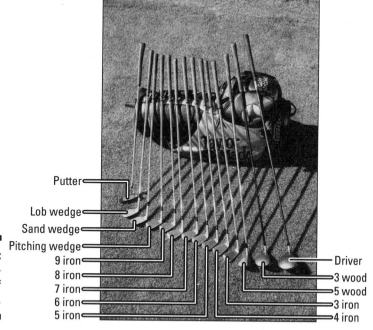

Figure 3-1:
My imple-
ments of
destruction.

Tradition versus Technology: Keep Tinkering with Success

Technology is the guiding light of fundamental change that is inherent to a capitalistic society in search of a more expensive way to hit the #$&!?*@ ball farther.* — Quote on the bathroom wall of the Wayward Soul Driving Range in Temecula, California

Technology and all its implications is a conversation topic that PGA Tour players visit quite often. Is the ball too hot? Are the big-headed titanium drivers giving the golf ball too much rebound? Is Tiger getting rich? I think that most players would answer these questions in the affirmative. Should golfers take a stance on the tenuous line between the balance of tradition and technology? "Probably not" would be the answer if all were polled.

To see where golf is today, you have to examine its past; then you can try to predict golf's future. Chapter 2 gives you the lowdown on how golf equipment developed into its modern forms; this section helps you gaze into the crystal ball to focus on what the future has to offer.

Whoever said that golf is played with weapons ill-suited for their intended purpose probably hadn't played with clubs made of titanium and other composite metals. These clubs allegedly act like a spring that segments of the golfing populace believe propels the golf ball — also enhanced by state-of-the-art materials and designs — distances it was not meant to travel. This phenomenon is called the *trampoline effect,* which some folks may mistake for a post-round activity for reducing stress. In fact, this effect is the product of modern, thin-faced metal clubs.

This recent phenomenon has fueled a debate pitting the forces of technology (the evil swine) against those of tradition (those languorous leeches who never see special-effects movies). Equipment that makes the game easier for the masses helps the game grow, the techno-wizards say. The traditionalists fret that classic courses may become obsolete, the need for new super-long courses may make the game cost more in both time and money, and golf may become too easy for elite players. Regardless of which side you agree with (you may, indeed, back both camps), one fact is undeniable: Improving golf equipment has been an unceasing process throughout the game's history.

People have been developing the golf ball and clubs for many years. In the last 100 years, however, science has played an increasing role in golf club development, with a strong influence coming from research into new metals, synthetic materials, and composites. Other developments worth noting include the following:

- ✔ The introduction of the casting method of manufacturing clubheads in 1963

- ✔ The introduction of graphite for use in shafts in 1973

- ✔ The manufacture of metal woods in 1979 (first undertaken by Taylor Made)

This last creation rendered persimmon woods obsolete, although a small number are still crafted.

The application of titanium to clubheads raised the bar in technological development (yet again) just a few years ago. Lighter than previous materials yet stronger than steel, titanium allows club manufacturers to create larger clubheads with bigger sweet spots, such as Callaway's Biggest Big Bertha and Taylor Made's Ti Bubble 2. Such clubs provide high-handicap golfers a huge margin for error — there's nothing quite like the feel of a mishit ball traveling 200 yards! But it is golf balls flying in excess of 300 yards that raise suspicions that these new clubs are making the ball too "excitable."

Golf balls have been under scrutiny for much longer, probably because each new generation of ball has had an ever greater impact on the game. Ball development makes golf easier and more enjoyable for the average person and thus cultivates more interest.

Nowadays, in addition to balata, balls made of surlyn, lithium, and titanium are available. Modern balls tout varied dimple patterns, multiple layers, and other features that attempt to impart a certain trajectory, greater accuracy, and better feel, as well as the ever-popular maximum distance allowed under the Rules of Golf established by the USGA. According to Appendix III in the rules, the Overall Distance Standard says that a ball "shall not cover an average distance of carry and roll exceeding 280 yards plus a tolerance of 6 percent." That means that no golfer should be able to average more than 296.8 yards with his or her best poke. But in 1998, John Daly averaged 299.4 yards on his measured drives on the PGA Tour. Uh oh.

Too bad all this progress hasn't cured the primary bane of a vast majority of recreational golfers: the dreaded slice. But golf manufacturers give their all to the task of reducing the troublesome left-to-right ball flight (for right-handers). They attempt to reduce slice with a number of adjustments, including adjusting shaft flex, adjusting inset (moving the hosel closer to the center of the clubface), and changing the face angle, center of gravity, and lie angle. If all this technology fails, golf lessons may prove helpful.

In the coming years, golf stands to become increasingly popular, and if history tells us anything, it's that technology is apt to contribute to the burgeoning number of converts. However, advances in golf equipment may occur at a relatively glacial pace. It's doubtful that the first decade of the 21st century could rival the first ten years of this century for technological impact or dramatic innovation.

Why? For one thing, scientists are running out of new stuff they can use to make clubheads — at least stuff that isn't edible. An expedition to Saturn may yield possibilities. Metallurgists are going to be challenged, although so far they're staying ahead of the game. New entries in the substance category include beta titanium, maraging steel, and liquid metal, all purportedly stronger and harder than current club materials.

Frank Thomas, technical director for the U.S. Golf Association, is one of the prominent folks standing in the way (somewhat reluctantly) of radical equipment enhancement. His job is to regulate the distance a golf ball should travel, yet he doesn't want to stifle technology altogether. The goal is to give the average golfer an advantage (whether it comes from the equipment itself or the joy of having better equipment) while keeping the game a challenge for the top players.

But someone is always trying to build a better mousetrap. And although everyone wants more distance, most performance-enhancing innovations are likely to come in putter designs. More than 600 putters went through the approval process at the USGA in 1998. If someone can invent a yip-proof blade, that person is going to make a fortune.

Golfers may also see changes in the ball, although again, dramatic alterations in ball design are unlikely. Customizing may become more commonplace. You may also see more layering of golf ball materials to help performance.

Also, not to be discounted are improvements in turf technology — an overlooked area boasting significant breakthroughs in the last 20 years. For example, in 1977, the average Stimpmeter reading for greens around the country (the Stimpmeter measures the speed of a putting surface — or any surface on a course) was 6.6. This means that a ball rolled from a set slope traveled 6 feet, 6 inches. Today, the average is closer to 8 feet. (Interesting note: At the 1998 U.S. Open at the Olympic Club in San Francisco, the fairways registered a 6.6 reading. That will put some roll on your rock, although this advantage was negated by the fairways at Olympic being only 2 feet wide.)

The biggest future breakthroughs in golf will probably come from humans. Physiological improvement and psychological refinement may be the surest paths to greater distance and lower scoring.

So hit the gym, take up yoga, hit your psychologist's couch, get in touch with your inner self, eat bran and all the spinach you can stand, drink 20 glasses of water a day, and take a stab at self-hypnotism if you have to. And if all that fails to add 10 yards off the tee, try a different ball. Ain't innovation great?

Clothing

The easiest way to date an old picture of a golfer, at least approximately, is by the clothes he or she is wearing. Sartorially, the game has changed enormously since the Scots tottered 'round the old links wearing a jacket, shirt, and tie.

The fabric of clothes has changed from those days of heavy wool and restricted swings. Light cotton and John Daly-like extra long arcs are what the splendidly smart golfer wears and aspires to today. Back at St. Andrews, the restraint of the clothing affected the golf swing. Those jackets were tight! In fact, I believe that was the single biggest influence on the early golf swings. You had to sway off the ball and then let your left arm bend on the backswing to get full motion. Also, golfers had to let go with the last three fingers of their left hands at the top of the swing. It was the only way they could get the shaft behind their heads. Put on a tweed jacket that's a little too small and try to swing. You'll see what the early golfers had to go through.

Styles have changed, too — even since I came on tour in the early 1970s. Back then, polyester was the fabric of choice. Bell-bottoms and bright plaids filled golf courses with ghastly ridicule. We've graduated to cotton fabrics — a softer, more humane existence on the course. Some guys on tour now wear expensive pants with more expensive belts. But most players wear off-the-rack clothes provided by clothing manufacturers.

Women have undergone an enormous fashion transformation on the course, too. Years ago, they played in full-length skirts, hats, and blouses buttoned up to the neck. All very restricting, I should imagine. Now, of course, they're out there in shorts and pants.

First of all, dress within your budget. This game can get expensive enough, especially if you try to outdress your playing partners. My general rule is to aim to dress better than the starter at the course. (The *starter* is the person in charge of getting everyone off the first tee.) The starter's style is usually a reflection of the dress standards at that particular golf course. If you're unsure about the style at a particular course, give the pro shop a call to find out the dress code.

Luckily, you don't have to go to great lengths to look good. Most retailers have cool golf gear these days. All you have to do is shop the malls or your local discount store, and you'll soon have a socially acceptable golf wardrobe that suits your style — and doesn't get you laughed out of town.

The bottom line is to dress comfortably and look good. If you dress well, you may appear as if you can actually play this game with a certain amount of distinction. People can be fooled. You never know!

Golf shoes are the final aspect of a golfer's ensemble. Shoes can be a fashion statement — alligator or ostrich. They can be comfortable — tennis shoes or sandals with spikes. The can take on the lore of the Wild West in the form of cowboy boots with spikes or, as my mentor Fairway Louie used to highlight is golfing attire, they can be military combat boots, which were an extension of his Zionist dialogue.

What's on the bottom of the shoe is all the rage now. The traditional metal spikes have been replaced with all sorts of *soft spikes*. Soft spikes are preferable to metal spikes because they reduce spike marks and wear and tear on the greens. Soft spikes are also easier on the feet. If the style of shoes is worthy, you can even go directly from the golf course to the nearest restaurant without having to change shoes. The golf world is becoming a simpler place to live.

Accessories

When it comes to accessories, a whole golfing subculture is out there. By accessories, I mean things like

- Covers for your irons
- Plastic tubes that you put in your bag to keep your shafts from clanging together
- Tripod tees to use when the ground is hard
- Golf watches that keep your score
- Rubber suction cups that allow you to lift your ball from the hole without bending down

I've even seen a plastic clip that fits to the side of your bag so that you can "find" your putter quickly. You know the sort of things. On the surface, accessories all appear to be good ideas, but then you often use them only once.

The place to find all this sort of stuff is in the classified advertising sections of golf magazines. But take my advice: Don't bother. Real golfers — and you want to look and behave like one — don't go in for that stuff. Accessories are very uncool. The best golf bags are spartan affairs and contain only the bare essentials:

- ✔ Six balls (or so)
- ✔ A few tees (wooden)
- ✔ A couple of gloves
- ✔ A rain suit
- ✔ A pitch mark repairer
- ✔ A few small coins (preferably foreign) for markers

  Two or three pencils
- ✔ A little bag (leather is cool) for your wallet, money clip, loose change, car keys, rings, and so on

Your bag should also have a towel (a real, full-size one) hanging from the strap. Use your towel to dry off and wipe clean your clubheads. Keep a spare towel in your bag. If it rains, you can't have too many towels.

I mentioned headcovers. Keep them only on your woods or metal woods. You have a wide range to choose from. You have your cuddly animal devotees. Other players like to be identified with a particular golf club, educational establishment, or sports team. Some players are content merely to advertise the manufacturer of the club they are using.

Bottom line? I recommend that you get headcovers with which you readily identify. Create your own persona. For example, PGA Tour player Craig "the Walrus" Stadler has walrus headcovers. Australian Steve Elkington doesn't use headcovers.

As for your golf bag, don't get a large tour-sized monstrosity with your name on the side. I do that because I play professionally and someone pays me to use their equipment. Go the understated route. Especially if you're going to be carrying your bag, go small and get the kind that has legs that fold down automatically to support the bag. First, you don't want to be loaded down on a hot day. And second, the last thing you want to do is draw attention to yourself. Blend in. Be as one with the environment.

✔

Chapter 4
Getting and Staying in Golf Shape

. . . .

In This Chapter

▶ Understanding why physical fitness is important in golf
▶ Finding a golf-specific fitness-training program for you

. . . .

*B*oth hands on the club, my body tense in anticipation of flush contact. Eyes preoccupied with a distant stare of the uncertainty of the golf ball's destination. I realize that the swing sequence has begun, and I put all available resources into sending the ball on a wanton mission of distance collection. I sense the fluid nature of Fred Couples's swing, the mass chaos of Tiger Woods's hips as they rotate through the hitting area, the silent stare of John Daly's gallery as they try to interpret what they just saw. I'm awakened from my trance by the dull thud of contact: It hurts, it's sickly, and I hear voices from nearby, questioning my masculinity. Impact has all the compression of a gnat flying into a wall of warm butter. My body is vibrating like a marked-down, used Ford Escort, and I nearly pass out from the physical exertion.

Once I get back on my feet to review the moment and wait for the laughter to die down, I realize that the instrument swinging this club has been totally neglected and is in a state of sad disrepair. My "exercise regimen" up to this point has been to get in a bathtub filled with lukewarm water, pull the drain cord, and then fight the current. It's time to end this madness. I'm going to exercise!

—Fairway Louie, circa 1987, after hitting his opening tee shot in the La Fiesta Restaurant's annual Dos Gringos Alternate (Tequila) Shot Tournament

 GARY SAYS

My expertise in regard to exercise is minimal at best, and the area of physical therapy is beyond my scope of knowledge. Therefore, I would like to introduce you to a friend of mine: Paul Callaway, PT, a licensed physical therapist. I met Paul in 1984 when he was the first Director of Physical Therapy we had for the PGA Tour. On the PGA Tour and Senior Tour, we have large vans that accommodate physical conditioning apparatuses supervised by physical therapists. This program was started for the betterment of physical conditioning on the tour. Paul is a guy I go to frequently when my Senior Tour body heads out-of-bounds.

Paul is the creator of Body Balance for Performance — a complete golf health and fitness-training program. The Illinois Section of the PGA has endorsed his program and techniques. If you would like more information about this subject, have other questions related to golf health and fitness training, or are interested in locating an officially licensed Body Balance for Performance center near you, call ProDynamics, Inc. (a division of Callaway Physical Therapy, Ltd. in Oak Brook, Illinois) at 888-FIT-GOLF (888-348-4653), or refer to the Body Balance for Performance Web page at www.fitgolf.com.

Understanding Why New Golfers Often Give Up

Golf is becoming the vogue thing to do. More than 26 million Americans are now screwing up their lives by taking up this game. There will be no sanity left for them after they start playing golf. But then again, for bowling you have to rent shoes, tennis is good if you're 17 years old, and I still don't understand squash, so golf seems like the right thing to do if I've got the rest of my life to do it.

This is a very hard game, and if you take it too seriously, it frustrates you enough that you'll start wearing your shoes backwards. I know. . . . Also, any lingering pain you have while playing discounts your ability to play well and sends you to the snack bar to pick up an adult beverage more often than you should. There's a lot of attrition going on in golf, for two main reasons, as I see it:

- ✔ Frustration from lack of improvement
- ✔ Injury

If you're going to have fun playing this game, you have to get your body ready to play golf for a lifetime. So let's get physical.

The purpose of this chapter is to embarrass you into getting into shape so that you can hit a little white ball around 150 acres of green grass without falling down. How tough can that be? I identify five essential elements of golf performance and specifically elaborate on the physical requirements for performing at your best while reducing your risk of doing something that hurts you. The motivation here is to get you out of the chair where you watch The Golf Channel and into a program that helps you feel better, hit the ball farther, and run circles around your kids in front of their friends. Well, the last one may be a stretch, but the other ones are a go.

Figuring Out the Five Essential Ingredients

Here's a list of five things that everybody should utilize for good performance in anything they do (anything!):

- ✔ A customized and sport-specific physical training program. Beer curls are not considered specific.
- ✔ Professional instruction in your chosen sport. I personally have an aprés-ski instructor.
- ✔ Proper mental skills. Enough said.
- ✔ Using training equipment. Please, no Speedos.
- ✔ Having talent to enjoy the sport.

All of these have to be blended into reaching your goal of playing your best. When this process is learned and practiced, it is called *integrated performance enhancement,* or "you da man," as I call it.

If you're going to play on the highest level, you have to have some balance between talent, physical conditioning, mental awareness, instruction, and good ol' perseverance. Simply going out and buying new drivers that are touted to hit the ball 50 yards farther is not going to cut it. Remember, you have to have proper mental skills; use them in this case. Promise me.

The new millennium golfers are getting into great physical shape. Gary Player was the first guy on the Tour who I saw preaching the benefits of being in good shape. At well over 60 years of age, he can physically do most things the kids on the regular Tour can do, except perhaps, catching some big air on a snowboard.

Tiger Woods and David Duval are into rigorous physical exercise programs that will keep them strong into the later stages of the year, when a lot of players tire from so much wear and tear on the body. Both of these guys can hit the ball into the next zip code, and that's not bad for incentive, either.

Considering the Three Key Concepts

Now that I've defined the elements of integrated performance enhancement (you da man), take a look at three concepts that are important for a good training program.

Structure governs function

This heading, simply put, translates to: Your physical structure affects the way you play this game. If your range of motion is like the Tin Man's, your golf swing will not look very athletic and could actually rust. You need to address problem areas with physical conditioning. It's that simple, so get off your wallet and do something, now!

Here are five areas you can address to help your golf game:

- Balance
- Control
- Flexibility
- Posture
- Strength

If you're deficient in one of these areas, you may develop some bad habits in your golf swing to compensate. Not only will your golf game suffer, but your body may break down from bad swing mechanics. Fix it now or fix it later; it's your choice.

Several things can cause structural imbalances. Typical factors include inherited body characteristics and the natural aging process, Dick Clark excluded. Imbalance can occur over a long period of time from consistent thumping of the golf ball.

Regardless of the causes for your body's structural imbalances, the connective tissue system in your body, called the *fascial system,* can develop restrictions that compress and/or pull on muscles, tendons, ligaments, nerves, bones, everything. Left uncorrected, these unbalanced forces within your fascial system will leave you in a mangled mess and adversely affect your performance.

You'll start to compensate for these restrictions in your golf swing, and pretty soon your golf game will stink. So go see a health and performance expert who is specifically trained to work with golfers, and cut out the middleman: bad golf.

Physical training improves structure

How can you improve your structure to play better and safer golf? A quick physiology lesson is at hand.

Earlier, I talked about fascia. More specifically, your body's fascial system contributes to your flexibility, mobility, posture, and function. Fascia, or connective tissue, is everywhere; it is the net that your body is in.

Fascia's main job is to retain your body's normal shape, providing resistance to various stresses. In order to change your body structure and improve your ability to play golf, you benefit most by following a specific sequence of physical training, called Release, Reeducate, and Rebuild, or the story of Gary McCord's career.

✔ **Release:** First, you must release your connective tissue restrictions. Specially designed flexibility exercises help reduce tension in the inelastic portion of the fascial system that is resistant to lengthening. You must perform these stretching exercises at low intensity but for a prolonged duration. Many people with significant fascial tightness need to sustain a single flexibility exercise for a minimum of three to five minutes before the layers of fascia begin to relax. A gentle, sustained stretching technique is far more effective than a short-duration, intense stretch because it more effectively and permanently lengthens the tough connective tissue of the body.

✔ **Reeducate:** As the fascial restrictions are being reduced, you need to reeducate your structure by doing specialized exercises aimed at improving posture, balance, stability, and control. These reeducation exercises help you capitalize on your improved flexibility by teaching you how to feel the positions in which your body is most functional. The goal for each golfer is to develop a new postural identity that produces a posture at address and swing mechanics that are safe, efficient, reproducible, and highly effective.

✔ **Rebuild:** Lastly, you undergo a program of rebuilding exercises, or strengthening exercises designed to solidify and then reinforce your physical structure and dynamic swing motion. These exercises can also improve your swing speed for added distance and improve muscular endurance for better swing control and performance toward the end of a round and/or during longer practice sessions.

This is a must for you prospective golfers. Enhance your structure and improve your game!

Exercise programs must be golf-specific and, ideally, customized

For an exercise program to be most helpful, it must be golf-specific. Warming up by throwing a shot put is not going to help your golf game. Fitness programs for other sports aren't designed around the specific muscles, movement patterns, and physical performance factors that support the golf swing.

Of equal importance to golf-specific training is personally customized fitness training. If you start an exercise program that isn't designed around your personal physical weaknesses, isn't tailored to the special demands of golf, and isn't designed to accomplish your personal performance goals, then the chance that the exercise program will help is nil.

Go out and find a specialist to work with and then ask what sort of initial physical performance evaluation will be performed. They will design their program from their findings. The elements of the evaluation should include at least the following:

✔ Health history of past medical problems, pain problems, injuries related to golf, and so on

✔ Tests to identify postural, structural, or biomechanical imbalances that may interfere with your ability to swing

✔ Balance assessment

✔ Muscle and joint flexibility testing

✔ Muscle strength, endurance, and control testing

✔ Biomechanical video analysis of the golf swing

✔ Golf skills evaluation (measurement of current swing and scoring performance potential, including elements of the swing such as clubhead speed and swing path, as well as driving distance, greens and fairways in regulation, handicap, and so on)

✔ Goals assessment (evaluation of performance goals, purpose for playing golf, and deadlines for reaching goals)

I'm proud of you. Following these steps helps you and your specific golf muscles perform better, and it beats watching Judge Judy during the day. Your physical abilities and conditioning will merge, and you will become a force to be reckoned with out on the links. Enjoy your new outlook on golf.

Sample Physical Tests and Corrective Exercises

I'm going to give you the sample "laboratory white mice" tests before the initial performance tests you'll be consulting a specialist for, right? From these tests, you'll be able to tell how much you need serious conditioning help.

Please remember, if you are unable to perform any portion of these simple tests or recommended corrective exercises easily and comfortably, you're not alone. I seized up during most of them! Go about it slowly, and if you can't perform one or the other, stop and turn on Judge Judy.

Test #1: The club behind the spine test

The club behind the spine test is a very helpful evaluation tool because it can identify several areas of physical weakness and/or imbalance. First, you know that having adequate rotation flexibility in the spine is one of the most essential physical requirements to perform a good golf swing. The area of the spine from which most rotation should come is the middle section known as the *thoracic* spine. To have maximal flexibility to turn during the swing, you must also have the physical potential to achieve a straighter thoracic spine at address, which is the way you set up to the ball (see Figure 4-1). In contrast, a bent thoracic spine at address blocks your ability to turn (see Figure 4-2). Therefore, one important purpose of this test is to determine your physical ability to achieve and maintain the ideal, straighter thoracic spine angle at address through adequate chest and middle spine flexibility.

Figure 4-1: A straight thoracic spine gives you maximal flexibility to turn during your swing.

Figure 4-2:
A bent
thoracic
spine
hinders
your ability
to turn.

In addition, this test measures (to a degree) the muscle strength of your lower abdominals, hips, thighs, middle and upper back, and shoulder blades — all essential muscle groups for achieving and maintaining proper posture at address. Furthermore, this test can identify tightness in your hamstring muscles (the muscles in the backs of your legs).

Perform the club behind the spine test as follows:

1. Stand upright while holding a golf club behind your back.

2. In one hand, hold the head of the club flat against your tailbone. In your other hand, hold the grip of the club against the back of your head. (See Figure 4-3.)

3. Bend your hips and knees slightly (10 to 15 degrees) and contract your lower abdominal muscles, as needed, to press the small of your back into the shaft of the club.

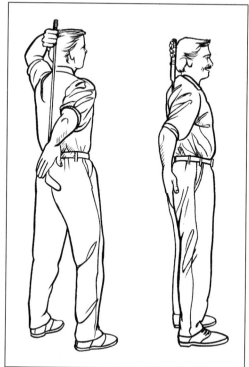

Figure 4-3:
The
beginning
position of
the club
behind the
spine test.

4. While keeping your lower back in complete contact with the clubshaft, straighten and vertically elongate the middle and upper portions of your spine and neck. The goal is to make as much complete contact between the shaft and the entire length of your spine and back of your head as possible. (See Figure 4-4.)

5. Attempt to bend forward from your hips and proportionately from your knees while maintaining club contact with your spine and head. Continue to bend forward until you are able to comfortably see a spot on the ground in front of you where the golf ball would normally be positioned at address. (See Figure 4-5.)

6. Remove the club from behind your back and grip it with both hands in your normal address position while attempting to maintain all the spine, hip, and knee angles that you just created. (See Figure 4-6.)

Figure 4-4:
Keep as much of your spine and back of your head in contact with the clubshaft as possible.

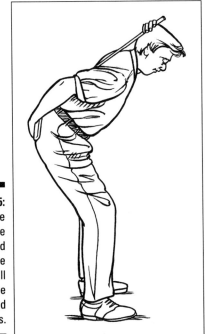

Figure 4-5:
Find the spot on the ground where the ball would be positioned at address.

Figure 4-6:
The ideal
address
position.

If properly executed, the club behind the spine test positions you so that
you feel comfortably balanced over the ball with muscle activity appropri-
ately felt in your lower abdominals, thighs, hips, upper back, and shoulder
blades. You achieve a straighter, more efficient thoracic spine angle and a
neutral, more powerful pelvic position for the golf address position with
proper degrees of hip and knee bend. In other words, you achieve a posture
at address with the greatest potential for producing a safe and highly
effective golf swing.

If you are unable to achieve the positions of this test easily and comfortably,
you may find the next three simple exercises helpful. Nevertheless, please
consult your physician before attempting to perform these or any of the
additional exercises suggested in this chapter. Although these exercises are
generally safe for most individuals, if you notice *any* discomfort while
performing these exercises, you should discontinue and consult with your
physician *immediately* before continuing.

Exercise #1: The recumbent chest and spine stretch

The recumbent chest and spine stretch can help golfers perform a very
important function within the initial phase of any proper exercise progres-
sion, called the *releasing* phase. This exercise specifically releases the
tightness in your chest, in the front of your shoulders, and in your lower

back. After you have mastered this exercise, you will have much better flexibility to achieve the club behind the spine test and, therefore, much better posture at address.

Perform this releasing exercise as follows:

1. Lie on a firm, flat surface with your hips and knees bent at a 90-degree angle. Rest your lower legs on a chair, couch, or bed, as shown in Figure 4-7.

   Depending on the degree of tightness in your chest, spine, and shoulders, you may need to begin this exercise on a softer surface (an exercise mat, blankets on the floor, or your bed) and place a small pillow or rolled-up towel under your head and neck to support them in a comfortable, neutral position. You may also need to place a small towel roll under the small of your back to support its arch.

2. As shown in Figure 4-8, bend your elbows to approximately 90 degrees and position your arms approximately 60 to 80 degrees away from the sides of your body so that you begin to feel a comfortable stretch in the front of your chest and shoulders. (This arm position looks a lot like a waiter's arms do when he carries a tray in each hand.)

   If you feel any pinching pain in your shoulders, try elevating your arms and resting them on a stack of towels or a small pillow so that your elbows are positioned higher above the floor than your shoulders.

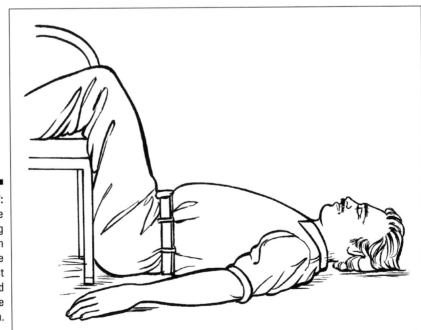

Figure 4-7:
The beginning position for the recumbent chest and spine stretch.

Figure 4-8:
Place your arms like this, so that you feel a comfortable stretch.

3. Relax into this comfortable stretch position for at least three to five minutes or until you experience a *complete* release of the tightness in your chest, front of your shoulders, and lower back.

   You're trying to get your back, spine, and shoulders completely flat on the floor.

Repeat this exercise daily for five to ten days until you can perform the exercise easily, feeling no lingering tightness in your body.

You may want to increase the degree of stretch in your body by removing any support or padding from under your body and/or arms — or even by adding a small towel roll under the middle portion of your spine (at shoulder blade level) in a position perpendicular to the direction of your spine (see Figure 4-9). Remember to *always* keep the degree of stretch comfortable and to support your head, neck, spine, and arms so that you don't put excessive stress on those structures while you perform this exercise.

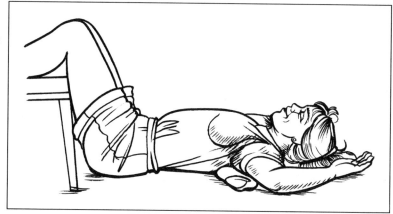

Figure 4-9:
Place a small, rolled-up towel under the middle of your spine to increase the stretch.

Exercise #2: The recumbent abdominal and shoulder blade squeeze

The recumbent abdominal and shoulder blade squeeze is designed to help reeducate your golf posture and begin rebuilding two key areas of muscle strength necessary for great posture at address: your lower abdominals and your shoulder blade muscles.

Perform this reeducation and rebuilding exercise as follows:

1. Assume the same starting position as for the recumbent chest and spine stretch (refer to Figure 4-8).

2. Contract the muscles of your lower abdominals and middle and lower shoulder blade regions so that you can feel the entire length of your spine, neck, and shoulders flattening firmly to the floor. If you are performing this exercise properly, you should feel a comfortable degree of muscle contraction while you maintain a normal, relaxed breathing pattern (see Figure 4-10).

3. Hold this contraction for three to five breaths, relax, and then repeat the exercise.

Perform this exercise at least once every other day for 2 to 3 weeks, starting with one set of 10 repetitions and building up gradually to one set of 50 repetitions as needed.

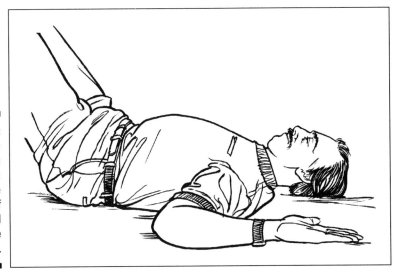

Figure 4-10:
Make sure that you feel a comfortable degree of stretch and can breathe normally.

Exercise #3: The prone torso lift

To advance the recumbent abdominal and shoulder blade squeeze exercise, you can further challenge your abdominal, spine, and shoulder blade muscles by trying the prone torso lift. This exercise provides the same golf-specific posture and structural reeducation and rebuilding benefits of the preceding exercise but to a more advanced degree.

Perform this exercise as follows:

1. Turn over on your stomach, place several large pillows under your body, and place your arms in the double "tray position" with your forehead resting on a towel roll, as shown in Figure 4-11.

2. Perform a pelvic tilt by squeezing your lower abdominal muscles, and rotate your pelvis forward.

3. Place your arms in the double "tray position," keeping your neck long and your chin tucked, and lift just your upper torso comfortably up off the pillows until you have achieved a straight spine (see Figure 4-12). Be sure to keep your neck tucked in and your lower back flat by contracting your lower abdominal muscles. Also remember to continue to breathe comfortably throughout the exercise. If you perform it properly, you should be able to achieve a lift position such that someone could place a golf club flat along your spine and have virtually no space between your spine and the clubshaft.

4. Hold the lift for three to five breaths, and then slowly relax and repeat.

Do this exercise at least every other day for 1 to 2 sets of 8 to 12 repetitions, and for about 2 to 3 weeks or until the exercise becomes very easy.

Figure 4-11:
Lie on your stomach and rest your forehead on a towel roll for the prone torso lift.

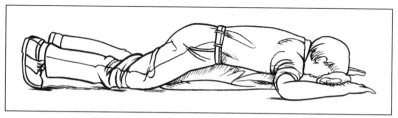

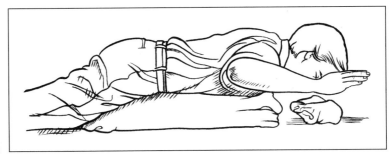

Figure 4-12:
Lift your upper torso to achieve a straight spine.

Test #2: The standing balance sway test

After posture, the next most important physical characteristic required to make an optimal and consistent golf swing is *balance*. The purpose of the standing balance sway test is to help you identify muscle and connective tissue tightness that may be pulling you out of ideal standing posture and balance, thus interfering with your posture and balance at address and during your full swing.

Perform the standing balance sway test as follows:

1. Remove your shoes and stand on a level surface with your arms hanging relaxed by your sides.

   If you have been prescribed customized orthotics (arch supports) for your shoes, please repeat this test with your orthotics in place and your shoes on.

2. Close your eyes and gently relax your body so that you can attempt to feel which direction your body would tend to drift, tip, or sway if you let it.

3. After five to ten seconds, open your eyes and identify the predominant direction of sway.

4. Repeat the test several times to determine whether you have a consistent direction of sway.

Much like a tent's center pole leaning toward a support guide wire that has been staked into the ground too tightly, the direction that you consistently feel is the first and/or strongest direction of sway is probably being caused by connective tissue and muscle tightness pulling your body in that direction. If left uncorrected, this tightness will also pull you out of posture and balance at address as well as during your swing. Any attempts to correct your swing motion without first reducing the physical causes of your posture and balance dysfunction can lead to inconsistent performance and/or injury.

Exercise #4: The single leg balance drill

Many excellent exercises can improve your standing balance as a golfer. One simple balance reeducation exercise is called the single leg balance drill.

Perform this balance reeducation exercise as follows:

1. Stand on a firm, flat surface in your bare or stocking feet.

   If you have been prescribed customized orthotics (arch supports) for your shoes, please repeat this exercise with your orthotics in place and your shoes on.

2. Place a club behind your spine as though you were attempting to perform the club behind the spine test (refer to Figure 4-4).

3. With your eyes open, attempt to stand and balance on your right leg only by lifting your left knee to approximately 90 degrees so that your left thigh is parallel to the floor (see Figure 4-13). In this position, do your best to maintain your balance for 10 to 15 seconds.

4. Repeat the exercise with your left leg down, lifting your right knee to 90 degrees.

Figure 4-13:
Attempt to balance in this position for 10 to 15 seconds.

Do this exercise 10 to 20 times with each leg at least once each day for 2 to 3 weeks or until you can easily perform the exercise without losing your balance on one foot in 15 seconds.

To increase the difficulty of this exercise and improve your golf balance even more, try the exercise with your *eyes closed!* You can imagine how much more balanced you'll feel over the ball at address and during your full swing when you can master this exercise with your eyes open and then with your eyes closed.

Test #3: The seated trunk rotation test

Adequate rotation flexibility in the spine and hips are two other essential physical performance requirements for optimal and safe golf. Without proper rotation flexibility in your hips and spine, you're unable to make a complete, well-balanced backswing and follow-through. Furthermore, movement compensations that you will most certainly make as a result will force typical biomechanical swing flaws such as reverse pivots, lateral sways, and coming over the top. Moreover, compensations from a lack of spine and hip rotation flexibility create stress in other body areas that aren't designed to rotate. If left uncorrected, this physical limitation will eventually spell disaster by causing an injury.

The next two tests can help you evaluate your rotation flexibility in these two body areas.

The first test is called the seated trunk rotation test. Perform this test as follows:

1. Sit forward in a chair so that your spine is not resting against the back of the chair.

2. Place a golf club across the front of your chest and shoulders (at the collarbone level) and hold the club securely to your chest and shoulders by crossing both hands in front of you (see Figure 4-14).

3. Sit as tall as possible in the chair, keep your feet flat on the floor, both knees pointing straight ahead, and turn your upper torso as far as comfortably possible to the right (see Figure 4-15).

4. When you have turned completely, look over your right shoulder and see where the end of the club is pointing behind you. Mentally mark the spot on the wall and estimate the approximate number of degrees of rotation that you have turned to the right.

5. Slowly return to the neutral starting position and then repeat the trunk rotation test to the left.

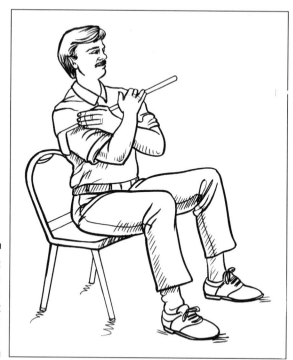

Figure 4-14:
Hold a club
securely to
your chest
and
shoulders.

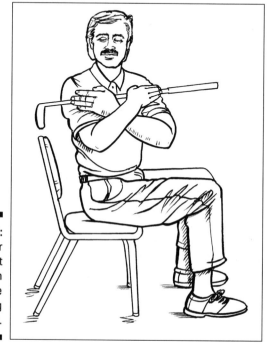

Figure 4-15:
Turn as far
to the right
as you can
while
remaining
comfortable.

Repeat this test in both directions three to five times to get a good estimate of the amount of trunk rotation in each direction and which direction you can rotate farther and/or easier.

Exercise #5: The supine trunk rotation stretch

The supine trunk rotation stretch is a good releasing exercise to help improve your ability to complete a stress-free backswing and follow-through. If the seated trunk rotation test (Test #3) identified limitations in one or both directions, this exercise can help you gain the needed flexibility in the proper region of your spine and enable a better turn.

Perform this releasing exercise as follows:

1. Lie on your back with your hips and knees bent so that your feet are flat on the floor and your arms rest comfortably away from your sides in the double "tray position" (see Figure 4-16).

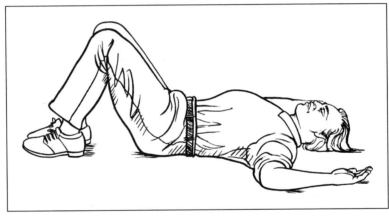

Figure 4-16: Lie on your back with your knees bent and your arms in the double "tray position."

2. Gently squeeze your shoulder blades and flatten your neck to the floor while you slowly and gently rotate your legs to the left.

3. Continue to slowly twist your body, keeping your right shoulder blade and forearm flat to the floor until you begin to feel a comfortable stretch in your spine and possibly in your right hip and the front of your right shoulder (see Figure 4-17).

4. Hold this position for three to five minutes or until you feel a *complete* release of the gentle stretch in your body. You can enhance the stretch in this position by bringing your left hand down from the "tray position" and gently pressing down on the top of your right thigh, as shown in Figure 4-17.

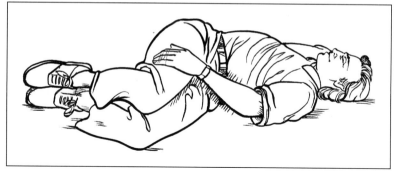

Figure 4-17: Twist your legs to the left until you feel a comfortable stretch.

5. Slowly return to the neutral starting position and then repeat the stretch, this time rotating your legs to the right.

Practice this releasing exercise at least once a day for two to three weeks until you can stretch equally well in both directions. If you evaluated that your spine was more stiff or limited in rotation when turning to your right during the seated trunk rotation test, you want to spend more time initially rotating your legs to the left. Likewise, if you evaluated that your trunk rotation flexibility was more limited when turning to your left, then initially rotate your legs to the right in this exercise. Your ultimate goal is *balanced* rotation in both directions.

Test #4: The seated hip rotation test

The seated hip rotation test is designed to measure the relative degree of rotation flexibility in your hips. This test can identify whether you may have significant tightness in one or both hips that may be interfering with your ability to rotate your hips during your golf swing. Poor hip rotation is one of the major causes of low back pain for golfers and can cause poor full swing performance and inconsistency.

Perform the seated hip rotation test as follows:

1. Sit forward in a chair so that your spine is not resting against the back of the chair.

2. Sit as tall as possible with your spine straight. Cross your right leg over your left knee so that the outer portion of your right ankle rests on the top of your left knee (see Figure 4-18).

3. Without losing your sitting posture, take both hands and gently apply downward pressure to the top of your right knee until you cannot comfortably push your shin any closer to a position parallel to the floor (see Figure 4-19).

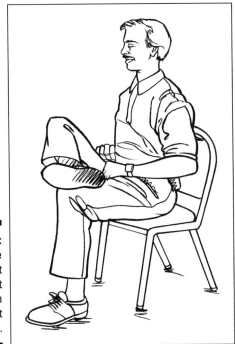

Figure 4-18:
Rest the outer part of your right ankle on your left knee.

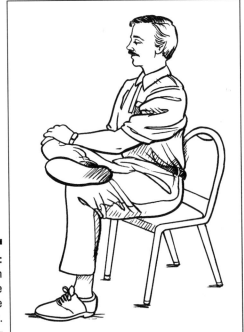

Figure 4-19:
Gently push your knee toward the floor.

4. When you have reached the limit of stretch for your right hip, observe your relative difficulty in achieving this position, the specific location and degree of tightness in your body, and the relative angle of your right shin compared to parallel with the floor.

5. Slowly release your right knee and repeat the test with your left ankle resting on your right knee.

6. Compare the results of testing both hips and determine whether one or both hips have rotation flexibility limitations.

Exercise #6: The supine hip rotation stretch

The supine hip rotation stretch is a safe and effective exercise to help you reduce your hip rotation tightness and, therefore, improve your ability to make a full turn around your hips during a full golf swing.

Perform this releasing exercise as follows:

1. Lie on your back close to a wall. Place both feet on the wall so that your hips and knees are bent to approximately 90 degrees. (See Figure 4-20.)

Figure 4-20:
Put your feet against a wall with your knees bent at a 90-degree angle.

2. Cross your right foot over your left knee and rest both hands on the top of your right knee.

3. Gently apply pressure to your right knee with your hands in a direction that is down and away from your right shoulder (see Figure 4-21) until you feel a light, comfortable stretch in the outer portion of your right hip and/or in the groin.

4. Hold this stretch for three to five minutes or until you feel a complete release of the original stretch in your right hip.

5. After the stretch is complete, slowly release the pressure on your right knee and repeat the stretch on your left hip.

Practice this releasing exercise at least once a day for two to three weeks or until you can stretch equally well in both hips. If you evaluated one hip to be tighter than the other during the seated hip rotation test, then initially spend more time stretching the tighter hip. Similar to the trunk rotation stretch, your ultimate goal is *balanced rotation* for both hips. Only by achieving complete and balanced hip rotation flexibility can you accomplish a full backswing and follow-through with each and every swing.

After you are balanced, you can advance this stretch simply by moving your body closer to the wall at the starting position. Doing so enables your hips and knees to bend at an angle greater than 90 degrees and enables a greater degree of stretch in your hips during the exercise.

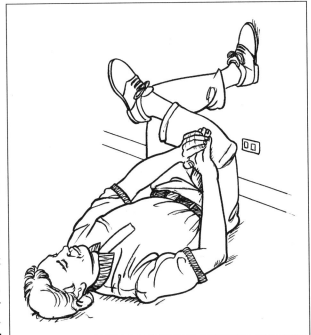

Figure 4-21:
Put gentle pressure on your knee until you feel a light stretch in your hip and/or groin.

Chapter 5

Should I Get a Formal Education?

. . . .

In This Chapter

▶ Keeping a record of how you've played

▶ Getting the most for your golf lesson money

▶ Knowing where to go for lessons

▶ Getting information from other sources

. . . .

Suppose that you just started to play golf by hitting some balls at the driving range. Your friends took you over to the range at lunch, and you launched a couple of balls into the sunshine and thought you might want to learn the game. Where do you go?

✔ **You can learn from books.** There are many books written on golf instruction that can lead you through the fundamentals of the game. You can go only so far by teaching yourself from a book, however.

✔ **You can learn from friends.** Most of us start out this way, which is why we develop so many swing faults. Friends' intentions are good, but their teaching abilities come under serious speculation.

✔ **You can learn by hitting balls.** I learned to play the game this way. The flight of the ball told me everything. I would go to the driving range and hit balls day and night. The pure act of swinging a golf club in a certain way made the ball fly in different trajectories and curves. This learning process is a very slow one because you have to learn through experimentation.

✔ **You can take lessons from a PGA golf professional.** This is the most expensive and most efficient way to learn the game. Lessons can cost as little as $8 an hour and as much as $250 an hour. The expensive guys are the ones you read about in *Golf Digest* and *Golf Magazine* and the ones you watch on TV. All golf professionals can help you with the basics of the game and get you started in the right direction.

Ten things a good instructor should have

1. Lots of golf balls
2. Patience
3. A sense of humor
4. Enthusiasm
5. An ability to teach players at all levels
6. An ability to explain the same thing in ten different ways

7. An encouraging manner
8. A method that he or she believes in
9. An ability to adapt that method to your needs
10. More golf balls

Finding Out What You Need to Work On

Keeping a record of how you've played for a few weeks before taking a lesson is a good idea. This information is invaluable for your pro. And don't track just your scores. Keep track of

- ✔ How many fairways you hit
- ✔ How many greens you hit
- ✔ How many putts you average
- ✔ How many strokes it ordinarily takes you to get the ball into the hole from a greenside bunker

Tracking all these things may seem like overkill, but doing so helps the pro quickly detect tendencies or weaknesses in your game. Then the pro knows where to look for your problems. If nothing else, tracking your play saves time — time you're paying for! Figure 5-1 shows how to keep track of these numbers on your scorecard.

Blue Tees	White Tees	Par	Hcp	JOHN			HOLE	HIT FAIRWAY	HIT GREEN		NO. PUTTS		Hcp	Par	Red Tees
Men's Course Rating/Slope Blue 73.1/137 White 71.0/130													Women's Course Rating/Slope Red 73.7/128		
377	361	4	11	4			1	✓	✓		2		13	4	310
514	467	5	13	8			2	✓	0		3		3	5	428
446	423	4	1	7			3	0	0		2		1	4	389
376	356	4	5	6			4	0	0		2		11	4	325
362	344	4	7	5			5	0	✓		3		7	4	316
376	360	4	9	6			6	✓	0		2		9	4	335
166	130	3	17	4			7	0	✓		3		17	3	108
429	407	4	3	5			8	✓	✓		3		5	4	368
161	145	3	15	5			9	0	0		2		15	3	122
3207	2993	35		50			Out	4	4		22			35	2701
			Initial										**Initial**		
366	348	4	18	5			10	0	0		2		14	4	320
570	537	5	10	7			11	✓	0		3		2	5	504
438	420	4	2	5			12	✓	0		2		6	4	389
197	182	3	12	4			13	0	0		2		16	3	145
507	475	5	14	5			14	✓	✓		2		4	5	425
398	380	4	4	5			15	0	✓		3		8	4	350
380	366	4	6	5			16	✓	0		2		10	4	339
165	151	3	16	4			17	0	0		2		18	3	133
397	375	4	8	5			18	0	0		2		12	4	341
3418	3234	36		45			In	3	2		20			36	2946
6625	6227	71		95			Tot	7	6		42			71	5647
Handicap													**Handicap**		
Net Score													**Net Score**		
Adjust													**Adjust**		

Scorer   **Attested**   **Date**

Figure 5-1: Keep a record of how many fairways and greens you hit and how many putts you hit. Your teacher will then be able to identify any problem areas.

Getting the Most from Your Lessons

Much has been written in the last ten years or so about the relationship between Nick Faldo and his former teacher, David Leadbetter. Under Leadbetter's guidance, Faldo turned himself from a pretty good player into a great player. In the process, Leadbetter — quite rightly — received a lot of praise and attention. Ultimately, however, the teacher is only as good as the pupil. And Faldo, with his extraordinary dedication and total belief in what he was told, may have been the best pupil in the history of golf.

When you take lessons, you need that same kind of faith. There's no point in going to someone you don't believe in for lessons. If you find yourself doubting what you're being told, you're wasting everybody's time. Change instructors if that happens — if your instructor doesn't tell you to go elsewhere first.

Be honest

Okay, so you're on the lesson tee with your pro. What's the drill? The first thing you need to be is completely honest. Tell your instructor your problems (your *golf* problems), your goals, the shots you find difficult. Tell him or her what style of learning — visual, auditorial, or kinesthetic — you find easiest. For example, do you like to be shown how to do something and then copy it? Or do you prefer to have that same something explained in detail so that you understand it?

Gratuitous solicitation: At the Kostis/McCord Learning Center at Grayhawk Golf Course in Scottsdale, Arizona, our sports psychologist, Dr. Don Greene, has each student take a personality test of about 100 questions. He compiles the information on a computer and then personalizes the most efficient manner in which our instructors can teach each student. Our instructors save valuable time because they know which teaching technique is best for each student. By utilizing this type of information, they develop a much better relationship with their students.

No matter which technique you prefer, the instructor needs to know what it is. How else can the instructor be effective in teaching you something new? The bottom line is that the pro needs to know anything that helps create an accurate picture of you and your game. Don't be shy or embarrassed. Believe me, there's nothing you can say that your instructor hasn't heard before!

Listen to feedback

Now that you've done some talking, make sure that you let the pro reciprocate. Listen to what the pro has to say. After the pro has evaluated both you and your swing, he or she will be able to give you feedback on where you should go from there. Feedback is part of every good lesson. So keep listening. Take notes if you have to.

Don't rate the success or failure of a session on how many balls you hit. You can hit very few shots and have a very productive lesson. It depends on what you need to work on. An instructor may have you repeat a certain swing in an attempt to develop a *swing thought,* or feel. You will notice when the suggested change is becoming more effective. Let the professional tell you when to hit and which club to use.

Don't do what a lot of people do; don't swing or hit while the pro is talking. Imagine that you're a smart chicken crossing the road — stop, look, and listen!

Overcome your doubts

Take it from me: Five minutes into every lesson, you're going to have doubts. The pro will change something in your swing, grip, or stance, and you'll feel weird. Well, think about this: You should feel weird. What you've been doing wrong has become ingrained into your method so that it feels comfortable. Change what's wrong for the better, and of course it'll feel strange at first. That's normal. Don't panic. You'll probably get worse before you get better. You're changing things to improve them, not just for the heck of it. So give what you're told to do a proper chance. Changes rarely work in five short minutes. Give them at least a couple of weeks to take effect. More than two weeks is too long; go back for another lesson.

Ask questions

Ask questions during your lesson. The pro is an expert, and you're paying good money, so take advantage of the pro's knowledge while he or she "belongs" to you. Don't be afraid of sounding stupid. Again, your question won't be anything the pro hasn't heard a million times before. Besides, what's the point of spending good money on something you don't understand?

The professional is trained to teach, so he or she will know any number of ways to say the same thing. One of those ways will push your particular button. But if you don't tell the pro that you don't "get it," he or she won't know. Speak up!

Ten rules to follow while learning

1. Find a good teacher and stick with that person.

2. Follow a timetable. Discipline yourself to work on what you've been told.

3. Concentrate.

4. Learn from your mistakes. You'll make them, so you may as well make them work for you.

5. Relax. Take your time, and you'll learn and play better.

6. Practice the shots you find most difficult.

7. Have goals. Remember, golf is a target game.

8. Stay positive. Golf is hard enough. A bad attitude only hurts you.

9. Stop practicing when you get tired. That's how sloppy habits begin.

10. Evaluate yourself after each lesson: Are you making progress?

Stay calm

Finally, stay calm. Anxious people don't make good pupils. Look on the lesson as the learning experience it is, and don't get too wrapped up in where the balls are going. Again, the pro will be aware of your nervousness. Ask him or her for tips on swinging smoothly. Nervous golfers tend to swing too quickly, so keep your swing smooth. Give yourself "time" during your swing to make the changes. What's important at this stage is that you make the proper moves in the correct sequence. Get those moves right and understand the order, and good shots are a given.

Where to Go for Lessons

Golf lessons are usually available wherever balls are hit and golf is played. Driving ranges. Public courses. Resorts. Private clubs. The price usually increases in that same order — driving range pros usually charge the least. As for quality, if the pro is PGA qualified, you can be reasonably sure that he or she will know how to help you improve.

A qualified PGA teaching professional may charge between $25 and $50 per session, which can range from 30 minutes to an hour. A professional has a good sense of how much to tell you and at what rate of speed; not all lessons require a specific amount of time.

When checking out places that offer golf lessons, ask whether they have video analysis capabilities. I know this sounds like some kind of psychology experiment from your college days, but videotaping your lessons can be helpful. When you're able to watch yourself on video, you and your instructor can pinpoint problem areas for improvement. If nothing else, a video record is a great way to track and monitor your progress as you build your fundamental skills.

Golf schools

No matter where you live in the United States, a golf school should be fairly close by. Golf schools are set up for all levels of players. And a lot of them are aimed at those just learning the game. Appendix B contains a listing of recommended golf schools.

Golf schools are great for beginners. You'll find yourself in a group — anything from 3 to 20 strong, which is perfect for you. There's safety in numbers, and it's reassuring. You'll find that you're not the only beginner. And you never know: Watching others struggle and work with their own problems may help you with *your* game.

Most of the better golf schools advertise in golf magazines. Be warned, though. These schools tend to be relatively expensive. They did very well in the 1980s when the economy was perceived to be strong and people had more disposable income. Since then, however, golf schools haven't been so successful. Golf school lessons are big-ticket items, which makes them among the first things people omit from their yearly budgets.

Having said that, many people are still going to golf schools. Why? Because they work. You get, on average, three days of intensive coaching on all aspects of the game from a good teacher. Because the groups are usually small, you get lots of one-on-one attention, too. Then you have the experiences of others. You can learn a lot by paying attention to what your fellow students are being told. Don't feel that you have to be hitting shots all the time. Take regular breaks — especially if you're not used to hitting a lot of balls — and use the time to learn. Soak up all the information you can. Besides, regular breaks are the best way I know to avoid those blisters you see on the hands of golf school students!

Driving ranges

I used to work at a driving range in Riverside, California. I spent hours picking up golf balls on the range and hitting those same balls when I was off work. The range was bare of any grass, the balls were old, and the flood lights had lost their luminance. But it was a great spot to learn the travails of the game.

Driving ranges have changed a lot since then. They are very sophisticated, with two or three tiers and putting greens, and many have miniature golf courses attached to them. Some very good (and some not so good) instructors work at these facilities. Most of them can show you the basic mechanics of the swing and get you off on the right foot.

Inquire at your local driving range whether the pro is a PGA golf professional. If so, you can be assured that he or she is fully qualified to guide you through golf's lesson book. If not, he or she still may know a lot about the game, but proceed with caution.

Local clubs

Even if you're not a member, getting a lesson from the local club pro is usually possible. He or she will probably charge a little more than a driving range pro, but the facilities will likely be a lot better. Certainly, the golf balls will be. And chances are, you'll have access to a putting green and a practice bunker, so you can get short-game help, too.

Playing lessons

A playing lesson is just what it sounds like. You hire a professional to play any number of holes with you. This theme has three main variations, all of which can help you become a better golfer.

- **You can do all the playing.** The professional walks with you, observing your strategy, swing, and style, and makes suggestions as you go. I'd recommend this sort of lesson if you're the type of person who likes one-on-one direction.

- **You can both play.** That way, you get the chance to receive instruction and the opportunity to observe an expert player in action. If you typically learn more by watching and copying what you see, this type of lesson is effective. Pay particular attention to the rhythm of the pro's swing, the way he or she manages his or her game, and how you can incorporate both into your own game.

- **The pro can manufacture typical on-course situations for you to deal with.** For example, the pro may place your ball behind a tree, point out your options and then ask you to choose one and explain your choice. Your answer and the subsequent advice from the pro help make you a better player. Imagine that you have two escape routes — one easy, one hard. All the easy one involves is a simple little chip shot back to the fairway. Trouble is, because you won't be gaining any distance, you might feel like you wasted a shot. The difficult shot — through a narrow gap in the branches — is tempting because the reward will be so much greater. But failure will be disastrous. Hit the tree, and you could take nine or ten shots on the hole. Decisions, decisions! Remember, there's more to golf than just hitting the ball.

Gary's favorite teachers nationwide

These teachers will teach absolutely anybody who wants to be taught — male or female, young or old. They are expensive — $100 to $350 an hour. Some of them teach at schools, and some you can't find anywhere (like Mac O'Grady). But these are some of the best instructors.

Teacher	Location
Chuck Cook	Barton Creek Lakeside; Austin, Texas; 800-888-2257
Jim Flick	Nicklaus/Flick Golf School; Scottsdale, Arizona; 800-642-5528
Hank Haney	Hank Haney Golf Ranch; McKinney, Texas; 214-542-2221
Butch Harmon	Lochinvar Golf Club; Houston, Texas; 713-821-0220
Peter Kostis	Kostis/McCord Learning Center; Scottsdale, Arizona; 602-502-1800
David Leadbetter	Lake Nona Golf Club; Orlando, Florida; 407-857-8276
Jim McLean	Doral Golf Resort & Spa; Miami, Florida; 805-592-2000
Mac O'Grady	Planet Earth (sometimes — don't even try to make contact)
Phil Rodgers	Grand Cypress Academy of Golf; San Diego, California; 407-239-1975
Bob Toski	20914 Hamaca Ct.,Boca Raton, Florida; 33433; 561-483-7299

Other Sources of Information

There's little doubt that the golf swing is the most analyzed move in all of sports. As such, more has been written — and continues to be written — about the golf swing than about any other athletic move. Take a look in any bookstore under *Golf,* and you'll see what I mean. Maybe you have, since you're reading this book. (You made a great choice!)

Bookin' it

So where should you go for written advice? Lots more books are out there, and some are quite good. But most books, sad to say, are the same old stuff regurgitated over and over. Remember: There hasn't been any original thought since the 15th century!

Gary's favorite golf instruction books

An amazing number of books have been written on golf. Historians have tried to track every hook and slice throughout golf's existence. Many have documented the footsteps of the great players throughout their careers.

But instruction is the main vein of golf books nowadays. There are books on every method of golf instruction, from household tools used as teaching aids to scientific data compiled by aliens used on the planet Blothar. (Okay, so the data compiled by aliens is a stretch.)

Anyhow, here are my favorite golf instruction books, listed alphabetically by author. I have tried to help by reducing the list to my ten favorites, but I know that there are many more that should be included. The material is inexhaustible, so take your time and peruse this golf library with an open mind.

Author	Book	Date of Publication
Tommy Armour	*How to Play Your Best Golf All the Time* (published by Simon & Schuster)	1953
Percy Boomer	*On Learning Golf* (published by Knopf)	1992
John Duncan Dunn	*Natural Golf* (published by Putnam's)	1931
Arnold Haultain	*The Mystery of Golf,* which is totally out of print, but still my favorite (published by Houghton Mifflin Co.)	1908
Ben Hogan	*Five Lessons: The Modern Fundamentals of Golf* (published by Barnes)	1957
Horace Hutchinson	*Golf: The Badminton Library* (published by Longmans, Green)	1890
Ernest Jones	*Swing the Clubhead* (published by Dodd, Mead)	1952
Robert T. Jones, Jr., and O. B. Keeler	*Down the Fairway* (published by Minton, Balch)	1927
Jack Nicklaus	*Golf My Way* (published by Simon & Schuster)	1974
Harvey Penick	*Harvey Penick's Little Red Book* (published by Simon & Schuster)	1992

Note: Some of these books are real collector's items and may be hard to track down. For any you can't find, contact George Lewis, Golfiana, P. O. Box 291, Mamaroneck, NY 10543; 914-698-4579.

Here's another secret: Stay away from many of the books "written" by the top players. There's nothing inherently wrong with the information they impart, but if you think you're going to get some stunning insight into how your favorite plays, think again. In all likelihood, the author has had little to do with the text. Exceptions exist, of course, but the input of the "name" player is often minimal.

Monthly magazine fixes

The best instructional magazines are *Golf Digest, Golf Magazine,* and *Golf Tips.* They are published monthly and owe most of their popularity to their expertise in the instructional field. Indeed, most people buy these magazines because they think that the articles will help them play better. They all do a good job of covering each aspect of the game every month. If you're putting badly, for example, you'll find a new tip that you can try every month. Best of all, these magazines use only the best players and teachers to author their stories. So the information you receive is second to none.

But is the information in golf magazines the best? *Sometimes.* The key is to be careful of what you read and subsequently take to the course. Top teacher Bob Toski once said, "You cannot learn how to play golf from the pages of a magazine." And he's right. Use these publications as backups to your lessons. Nothing more. Do not try everything in every issue. You'll finish up hopelessly confused. Be selective.

Don't get the idea that I don't like these magazines. I've authored a few instruction pieces for *Golf Digest* over the years myself. But by definition, these stories are general in nature. They are not aimed specifically at *your* game. Of course, some stories will happen to be for you. But most stories won't. You have to be able to filter out those that aren't.

Videos: Feel the rhythm

As more and more Americans install VCRs in their living rooms, the popularity of instructional videos grows. Videos have a lot to offer instructionally. Because they can convey movement and rhythm so much better than their print counterparts, videos are perfect for visual learners. Indeed, watching a video of a top professional hitting balls before you leave for the course isn't a bad idea. The smoothness and timing in an expert's swing has a way of rubbing off on you.

You can buy golf instruction videos in any store that sells videos, including golf shops, and you can order some of them from the back of your favorite golf magazines.

Gary's favorite golf instruction videos

Like books, a bountiful supply of golf videos is on the market. They range from *Dorf on Golf* by Tim Conway to very sophisticated videos on the do's and don'ts of your golf swing. Here's a list of my favorites.

Author	Video	Description
Fred Couples	*Couples on Tempo*	Who could tell it better than Freddie for tempo?
Ben Crenshaw	*The Art of Putting*	This video is a must-see for golfers of any caliber.
Nick Faldo	*Nick Faldo's Tips and Drills*	Faldo shares his secrets about what to do when your swing needs adjusting.
David Leadbetter	*Faults and Fixes*	Pause the video and find your fault and cure.
David Leadbetter	*Leadbetter's Simple Secrets*	This video provides easy-to-understand explanations.
David Leadbetter	*The Full Golf Swing*	An overview from the master.
Harvey Penick	*Harvey Penick's Little Red Video*	The video that was born out of one of the most popular golf books ever written, *Harvey Penick's Little Red Book*.
Harvey Penick	*The Little Green Video*	Harvey Penick elaborates more on his "homey" style of golf instruction.
Rick Smith	*Rick Smith's Range Tips*	An up-and-coming golf instructor gives his version of remedies.
Donna White	*Beginning Golf For Women*	Simple, easy to understand, and well produced.

Instructional gizmos

A quick look at the classified section of any golf magazine will tell you that lots of little instructional gizmos are available. Most aren't very good. Some are okay. And a few are excellent.

GARY SAYS

Gary's favorite instructional gizmos

Gizmo	*Function*	*Where to Find It*
A 2-x-4 board	Lies on the ground to aid your alignment.	Hardware store or lumber yard
Balance board	A platform with a balance point in the middle. The only way you can swing and hit the ball is by staying in balance.	Mail order
Chalk line	A builder's tool used to help your putting stroke. The line is caked in chalk. You "snap" it to indicate the line you want to the hole.	Hardware store
"Flammer"	A harness across your chest with an attachment for a shaft in the middle. When you turn as if to swing, you get the feeling of your arms and body turning together because of a telescopic rod that connects the club to your chest.	Mail order
Head freezer	Attaches to your cap. You look through a rectangular frame so that you can check the amount your head is moving during your swing/stroke.	Mail order
Perfect swing trainer	A large, circular ring that you lay your shaft against as you swing. Helps keep your swing on plane.	Mail order
Putting connector	A device that fits between your arms, keeping them apart and steady during the stroke.	Mail order or a few golf shops
Sens-o-grip	Bleeps if you grip too tightly.	Mail order or most golf shops
Spray paint	A can of paint enables you to spray lines on the ground, which helps with alignment and swingpath.	Hardware store
Swing straps	Hook them on your body to keep your arms close to your sides during the swing.	Mail order or most golf shops

Chapter 6

Where to Play and Who to Play With

In This Chapter

▶ Warming up at driving ranges

▶ Reserving tee time on public courses

▶ Fitting in at country clubs

▶ Blending into your golf foursome

Golf is played in three places: on public courses, at private clubs, and on resort courses. Some courses have as few as 9 holes, and others have as many as six 18-hole courses at one facility. You can also hit balls at driving ranges, which is where you should start. If you rush to the nearest public course, tee up for the first time, and then spend most of the next few hours missing the ball, you're not going to be very popular with the group behind you. Pretty soon, they're going to get tired of watching you. Believe me, instead of watching you move large clumps of earth with every swing, they'd rather be contemplating whether to have that second glass of a cool beverage in the clubhouse.

Driving Ranges

Driving ranges are where to start. You can make as many mistakes as you want. You can miss the ball. Slice it. Duff it. Top it. Anything. The only people who'll know are the people next to you, who are probably making the same mistakes. And believe me, they won't care. They've got their own problems.

Driving ranges are basically large fields, stretching to as much as 500 yards in length. Which means, of course, that even the longest hitters of the golf ball can turn to turbo warp. But you don't have to hit your driver. A good driving range will have signs marking off 50 yards, 100 yards, 150 yards, and so on. You can practice hitting to these targets with any club.

Some driving ranges provide clubs for your use, but most expect you to bring your own. As for balls, you purchase bucketfuls for a few dollars. The bigger the bucket, the more it costs.

Public Courses

As you'd expect from their name, public courses are open to anyone who can afford the greens fee. As such, they tend to be busy, especially on weekends and holidays. Some golfers sleep in their cars overnight just so they can get an early tee time the next morning. Sleeping in a car may not sound like fun on the surface, but I'm told that it's a great bonding experience.

Tee-time policies

Most of the time, the course you want to play will have its own tee-time policy. Find out what it is. Many courses let you book a time up to a week in advance. Make sure that you book a starting time at least 24 hours in advance. Some courses even have a strange policy whereby you have to show up at a designated time midweek to sign up for weekend play. And some courses you can't book at all. You just show up and take your chance. Hence the overnight gang sleeping in their cars.

Okay, I'll assume that you've jumped through whatever hoops are necessary and you know when you are supposed to tee off. So you pull into the parking lot about an hour before your allotted time. What next? Most places have a clubhouse. You may want to stop there to buy a drink or food and change your clothes.

By all means, make use of the clubhouse, but don't change your shoes there. If you are already dressed to hit the greens, put on your spikes in the parking lot. Then throw your street shoes into the trunk. You won't look out of place knotting those laces with your foot on the car bumper. Everyone does it!

I'm here! Now what?

The first thing to do when you arrive at the clubhouse is to confirm your time with the pro or starter and then pay for your round. The pro is sure to be in one of two places: teaching on the practice range or hanging out in the pro shop. If the pro doesn't take the money, the starter adjacent to the first tee usually will. As for cost, the price depends on the standard of the course and its location. You can pay anything from $10 to $150.

After you have the financial formalities out of the way, hit some balls on the driving range to warm up those creaky joints of yours. You can buy a bucket of about 40 balls from either the pro or the starter.

Here's what I do when I'm playing in a Tour event. Your practice sessions won't be this long, but I need time to try to figure out how to beat Greg Norman. I don't think I'll ever have enough time!

I get to the golf course one hour before my starting time. I go to the putting green and practice short shots — chip shots and short pitches. (Chapter 10 covers these shots in detail.) Make sure that on your golf course you are allowed to pitch to the practice green; some courses don't allow it. This practice gives me an idea how fast the greens are and slowly loosens me up for full-swing shots.

Then I wander over to the practice tee and loosen up with some of the exercises that I describe throughout Part II. Start with the sand wedges and work your way up to the driver. I hit balls with my even-numbered clubs, starting with the wedge, 8-, 6-, 4-, and then 2-iron. I have no idea why!

Next, I hit my 3-metal wood. Then I proceed to bomb the driver. If John Daly is next to me, I quietly wait for him to finish and then hit my driver. Most of the people have left by then. Immediately after hitting the driver, ten balls at most, I hit some short sand wedge shots to slow down my metabolism.

I hit the putting green next, usually 15 minutes before I tee off. (See Chapter 9 for detailed information about putting.) I start with simple 2- to 3-foot putts straight up a hill so that I can build my confidence. Then I proceed to very long putts — not to the hole, but to the far fringe of the green. I do this because I don't want to become target conscious on the long putts. Putting the ball to the opposite fringe lets me work on speed. That's the last thing I do before going to the tee. (Well, I do go to the restroom first because I get real nervous.)

Country Clubs

In your early days as a golfer, you are unlikely to play much of your golf at country clubs. But if you do play at a country club, don't panic. You're still playing golf; it's just that the "goalposts" have been shifted slightly. In order not to commit a social faux pas, you must be familiar with a few formalities:

✔ **Time your arrival so that you have just over an hour to spare before you tee off.** You need to do a few things before you get that driver in your hands.

✔ **Before you leave home, make sure that you're wearing the right clothes.** It's unlikely that a sweatshirt announcing you as an avid follower of the Chicago Bulls or those cool (in your mind, anyway) cut-off jeans will work in this environment. Wear a shirt with a collar and, if shorts are allowed, go for the tailored variety that stops just short of your knees. Short shorts are a no-no at most country clubs. In fall and winter, slacks are acceptable for women. In the summer, shorts cut just above the knees are fine.

✔ **Get good directions to your destination.** It won't do your heart rate or your golf game any good to have a stressful journey during which you get lost six or seven times.

✔ **When you drive your car up the road toward the clubhouse, don't make the simple mistake of turning sharply into the parking lot.** Go right up to the clubhouse. A person will no doubt be waiting to greet you. Acknowledge his cheery hello as if this is something you do every day. Tell him who you're playing with — your host. Then get out of your car, pop the trunk, remove your spikes, slip him a couple of bucks and your keys, and stroll into the clubhouse.

Don't worry about your car or your clubs. The car will be parked for you, and the clubs will either be loaded onto a cart or handed to a caddie.

✔ **After you're inside the clubhouse, head for the locker room.** Drop your street shoes off next to your host's locker and then ask for directions to the bar, or to wherever your host is waiting.

Don't offer to buy your host a drink, for two reasons. First, he's the host. And second, you probably won't be able to buy anything, anyway. He'll most likely sign the tab and be billed at the end of the month. (The only place where your cash/plastic will be accepted is the professional's shop. The pro will sell you anything, but take my advice: Skip the purchase of that neat-looking shirt with the club logo on it. Every time you wear it, people will assume that you're a member there. The questions will soon get old.)

After your round, your clubs will probably disappear again. Don't worry. They'll be waiting in the bag drop when you finish your refreshing post-round beverage. Don't forget to tip the bag-handlers. Again, a couple of bucks is usually fine.

✔ **When you change back into your street shoes, you'll often find them newly polished.** That means another tip. And when you leave, your golf shoes will have been done, too. Aren't country clubs grand?

- ✔ **One more tip to go.** Give it to the person who delivers your car back to you and loads your clubs into the trunk.

- ✔ **On the course, be yourself.** And don't worry about shooting the best round of golf you've ever played. Your host won't expect that. Even if you happen to play badly, your host won't be too bothered as long as you look as if you're having fun and keep trying. Just don't complain or make excuses. Nobody wants to hear them, and you'll be branded as a whiner.

Resort Courses

You're on vacation, and you want to play golf. Where to go? To a resort course, of course. Some of my favorite resort courses include Kapalua (Maui, Hawaii), Doral (Miami, Florida), and Hilton Head Island (South Carolina).

The great thing about resort courses is that you don't have to be a member or even have one in tow. The only problem arises when you aren't staying in the right place. Some courses are for certain hotel guests only. And again, prices vary, depending on the course and its location. Generally, though, resort courses cost more than public courses.

Make a phone call ahead of time to find out when you can play. Then show up. Resort courses are a lot like public courses, but some have bag handlers and so on. Tip them as you would at a private club.

You'll probably have to use a cart, too. There are very few resort golf courses in the world that don't have mandatory carts. So enjoy the ride!

Introducing Yourself to the First Tee

Lots of interesting things happen on first tees. I cover the gambling aspect of this initial get-together in Chapter 16, but you should be aware of some other things as well.

If you're playing with your friends, you don't need any help from me. You know them, and they know you. You should be able to come up with a game by yourselves. And you'll be able to say anything to them, with no risk of offending anyone.

That's not the case if you show up looking for a game. Say you're at a public course and you have asked the starter to squeeze you in (a few bucks will usually get you off sooner rather than later). Tell the starter your present skill level. If you're a beginner, you don't want to be teaming up with three low-handicap players. Forget all that stuff about how the handicap system allows anyone to play with anyone. That propaganda doesn't take human nature into account.

This game, like life, has its share of snobs. And, generally speaking, the worst are single-digit handicappers. Most of them have no interest in playing with you, a mere beginner. They might say that they do, but they're lying. They see 18 holes with someone who can't break 100 as four to five hours of torture. The same is true on the PGA Tour. Some pros genuinely enjoy the Wednesday Pro-Ams — Mark O'Meara comes to mind — but a lot would gladly skip it given the chance. The only upside from their point of view is that it represents a practice round of sorts. Now that may seem an awful and despicable attitude — from a pro or an amateur — but it's a fact of golfing life. No one will actually say anything to you (people are generally much too polite), but the attitude is there. Get used to it.

Maybe I'm being a little harsh, but there's plenty of anecdotal evidence. It's a fact that the golfers of the world are more comfortable playing with their "own kind." Watch a few groups play off the first tee. You'll soon see a trend. Almost every foursome consists of four players of relatively equal ability. There's a reason for that. Make that two reasons. No one wants to be the weak link in the chain. And no one wants to play with those hackers who can't keep up.

So you're paired with Gary, Jack, and Arnold. Introduce yourself without giving away too many secrets. Tell them what you normally shoot, if and when they ask, and make it clear that you are a relatively new golfer. This information is impossible to conceal, so don't try. They'll know within a couple of holes anyway. But don't volunteer any further information. Save that for during the round. Besides, you'll find that most golfers are selfish in that they really don't care about your game. All they care about is their own game. They'll make polite noises after your shots, but that's the extent of their interest. You'll soon be that way, too. There is nothing — *nothing* — more boring than listening to tales about someone else's round or game. But that's part of the social order of this game. The stories are endless, and most embellished, but the bonding is done here.

When You're the Worst

Now, I've said a lot about who you should play with and who you shouldn't, but the fact is that, early in your golfing existence, almost everyone is better than you. So, chances are, you're going to be in a foursome in which you are certainly the worst player. What do you do? This section gives you some tips for getting through what can be a harrowing experience.

Pick up the ball

The worst thing you can do is delay play. After you have hit the ball, oh, ten times on a given hole, pick it up and don't finish the hole as a courtesy to your playing partners. There's always the next hole.

When you're actually scoring a game, you're required to finish out every hole — that is, you have to post a score for each hole. But beginners should feel free to skip that technicality. While you're learning, don't worry about scores.

Look for balls by yourself

This comes under the same "don't delay" heading. If you happen to hit a shot into the highest spinach patch on the course, don't let your companions help you look for it. Tell them to play on, and you'll catch up after a "quick look." They'll be relieved and see you as someone who, though having a bad day, would be worth playing with again. (If you don't find the ball soon, just declare it lost and don't score that hole.)

Don't moan

Don't become a pain in the you-know-what. Most golfers, when they're playing poorly, spend an inordinate amount of time complaining. That's bad — and boring for the other players. They don't want to hear how well you've been playing or about that great round you shot last week. All they care about is the fact that you are slowing things up. So no whining.

Don't analyze your swing

Analyzing your swing is another common trap. You hit a few bad shots — okay, more than a few. Then you start analyzing what you're doing wrong. Stuff like, "Maybe if I just turn a little more through the ball . . . ." This comment is not what the others want to hear. They don't want to waste time worrying about your game. So don't ask for tips. If one is offered, try it, but keep the fact that you are doing so to yourself.

When You're Not the Worst

There is, of course, the other side of the coin. How do you behave when another member of your group can't get the ball above shin height? Here are some pointers:

✔ **Say nothing.** Whatever you do, do not attempt to be encouraging as your pal's game slips further into the mire. After a while, you'll run out of things to say. And your pal will be annoyed with you. And never give advice or swing tips to anyone. You'll be blamed for the next bad shot.

✔ **Talk about other stuff.** The last thing you should talk about is your pal's awful game. Find some common interest and chat about that. Anything to get the subject off that 20-yard dribbler your pal just hit.

Who Not to Play With

As I said earlier, most foursomes are made up of players of roughly equal ability. That's what you should strive for, if at all possible. In fact, the best possible scenario is to find three golfers who are just a little bit better than you. Then you can feed off their fairly recent experiences and have a reasonable target to aim for in your own game.

Anyway, I digress. Those are the sorts of people you should be playing with. Who you *shouldn't* be playing with are those people who play a "different game." That means anyone who shoots more than 20 shots less than you on an average day. All someone like that will do is depress you. Stay away — at least for now. When you get better, playing with and watching someone who has more skill than you helps you become better.

Part II

You Ain't Got a Thing If You Ain't Got That Swing

In this part . . .

How can something that takes only one second to perform, the golf swing, be so complicated to learn? Do you need to go back to school and study theoretical physics? No. Just enroll here, and I'll make it easy for you.

This part shows you how to swing a golf club without falling down. I show you how to find your swing and then show you how to do everything from teeing off on the opening tee to brushing that 3-foot putt into the hole for your par.

Chapter 7

Getting into the Swing of Things

In This Chapter

▶ Understanding the importance of good balance

▶ Types of golf swings

▶ Getting into position

▶ Mastering your swing

▶ Swinging from head to toe

*W*hat is a golf swing? That's a very good question, one that has any number of different answers for any number of people. For most of us, a golf swing means "nonsequential body parts moving in an undignified manner."

In simple terms, though, a golf swing is a coordinated (hopefully), balanced movement of the whole body around a fixed pivot point. If done correctly, this motion swings an implement of destruction (the club) up, around, and down so as to hit a ball with an accelerating blow and with the utmost precision (on the center of the clubface).

I'm starting to feel dizzy. How about you?

The Importance of Maintaining Balance

The key to this whole swinging process is maintaining balance. You cannot hit the ball with consistency if at any time during your swing, you fall over. In contrast, when your swing consists of a simple pivot around a fixed point, the clubhead strikes the ball from the same downward path and somewhere near the center of the clubface every time. Bingo!

You're probably wondering where this fixed point in your body is. Well, it isn't your head. One great golf myth is that the head must remain perfectly still throughout the swing, which is very hard to do. I don't advise keeping your head still . . . unless your hat doesn't fit.

The fixed point in your golf swing should be between your collarbones and about 3 inches below them, as shown in Figure 7-1. You should turn and swing around that point. If you get that pivot point correct, your head will swivel a little bit as you turn back and then through on your shots. If your head appears to move like Linda Blair's did in *The Exorcist,* you've got it wrong.

Different Strokes for Different Folks

You can swing the golf club effectively in many ways. For example, you can have long swings and short swings. Imagine that you backed into a giant clock. Your head is just below the center of the clock. If at the top of your swing, your hands are at 9 o'clock and the clubhead is at 3 o'clock, you are in the standard position for the top of your backswing. The shaft is parallel to the ground.

At the top of John Daly's swing, which is a long swing, his hands are at 12 o'clock, and the clubhead is approaching 5 o'clock. Does your chiropractor have a toll-free number? Other swings have a shorter arc or circle. John Cook on the PGA Tour and Amy Alcott on the LPGA Tour, for example, have short swings. Their hands only get to 8 o'clock, and the clubhead gets to 1 o'clock.

Physical constraints dictate the fullness and length of your swing; the distance the club travels is unimportant.

Golf swings differ in other ways, too.

- ✔ Some players swing the club more around their bodies — like you would swing a baseball bat.
- ✔ Others place more emphasis on the role of their hands and arms in the generation of clubhead speed.
- ✔ Still others place that same emphasis on the turning of the body.

Physique and flexibility play a major role in how you swing a golf club. If you are short, you swing more around, or flatter, because your back is closer to perpendicular at address. (Address is the motionless position as you stand ready to hit the ball.) If you are tall, you must bend more from the waist at address, so your swing is automatically more upright. Remember, the left arm always swings about 90 degrees to the angle of the spine. Stand straight up and put your left arm straight out, away from your body. Now start bending at the waist. See how your arm lowers? It's staying 90 degrees to your back as you bend down. I wish I would have taken more geometry in school!

Your "fixed point" is 3 inches below the middle of your collarbones.

Your head swivels to the right as you swing back . . .

then through . . .

all the way to the finish.

Figure 7-1: What doesn't move in your golf swing.

Adding more power to the female stroke

I've seen plenty of female golfers, and not just playing the LPGA Tour, with tremendous power for driving the ball several hundred yards — women like Mickey Wright and Laura Davies, just to name a few. But for the most part, the average woman simply doesn't possess the same upper body, forearm, and wrist strength as a man. And much to her dismay, she cannot drive the ball 300 yards like John Daly.

By following a few simple strengthening and conditioning exercises (see Chapter 4), lady golfers — or golfers at any level — can strengthen their upper bodies, wrists, and forearms and ultimately improve the power in their swings.

Here's one simple exercise for women that improves wrist strength — and you can do it almost anywhere: Take a tennis ball in your hand and grip it until it hurts. Then switch hands and do the same thing. You don't have to give yourself carpal tunnel syndrome, but repeat this exercise for at least five minutes with each hand. You'll notice gradual improvement in your wrist and forearm strength, which helps you avoid wrist injury and overall arm fatigue.

Factors of Flight

Although you can swing a golf club in many ways, in order to hit the ball squarely, all good swings have a few common denominators. But before I get to that, I want to break down the factors of flight:

- ✔ First, you want to hit the ball.
- ✔ Second, you want to get the ball up in the air and moving forward.
- ✔ Third, you want to hit the ball a long way.
- ✔ Fourth, you want to hit the ball a long way while your friends are watching.
- ✔ And last, you become obsessed, just like the rest of us.

Hitting the ball

You would think hitting the ball would be easy. But golf isn't tennis or baseball, where you can react to a moving ball. In golf, the ball just sits there and stares at you, beckoning you to make it go somewhere.

Here's your first thought: "I won't turn my body too much; I'll just hit the thing with my hands." That's natural — and wrong. You're worried about losing sight of the ball in your backswing and hitting nothing but air. You're not alone. We've all been through this sweat-drenched nightmare of flailing failure. Don't worry. You will evolve! You will make contact!

Getting the ball airborne

Okay, after a few fairly fruitless attempts, you're finally hitting more ball than air in your search for flight. You need a lesson in the aerodynamics of the game. The only time you want the golf ball to be on the ground is when you get close to the hole. To have any kind of fun the rest of the time, you want air under the ball; you need the ball to fly! Then you can stare with horrified fascination at the ridiculous places the ball ends up, which is the essence of the game.

One of my *Golf For Dummies* secrets is that the only time you should lift something is when you rearrange your living-room furniture. Never try to lift a golf ball with your club. You should hit down with every club except the driver and the putter, as shown in Figure 7-2. And when you do hit down, don't duck or lunge at the ball; hit down but keep your head up.

When you use your driver, the ball is set on a tee about an inch above the ground; if you hit down, the ball will fly off the top edge of the club. As a result, the shot will be high and short — not my favorite combination! With the driver, you want the clubhead coming into the ball from a horizontal path to slightly up when you make contact.

When you putt, you don't want the ball airborne. A putter is designed to roll the ball along the ground, not produce a high shot. So you need to foster more of a "horizontal hit" with that club. See Chapter 9 for information on putting.

Figure 7-2:
Hit down on all clubs except the driver.

If the club in your hands is a fairway wood or an iron, hit down.

Creating the power

As soon as the ball is in the air, your ego kicks in. Power with a capital *P* becomes your concern. Power intoxicates your mind. Power makes legends out of mere mortals. Power makes you want to get a tattoo. Power also sends the ball to the far corners of your little green world if you don't harness it properly.

Some professional golfers can create as much as $4^1/_2$ horsepower in their swings. That's some kind of giddy-up. This power comes from a blending of the body twisting around a slightly moving pivot point with a swinging of the arms and hands up and around on the backswing and then down and around in the forward swing. All of which occurs in the space of about one second!

The key to gaining your optimum power is to try to turn your back to the target on your backswing, as shown in Figure 7-3. Which involves another *Golf For Dummies* must-do: On the backswing, turn your left shoulder under your chin until your shoulder is over your right foot. Make sure that you turn your shoulders far enough. Don't just raise your arms. Turning your shoulders ensures that you have power for the forward move. Turn for power. The unwinding of the hips and the shoulders on the downswing creates the power surge.

Turn your left shoulder "over" your right foot.

Figure 7-3:
At the top
of the
backswing.

The same swing principles apply for women. However, to build momentum for the swing speed, ladies can rely on a longer backswing. A long backswing allows complete rotation in the left shoulder, which enables the left arm to extend fully and cocks the wrist to help release the power.

Building Your Swing

To become a golfer, you must master the building blocks of your swing. How do you hold on to the club so that you can give the ball a good whack? After you have a good grip, how do you align yourself to the target so that the ball goes somewhere close to where you aimed? What should your posture look like? How much knee flex should you have, and where in the world is the ball located in your stance? Should you look at the ball or somewhere near the sun? This section has the answers.

For natural left-handers, perfecting the golf swing can be tricky. In the past, there weren't many clubs designed for the lefty, and most course designs put left-handed golfers at a disadvantage. As a result, many lefties were taught to play right-handed. Today, however, technology has advanced to the point where some clubs are designed especially for left-handers.

Whether you swing left-handed or right-handed, it basically all comes down to which side has the stronger, most natural-feeling swing. To find out what works best for you, try swinging the club like a baseball bat from each side (keeping a safe distance from all breakable objects and small children). The muscles used in swinging a bat are similar to the range of motion in a golf swing. Of course, if you still have trouble hitting a straight shot, you can always blame the equipment. I do.

The grip

Although the way in which you place your hands on the club is one of the most important parts of your method, it is also one of the most boring. Few golfers who have played for any length of time pay much attention to hand placement. For one thing, your grip is hard to change after you get used to the way your hands feel on the club. For another, hand placement simply doesn't seem as important as the swing itself. That kind of neglect and laziness is why you see so many bad grips.

Get your grip correct and close to orthodox at the beginning of your golfing career. You can fake about anything, but a bad grip follows you to the grave.

Ladies tend to have smaller hands than men, so for them, it's important to have the right grip size on the club. Another tip for ladies is to use the closed-face grip position, which can help square the clubface during the swing.

Here's how to sleep well in eternity with the correct grip. Standing upright, let your arms hang naturally by your side. Get someone to place a club in your left hand. All you have to do is grab the club. Voilà! You've got your left-hand grip (see Figure 7-4).

Stand upright, letting your arms hang . . .

and then grab the club.

Figure 7-4:
Your left-hand grip.

Well, almost. The grip has three checkpoints:

1. **First is the relationship between your left thumb and left index finger when placed on the shaft.**

   I like to see a gap of about three quarters of an inch between the thumb and index finger. To get that gap, you have to extend your thumb down the shaft a little. If extending your thumb proves too uncomfortable, pull your thumb in toward your hand. Three quarters of an inch is only a guide, so you have some leeway. But remember: The longer your thumb is down the shaft, the longer your swing. And the opposite is also true. Short thumb means short swing. (See Figure 7-5.)

Figure 7-5: What length thumb?

2. **Check to see that the clubshaft runs across the base of your last three fingers and through the middle of your index finger, as shown in Figure 7-6.**

   This placement is important. If you grip the club too much in the palm, you hinder your ability to hinge your wrist and use your hands effectively in the swing. More of a finger grip makes cocking the wrist on the backswing, hitting the ball, and then recocking the wrist on the follow-through much easier. Just be sure that the "V" formed between your thumb and forefinger points toward your right ear.

3. **Okay, your left hand is on the club. Complete your grip by placing your right hand on the club.**

   You can fit the right hand to the left by using one of three grips: the overlapping (or Vardon) grip, the interlocking grip, or the ten-finger grip.

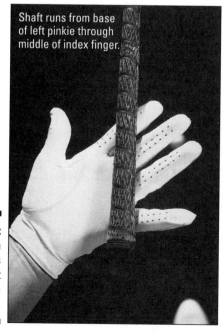

Figure 7-6: Grip more in the fingers of the left hand than in the palm.

Vardon grip

The Vardon grip is the most popular grip, certainly among better players. The great British player Harry Vardon, who still holds the record for most British Open wins — six — popularized the grip around the turn of the century. Old Harry was the first to place the little finger of his right hand over the gap between the index and next finger of the left as a prelude to completing his grip, as shown in Figure 7-7. Harry was also the first to put his left thumb on top of the shaft. Previously, everybody had their left thumbs wrapped around the grip as if they were holding a baseball bat.

Try the Vardon grip. Close your right hand over the front of the shaft so that the V formed between your thumb and forefinger again points to your right ear. The fleshy pad at the base of your right thumb should fit snugly over your left thumb. The result should be a feeling of togetherness, your hands working as one, single unit.

This grip is very cool; probably 90 percent of Tour players use the Vardon grip.

Figure 7-7:
In the Vardon grip, the right pinkie overlaps the left index finger.

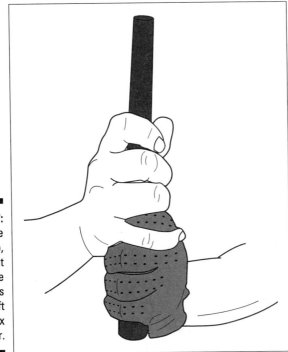

Interlocking grip

The interlocking grip is really a variation on the Vardon grip. The difference is that the little finger of your left hand and the index finger of the right actually hook together (see Figure 7-8). Everything else is the same. You may find this grip more comfortable if you have small hands. Tom Kite and Jack Nicklaus, possibly the game's greatest player ever, both use this grip for that reason. Many of the top women players use this grip, too.

Figure 7-8: An alternative is to interlock the right pinkie and left index finger.

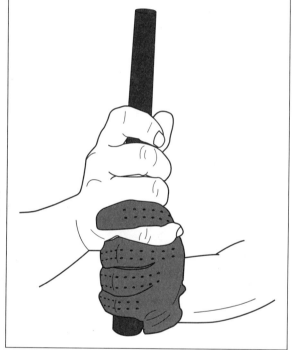

Ten-finger grip

The ten-finger grip used to be more common, but you still see it occasionally. PGA Tour player Dave Barr from Canada uses this grip. The ten-finger grip is what the name tells you it is. You have all ten fingers on the club. No overlapping or interlocking occurs; the little finger of the left hand and the index finger of the right barely touch (see Figure 7-9). If you have trouble generating enough clubhead speed to hit the ball as far as you would like, give this grip a try. Keep in mind that controlling the clubhead is more difficult with this grip because more "cocking" of the hands occurs.

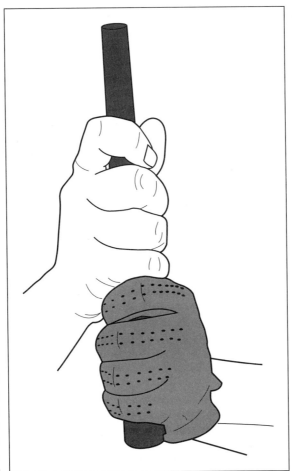

Figure 7-9:
Or you can place all ten fingers on the club.

Completing your grip

Put your right hand on the club, the palm directly opposite your left hand. Slide your right hand down the shaft until you can complete whatever grip you find most comfortable. Your right shoulder, right hip, and head lean to the right to accommodate the lowering of the right hand. Your right earlobe moves closer to your right shoulder.

Your grip pressure should never be tight. Your grip should be light. You should exert only as much pressure as you would when picking up an egg from a spotted owl. Lightly now! Spotted owls are becoming extinct!

Aiming

I played on the PGA Tour for 21 years, which means I took part in a lot of Pro-Ams. (In a Pro-Am, each professional is teamed with three or four amateurs.) And in every single one of those rounds, I saw someone misaligned at address. Sometimes that someone was me! Aiming properly is that difficult.

Generally speaking, right-handed golfers tend to aim to the right of the target. I don't see many of them aiming left — even slicers, whose shots commonly start left and finish right. Invariably, people tend to aim right and swing over the top on the way down to get the ball started left. (For information on fixing common faults, see Chapter 13.)

So what makes aiming so difficult? Human nature is part of it. Getting sloppy with your aim is easy to do when your mind is on other things. That's why discipline is important. Taking the time and trouble to get comfortable and confident in his alignment is one reason Jack Nicklaus was as great as he was. Watch him even now. He still works his way through the same aiming routine before every shot. And I emphasize routine. First he looks at the target from behind the ball. Then he picks out a spot about a couple of feet ahead of his ball on a line with that target. That spot is his intermediate target. Then he walks to the ball and sets the clubface behind it so that he's aiming at the intermediate point. Aligning the club with something that is 2 feet away is much easier than aiming at something 150 yards away.

How Nicklaus aims is exactly how you must work on your aim. Think of a railroad track. On one line is the ball and in the distance, the target. On the other line is your toes. Thus, your body is aligned parallel with but left of the target line. If you take nothing else away from this section on aiming, remember that phrase. Cut out Figure 7-10 and place it on the ceiling over your bed. Stare at it before you go to sleep.

Don't make the mistake that I see countless golfers making: aiming their feet at the target. If you aim your feet at the target, where is the clubface aligned? Well to the right of where you want the ball to go. This type of alignment will usually sabotage the flight of your ball.

The stance

Okay, you're aimed at the target. But you're not finished with the feet yet. Right now, your feet are not pointing in any direction; you're just standing there. All the books tell you to turn your left toe out about 30 degrees. But what's 30 degrees? If you're like me, you have no clue what 30 degrees looks like or — more important — feels like, so think of 30 degrees this way:

Far too many golfers align their feet to the right of the target.

Aim the clubface where you want the ball to go. Your toe line should be parallel to your target line.

Figure 7-10: Aiming correctly.

We all know what a clock looks like, and we know what the big hand is and what the little hand does. If you are well versed in recognizing time pieces, you should be able to build a stance.

Your left foot should be pointed to 10 o'clock, and your right foot should be at 1 o'clock. However, this does not work during daylight saving time. You're on your own then.

Figure 7-11 demonstrates this stance. Keep it simple and always be on time.

Width of stance is easy, too. Your heels should be shoulder-width apart, as shown in Figure 7-12. Not 14 inches, or 18 inches. Shoulder-width. Let the shape of your body dictate what is right for you.

Knee flex

Moving on up, the next stop is the knees. Again, you can read all sorts of books that tell you the precise angle at which your knees should be flexed at address. But that knowledge isn't going to do you much good when you're standing on the range without a protractor. What you need is a feel.

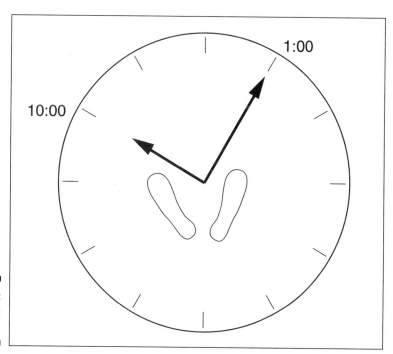

10:00

1:00

Figure 7-11:
A standing
start.

With a driver, the gap between your knees
should be shoulder width.
Think "bow-legged."

Figure 7-12:
Knees
should be
as wide
as the
shoulders.

Think of your knee flex as a "ready" position. You've got to be set so that movement is possible. So, from an upright start, flex your knees and bend forward until your arms are hanging vertically, as shown in Figure 7-13. That's where you want to be. Just like a quarterback waiting for a snap. Or a soccer goalkeeper facing a shot. Or a shortstop ready for a ground ball. You're ready to move. Left. Right. Back. Forward. Whatever. You're ready. And remember, maintaining balance is the key.

Flex knees and bend forward until arms hang vertically.

Figure 7-13: Get "ready."

Ball position

Where is the ball positioned between your feet? It should be positioned opposite your left armpit with a driver, which also should be opposite your left heel, and steadily moved back with each club until you get to the middle of your stance with a wedge (see Figure 7-14).

You are trying to hit up on the driver; that's why the ball is forward in your stance (toward the target). You hit down with all other clubs, which is why you move the ball back in your stance (away from the target) as the golf club increases with loft. When the ball is played back in your stance, hitting down is much easier.

For a driver, place the ball opposite your left armpit.

Figure 7-14:
Ball
position.

The bottom of the swing

The bottom of the swing is an important yet frequently neglected aspect of golf. The bottom of the arc of the swing has to have a low point; hopefully, that low point is where your golf ball will be as you swing an iron. (Remember, the driver must be hit on the upswing.) If you don't know where the bottom of your swing is, how do you know where to put the ball in your stance? You can make the best swing in the world, but if the ball is too far back, you'll hit the top half of it. Too far forward is just as bad, and you'll hit the ground before the ball. Neither is too good an idea.

Fear not; such shots are not going to be part of your repertoire. Why? Because you're always going to know where the bottom of your swing is: directly below your head.

Think about it. I've already discussed how the ball is positioned opposite the left armpit for the driver. That position automatically puts your head "behind" the ball. In other words, the ball is nearer the target than your head. All of which means that you are going to strike the ball on a slightly upward blow. The bottom of the swing is behind the ball, so the clubhead will be moving up as it hits the ball, as shown in Figure 7-15. That's all right because the ball is off the ground perched on a tee. The only way to make solid contact (and maximize your distance) is to hit drives "on the up."

If it's on a tee, you better hit up or your club will go under.

Figure 7-15:
Hit up.

The situation for an iron shot from the fairway differs from that of hitting a driver from the tee. Now the ball is sitting on the ground. Plus, the club you are using has more loft and is designed to give best results when the ball is struck just before the ground. So now your head should be over the ball at address and impact. In other words, something has to move.

That something is the ball. Start from the middle of your stance, which is where the ball should be when you are hitting a wedge, one of the shortest and most lofted clubs in your bag. Move the ball steadily forward — all the way to opposite your left armpit for the driver — as the club in your hands gets longer. (See Figure 7-16.)

So for me, the distance between my left armpit and chin is about 6 inches. With the driver, the ball is opposite my left armpit, and with the shorter irons, it's opposite my chin (that is, where my head is). In my case, the ball moves about 6 inches. Most golf courses are about 7,000 yards, so 6 inches shouldn't have much significance. Practice this part early in your development and then worry about the 7,000 yards that you have to play.

You may be a little confused by all of that. On its face, it may sound weird that the more lofted clubs (which hit the highest shots) are back in your stance so that you can hit down on the ball more. But the explanation is a simple one. The more the clubface is angled back from vertical, the higher the shot will be. Thus, the only way to get a ball that is lying on the ground up in the air is by exerting downward pressure.

When you use a wedge, place the ball in the middle of your stance.

As the club gets longer, the ball moves targetward.

Figure 7-16:
The ball moves!

The eyes have it

I see a lot of players setting up to shots with their chins on their chests. Or, if they've been told not to do that, their heads are held so high they can barely see the ball. Neither, of course, is exactly conducive to good play (see Figure 7-17).

TIP

So how should you be holding your head? The answer is in your eyes. Look down at the ball, which is in what optometrists call your gaze center. Your gaze center is about the size of a Frisbee. Everything outside your gaze center is in your peripheral vision. Now lift your head or drop it slightly. As your head moves, so do your eyes, and so does the ball — into your peripheral vision. Now you can't see the ball so well. Keep your head steady enough to keep the ball inside the Frisbee, and you can't go too far wrong (see Figure 7-18).

Don't put your chin on your chest.

But don't lose sight of the ball either!

Figure 7-17:
Chin up!
Or down?

Keep the ball in the middle of your "gaze center."

That dictates the position of your head.

Figure 7-18:
Stay
focused.

One hand away

One last thing about your address position. Let your arms hang so that the butt end of the club is one hand away from the inside of your left thigh, as shown in Figure 7-19. You should use this position for every club in the bag except for your putter.

The butt end of the club is a useful guide to check whether the relationship between your hands and the clubhead is correct. With a wedge, for example, the butt end of the club should be in line with the middle of your left thigh. For a driver, it should be opposite your zipper. As before, every other club is between those parameters.

The club should be one hand from your body.

Figure 7-19:
Your hands
and the
club.

The shaft of a wedge should point at the crease in your left pant leg (or the middle of your thigh).

A driver should point at your zipper.

Well, I've talked about a lot of stuff, and I haven't even taken a cut at it yet. Work hard on these preswing routines. After you get yourself in position to move the club away from the ball, forget your address position and concentrate on your swing. It's now time to do what you were sent here to do: create some turbulence. Now I'll get on with the swing.

Starting the Swing: Train Hands/Arms First

Many people think that the most effective way to develop a consistent golf swing is to stand on the range whacking balls until you get it right. But the best way to develop a consistent golf swing is to break the swing down into pieces. Only after you have the first piece mastered should you move on to the next one. I start with what I call miniswings.

Miniswings: Hands and arms

Position yourself in front of the ball as I described earlier in this chapter. Now, without moving anything except your hands, wrists, and forearms, rotate the club back until the shaft is horizontal to the ground and the toe of the club is pointing up. The key to this movement is the left hand, which must stay in the space that it is now occupying, in its address position (see Figure 7-20). The left hand is the fulcrum around which the "swing" rotates. The feeling you should have is one of the butt of the club staying in about the same position while your hands lift the clubhead.

After you get the hang of that little drill, graduate to hitting shots with your miniswing. Let the club travel through 180 degrees, with the shaft parallel to the ground on the backswing and then back to parallel on the through-swing; your follow-through should be a mirror-image of the backswing. The ball obviously doesn't go far with this drill, but your hands and arms are doing exactly what you want them to do through impact on a full swing. Cock the wrists, hit the ball, recock the wrists.

After you have this down, it's time to turn on the horsepower and get your body involved in the action.

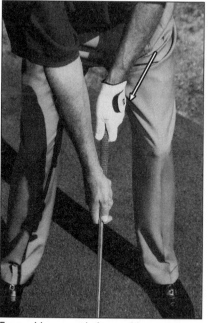

Figure 7-20:
Push
down —
pull up.

From address, push down with your left hand as you pull up with your right.

Rotate the club back until the shaft is horizontal, the toe pointing up.

The body

GARY SAYS

One of the most effective ways for your brain to master something like the golf swing is to set the motion to music. We all learned our ABCs by putting the letters to song. I have played some of my best golf while internally humming a Hootie and the Blowfish single. Music plays a definite role in the learning process.

When you start to move the club and your body into the swing, think of a melody. Make the song real music. Rap, with its staccato rhythm, is no good. To me, that suggests too much independent movement. The golf swing should be a smooth motion, so your song should reflect that smoothness. Think of Tony Bennett, not Coolio.

Anyway, here's the first step toward adding body movement to the hands and arms motion described in the preceding section. Stand as if at address, your arms crossed over your chest so that your right hand is on your left shoulder and your left hand is on your right shoulder. Hold a club horizontally against your chest with both hands, as shown in Figure 7-21.

Figure 7-21:
Turn your
body. Left hand on right shoulder, right hand on left shoulder, place a club across your chest.

Then turn the club with your shoulders through 90 degress.

Now turn as if you are making a backswing. Turn so that the shaft turns through 90 degrees, to the point where the shaft is perpendicular to your toe line. As you do so, allow your left knee to move inward so that it points to the golf ball. But the real key is that your right leg must retain the flex that you introduced at address. Retain the flex, and the only way to get the shaft into position is by turning your body. You can't sway or slide to the right and create that 90-degree angle artificially.

The turning to the right in your backswing should feel as if you are turning around the inside of your right leg so that your back is facing the target. That's the perfect top-of-the-backswing position.

Unwinding

From the top (note that your spine angle must also remain in the same position from address to the top of the backswing), you must learn the proper sequence so that your body unwinds back to the ball.

The uncoiling starts from the ground and moves up. The first thing to move is your left knee. Your knee must shift toward the target until your kneecap is over the middle of your left foot, where it stops. Any more and your legs start to slide past the ball. A shaft stuck in the ground just outside your left foot is a good check that this move hasn't gone too far. If your knee hits the shaft, stop and try again.

Next, your left hip slides targetward until it is over your knee and foot. Again, the shaft provides a deterrent to your hip going too far.

Pay particular attention to the shaft across your chest in this phase of the swing (work in front of a mirror if you can). The shaft should always parallel the slope of your shoulders as you work your body back to the ball.

Finishing: Looking the part

"Swing" through the impact area all the way to the finish. Keep your left leg straight and let your right knee touch your left knee, as shown in Figure 7-22. Hold this position until the ball hits the ground to prove that you have swung in balance.

If you can do all these things, you're going to look like a real player pretty quickly. Looking the part at least is important. Think about it. Get up on the first tee looking like a schlep who doesn't know how to stand to the ball or make a balanced follow-through, and you're expected to play badly. You don't need excuses. But if you get up to the tee and make the swing I described, passersby are going to stop and watch. And you can have a lot of excuses if you look good. People think you're just unlucky, especially if you look shocked that your shot hit a pedestrian going to the mall three blocks away.

Putting everything together

Practice each of these exercises for as long as you need to. After you put them together, you have the basis of a pretty good golf swing, one that is a combination of hands/arms and body motion.

- ✔ Practice your miniswing.
- ✔ Hum a mellow tune.
- ✔ Turn your shoulders so that your back is facing the target.
- ✔ Put a shaft in the ground — don't slide.
- ✔ At finish, keep your left leg straight and your right knee toward left.

Instead, turn
your left hip
inside the shaft.

Don't slide
into the shaft
outside your
left leg.

Figure 7-22:
Turn
through —
don't slide.

Wrong   Right

Coordinating all these parts into a golf swing takes time. The action of the parts will soon become the whole, and you will develop a feel for your swing. Only repetition from hitting practice balls will allow the student to gain this information. Knowledge, in this case, does not come from reading a book. So get out there and start taking some turf!

Key on the rhythm of your swing. There comes a point in every golfer's life where you just have to "let it go." You can work on your mechanics as much as you want, but the moment to actually hit a ball arrives for all of us. And when that moment comes, you can't be thinking about anything except, perhaps, one simple swing key, or swing thought. That's why top golfers spend most of their time trying to get into what they call "the zone."

Fast-, slow-, and medium-paced swings

Here's a short list of fast-, slow-, and medium-paced swings on the PGA Tour, past and present. In each case, the player's personality fits his or her swing speed.

Fast	Medium	Slow
Ben Hogan	Steve Elkington	Ben Crenshaw
Dan Pohl	Lee Janzen	Jay Haas
Nick Price	Davis Love III	Nancy Lopez
Annika Sorenstam	Jack Nicklaus	Larry Mize
Lanny Wadkins	Sam Snead	Scott Simpson
Tom Watson		

The zone is a state of uncluttered thought, where good things happen without any conscious effort from you. You know the kind of thing. The rolled-up ball of paper you throw at the trash can goes in if you just toss the wad without thinking. The car rounds the corner perfectly if you are lost in your thoughts.

In golfing terms, getting into the zone is clearing your mind so that your body can do its job. The mind is a powerful asset, but it can hurt you, too. Negative thoughts about where your ball might go are not going to help you make your best swing. Of course, getting into the zone is easier said than done.

So how do you get to the zone? Perhaps the best way is to focus on the rhythm of your swing as opposed to mechanics or possible screw-ups. By rhythm, I don't mean speed. We've seen fast swings and slow swings and a lot in between, and all can have good rhythm. For example, the 1994 British Open champion Nick Price has a very fast swing motion. Blink and you miss it. In contrast, 1987 Masters winner Larry Mize has an extremely slow method. Congress works faster. Yet each has the perfect rhythm. And that perfect rhythm is the key. The rhythm of your swing should fit your personality. If you are a fairly high-strung, nervous individual, your swing is probably faster than most. If your swing is much slower, then you're probably more laid-back and easygoing. The common factor is that the potential for smoothness is within each individual.

Waggle/swing trigger

Good rhythm during your swing doesn't just happen. Only on those days when you are in the zone will you not have to give your swing encouragement. The rest of the time, you need to set the tone for your swing with your waggle. A waggle is a motion with the wrists in which the hands stay pretty much stationary over the ball and the clubhead moves back a foot or two as if starting the swing (see Figure 7-23). In fact, a waggle is a bit like the mini-swing drill I described in the section "Miniswings: Hands and arms," earlier in this chapter.

Waggling the club serves two main purposes.

- ✔ Waggling is a rehearsal of the crucial opening segment of the backswing.

- ✔ If done properly, waggling sets the tone for the pace of the swing. In other words, if you have a short, fast swing, make short, fast waggles. If your swing is of the long and slow variety, make the same kind of waggles. Keep within your species.

- ✔ Make that three purposes. In golf, you don't want to start from a static position. You need a "running" start to build up momentum and to prevent your swing from getting off to an abrupt, jerky beginning. Waggling the clubhead eases tension you may be feeling and introduces movement into your setup.

Figure 7-23:
Get in
motion.

But the waggle is only the second-to-last thing you do before the backswing begins. The last thing is your swing trigger. Your swing trigger can be any kind of move. For example, 1989 British open champion Mark Calcavecchia shuffles his feet. Gary Player, winner of nine major championships, kicks his right knee in toward the ball. A slight turning of the head to the right is Jack Nicklaus' cue to start his swing. Your swing trigger is up to you. Do whatever frees you up to get the club away from the ball. Create the flow!

After you play golf a while, you can identify players you know from hundreds of yards away by their mannerisms, preshot routine, waggle, and swing trigger. In fact, you can set your watch by good players. Good players take the same amount of time and do exactly the same things before every single shot. And that consistency should be your goal, too. Make yourself recognizable!

When I started working with Kevin Costner on his golf game for the movie *Tin Cup,* one of the first things we talked about was a preshot routine. Teaching Kevin about the preshot routine this early in his education as a golfer got him to do the same thing every time he approached the ball. We had to get him to look like a real touring pro, and every one of them has his own routine.

Kevin picked up the preshot routine real fast. He would get behind the ball about 6 feet and look at the ball and then the target (seeing the target line in his mind's eye). He would then walk up and put his clubface right behind the ball and put his feet on a parallel line to his target line, which is the best way to establish the correct alignment procedure. He would then look at the target once, give the club a little waggle, and then whack, off the ball went. I made him repeat this routine from the first day we started on his swing.

By the time the golf sequences were shot for the movie, Kevin had the look of a well-seasoned touring pro. In fact, as we were walking down the second hole together in the Bob Hope Chrysler Classic, I asked Kevin where he got all those mannerisms of tugging on his shirt, always stretching his glove by pulling on it, and pulling his pants by the right front pocket. He looked at me and said, "I've been watching you for the past three months." I had no idea I was doing all those things in my preshot routine, so you see that your mannerisms become automatic if you do them enough. By the way, my preshot routine looks a lot better when Kevin Costner does it!

Visualizing shots

As you practice your swing and hit more and more shots, patterns — good and bad — emerge. The natural shape of your shots becomes apparent. Few people hit the ball dead-straight; you'll either fade most of your shots (the ball flies from left to right, as shown in Figure 7-24) or draw the majority (the ball moves from right to left in the air). If either tendency gets too severe and develops into a full-blooded slice or hook (a slice is a worse fade, and a hook is a worse draw), stop. Then go for lessons. At this stage, your faults tend to be obvious, certainly to the trained eye. So one session with your local pro should get you back on track.

A lesson is important. Faults left to fester and boil soon become ingrained into your method. When that happens, eradicating them becomes a lengthy, expensive process. The old adage comes to mind: "Pay me now, or pay me later." Pay him early so it's easier to fix. Chapter 3 offers valuable information regarding golf lessons. For a listing of golf schools, see Appendix B.

Anyway, after you've developed a consistent shape of shot, you can start to visualize how that shape fits the hole you're on. Then, of course, you know exactly where to aim whether the hole is a dogleg right (turns right), dogleg left (turns left), or straight away. You're a real golfer. Get some plaid pants!

Roll the film — take 83 — action!

When you put together all the connected parts I discuss in this chapter, they should flow into a swing. The first time you see yourself swinging on a picture or a tape, you will swear that that person is not you. What your swing feels like versus what really occurs can be deceiving.

The golf swing is nothing more than a bunch of little motions that are learned, becoming a total motion that is remembered. The tempo and rhythm are applied to the motion through your personality. Those individuals who go fast in life swing fast; those who go slow swing accordingly.

If you can gain the basic mechanics through this book and then apply your own personality, your swing should bloom into something unique. Work hard to understand your swing and watch how other people swing at the ball. The great Ben Hogan told me he would watch other players that he played with. If he liked something they did with their swing, he would go to the practice tee and incorporate that particular move into his swing to see if it worked. What finally came out was a mix of many swings blended to his needs and personality. A champion works very hard.

My golf swing is not the one I used on tour. In 1986, at the age of 38, I started working with Mac O'Grady to revamp my entire swing. Mac gave me a model that I used and blended with my existing swing, shown in the nine photos of Figure 7-25. What came out is a pretty good-looking golf swing, if I do say so myself. Thanks, Mac, for at least making me look good!

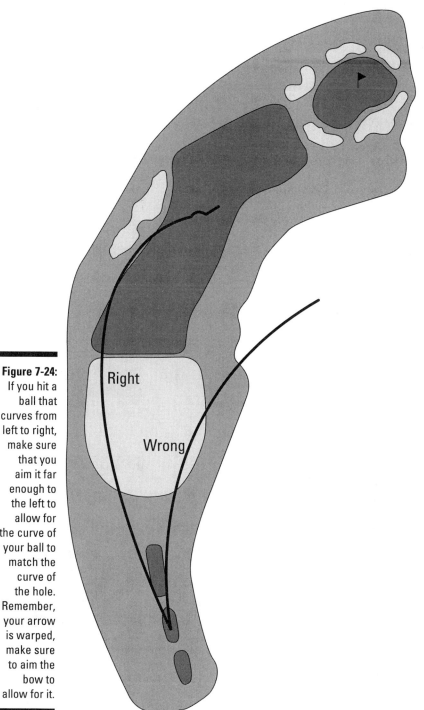

Figure 7-24:
If you hit a
ball that
curves from
left to right,
make sure
that you
aim it far
enough to
the left to
allow for
the curve of
your ball to
match the
curve of
the hole.
Remember,
your arrow
is warped,
make sure
to aim the
bow to
allow for it.

Right

Wrong

Address: The calm before the chaos. All systems are go and flight is imminent.

Monitor your swing speed at this time. Checking to see if my seatbelts are fastened.

Turn and stay balanced over your feet. Feel the sun and breeze on your face.

I've reached the top. I'm in attack mode, my swing is growing teeth.

The start down is a slooooooow accumulation of speed. At this time, I've forgotten the sun and wind on my face.

I've organized my chaos. Liftoff is precise. My soul feels the ball.

Figure 7-25: Not a bad-looking golf swing!

The hit is relayed up from the shaft to my hands, through my arms into my command center. Post-impact, I feel I've been here forever.

My first glimpse at the sphere that is targetbound. The anxieties of flight and destination consume my brain.

Who cares where it went? I look good enough to be on the top of a golf trophy.

Chapter 8

Developing Your Own Swing

. . . .

In This Chapter

▶ Defining your golf personality

▶ Checking out your swing plane

. . . .

This chapter comes with the golfing equivalent of a government health warning. The information on the next few pages isn't for everyone. That's not to say that anything in this chapter is incorrect; it isn't. But for a lot of you — especially if you're at an early stage of your development as a golfer — it will be too much to assimilate. Brain warp. Little puffs of smoke will be coming from your ears.

So you need to know yourself psychologically and how much information you are able to retain. Say you just bought a personal computer with 450 MHz Pentium processor, 128MB RAM, and 14GB on your hard drive. You're sailing with a 3-D accelerator card and a DVD-ROM drive and have 56K modem capabilities. You're ready to rumble. You get home in a flash and start tearing the boxes to pieces. You hook this cable to that port and put this on top of that. You're flying by the seat of your pants and have no idea what you're doing, but you do it anyway. Gone is the idea of looking at the instructions or reading any print data on how to assemble this new computer.

If that scenario sounds like you, skip this chapter. You already know all you need to know about the golf swing — at least for now.

If, however, you are the type who takes a computer home, reads everything in the box, and goes from page 1 to the end of the instruction manual as you piece the computer together, then you're going to want to know more about the golf swing before you can play with confidence. Read on to better understand the complexities of the swing.

What Type of Golfer Are You?

My friend, renowned teacher Peter Kostis, breaks golfers into four types:

- **Analytics** are organized types. You can always spot their desks — the neat ones — in the office.

- **Drivers,** as you'd expect, like to work. They do whatever it takes to get something done.

- **Amiables** are easy to deal with. They accept whatever advice you offer without asking too many questions.

- **Expressives** don't mind any environment they happen to find themselves in; they adjust to whatever comes their way.

In golfing terms, an analytic is someone like Nick Faldo or Bernhard Langer. Jack Nicklaus, Tom Kite, and Tom Watson are drivers. Nancy Lopez, Fred Couples, and Ben Crenshaw are amiables. And Fuzzy Zoeller and Lee Trevino are classic expressives.

Drivers and analytics don't play like amiables and expressives. For a driver or analytic to score well, he needs confidence in his mechanics. An amiable or expressive doesn't. If he feels like he's playing okay, then his swing must be okay, too.

The following situation clarifies these differences. Four of the greatest golfers of our time are playing an exhibition. Lee Trevino, Ben Crenshaw, Jack Nicklaus, and Nick Faldo are scheduled to tee off at Running Rut Golf Course precisely at 11 a.m. Because of a mix-up with the courtesy cars that pick up the players and deliver them to the golf course (Jack and Nick don't like the color of their car; Freddy and Ben could care less), the players are late getting to Running Rut Golf Course.

When the players arrive, with only ten minutes to tee off, the analytic (Faldo) and the driver (Nicklaus) run out to hit balls before playing. Faldo has to swing to gain confidence, and Nicklaus has to hit balls because he likes to work at it.

The other two guys are in the locker room putting on their golf shoes. Trevino is in deep conversation with the locker room attendant about the virtues of not having to tune up his Cadillac for 100,000 miles due to the technologies of the North Star System. Crenshaw is puffing on a cigarette, telling a club member that he was totally flabbergasted yesterday when three 40-foot putts lipped out and just about cost him his sanity. The expressive (Trevino) and the amiable (Crenshaw) don't have to hit balls to get ready. They just go about their business and don't worry about much.

By the way, the match is called off when Faldo and Nicklaus refuse to come to the tee because Nick finds something on the practice tee that he wants to work on and Nicklaus ends up redesigning the practice range. I was told later that the locker room attendant bought Trevino's old Cadillac.

At this stage of your development, being an amiable or an expressive is to your advantage. Because of the enormous amount of new information that you have to absorb, anything that prevents confusion is good.

Having said that, this chapter is for all you analytics and drivers out there. Amiables and expressives, see you in Chapter 9.

Establishing Your Swing Plane

The *swing plane* at its most basic is the path the clubshaft follows when you swing. Unfortunately, other factors affect your swing plane, including your height, weight, posture, flexibility, the thickness of your torso, and the dew point. The plane of your swing can get complicated — especially if you want to cover all the possible variations in the plane from address to the end of the follow-through.

At this point, for all you amiables and expressives, let me expound on the idea of not thinking about the plane of your swing but about the shape of your swing. Two of the best players in the game today — Greg Norman and Bruce Lietzke — have totally different planes to their swings. The golf swing consists of different planes that are shifted during the course of the swing. For example, Greg Norman shifts the plane of his swing initially on the backswing to the outside a little, and then shifts the plane on the downswing to the inside to hit the ball for his particular curve of the ball *(draw)*. Bruce shifts the plane of his swing initially on the backswing to the inside and then shifts the plane on the downswing to the outside to hit the ball for his particular curve of the golf ball *(fade)*.

So you can see in all this nonsense that there is no one plane in the golf swing. The plane is always shifting in the swing. The swing is an ongoing thing that can get real complicated. Because I'm an expressive, I like to think of the swing not on a plane but in a certain shape. I like to have a picture in my mind of a certain swing shape and forget about the plane of my swing. One picture is geometry, and one is art. I was never good at geometry.

I feel better having said that, so now all you analytics and drivers out there can chew on this plane thing.

The plane of your swing is dictated to a large extent by the clubshaft's angle at address. The swing you make with a wedge in your hands is naturally more upright — or should be — than the swing you make with a driver. The driver has a longer shaft than the wedge and a flatter *lie* (the angle at which the shaft emerges from the clubhead).

For this book, I'm assuming that you maintain the plane you establish at address throughout the swing. For most players, this assumption isn't always the case. If a player's favored shot is one that bends a great deal in the air, the swing plane is tilted either to the right or to the left to compensate for the ball's flight. But if you're trying to hit straight shots, one consistent plane is the way for you.

Mastering the checkpoints

The easiest way to ensure that you maintain your swing is on plane is to have a series of checkpoints, as shown in Figure 8-1. By the way, I'm assuming that you're swinging a driver and that you are right-handed. (To analyze your swing, use a video, a stillframe, or a mirror, or have someone watch you.)

✔ The first checkpoint is at address. The shaft starts at a 45-degree angle to the ground.

✔ Now swing the club back until your left arm is horizontal. At that point, the club's butt end (the end of the grip) points directly at the target line. (The target line is the line that exists between the target and the ball. That line also continues forward past the target in a straight line and beyond the ball going in the opposite direction in a straight line. What I'm talking about in this case is one long, straight line.) If the end of the grip is pointing to the target line, you're on plane. If the end of the grip points above the target line, your swing is too flat, or *horizontal;* if the grip end is below the target line, your swing is too upright, or *vertical.*

✔ At the top of your backswing, the club should be parallel with a line drawn along your heels. That's on plane. If the club points to the right of that line, you have crossed the line and will probably hook the shot. A club pointing to the left of that line is said to be *laid off.* In that case, expect a slice.

✔ Halfway down, at the point where your left arm is again horizontal, the shaft's butt end should again point at the target line. This position and the one described in the second bullet in this list are, in effect, identical in swing plane terms.

Start with the shaft at 45 degrees to the ground.

At the top, the shaft should be parallel with a line along your heels.

Impact should look a lot like address, except that the hips are opening to the target.

Figure 8-1: The swing plane.

✔ Impact is the most important point in the golf swing. If the clubface is square when it contacts the ball, what you do anywhere else doesn't really matter. But if you want to be consistent, try to visualize impact as being about the same as your address position, except your hips are aimed more to the left of the target than at the address position, and your weight is shifting to the left side.

Now remember, this method of mastering your checkpoints is a perfect-world situation. Your size, flexibility, and swing shape will probably produce different results. Don't be alarmed if you don't fit this model; not more than a dozen players on the Tour fit this model. Like anything else, there's room for deviation.

At the top

Take a closer look at the top of the backswing. If you can get the club on plane at the top of the backswing, a good shot is more likely.

Look for four things in your backswing:

✔ Your left arm and your shoulders must be on the same slope. In other words, your arm and shoulders are parallel.

✔ The top of your swing is basically controlled by your right arm, which forms a right angle at the top of the swing (see Figure 8-2). Your elbow is about a dollar bill's length away from your rib cage.

Your right arm should form a right angle at the elbow.

Figure 8-2: Checkpoint.

✔ Your shoulders turn so that they are at 90 degrees to the target line.

✔ The clubface is angled parallel to your left arm and your shoulders. Your left wrist controls this position. Ideally, your wrist angle remains unchanged from address to the top. That way, the relationship between the clubface and your left arm is constant. If your wrist angle does change, the clubface and your left arm are going to be on different planes — and that's a problem.

If your wrist does change, it is either bowed or cupped (see Figure 8-3). A *bowed* (bent forward) left wrist at the top causes the clubface to look skyward in what is called a *closed* position. From that position, a hook is likely. A *cupped* (bent back) wrist means that the clubface is more visible to someone looking you in the face. A cupped wrist leads to an open position, which probably results in a slice.

Of course, playing good golf from an open or closed position at the top of the backswing is possible but more difficult. To do well, your swing has to have some kind of built-in compensation, which is the only way you can square the clubface at impact. And compensations take a lot of practice. Only if you have the time to hit hundreds of balls a week can you ever hope to improve from an inherently flawed swing. Even then, that compensated swing is going to be tough to reproduce under pressure. For examples, watch Corey Pavin (open) and Lee Trevino (closed).

Anyway, swing sequences tend to show three very different methods. The legendary Sam Snead crosses the line at the top and comes over every shot to get the ball to go straight. Solheim Cup player Annika Sorenstam is the opposite. She lays the club off at the top. And 1995 PGA champion Steve Elkington is on plane. Make his swing your model, and you can't go too far wrong.

Figure 8-3:
Wristy
business.

When your left wrist is "bowed," watch out for a hook.

When your left wrist is "cupped," watch out for a slice.

Going Where Others Have Gone Before

No matter what your playing level, a great way to improve is to watch other players, particularly those with some of the same characteristics that you have. Watch for similarities in body size, pace, and shape of swing — even the kinds of mistakes they make under pressure.

One way to start is to identify your goals. Do you want to emulate the master of the long game, John Daly, who regularly blasts drives beyond 300 yards? Or do you want to concentrate on following some experts in the short game, such as Seve Ballesteros, Walter Hagen, and Patty Sheehan? Phil Mickelson has a great lob wedge and sand wedge. Phil Rodgers, with his unique chipping techniques, is a short-game guru.

If you want to follow some really fine putting, keep your eyes peeled for Isao Aoki of Japan, who displays a unique putting stroke acutely tailored to Japanese grass. Former PGA champion Jacki Burke was one of the greatest short putters of all time. Some of the best putters in the world today are Ben Crenshaw and Phil Mickelson, with their long, slow putts, as well as Jim Furych, David Duval, and Mark O'Meara. Nancy Lopez was another great putter in her heyday.

Maybe you want to work on something much more specific. In terms of different swing shapes, every golfer has something to illustrate. Keep a close eye on the golfers who swing like you do, and you may notice something about them that makes their drives sail those 300 yards down the fairway.

Look at those people who have short swings (the club doesn't get to parallel at the top of their swings): Amy Alcott, Lee Trevino, and John Cook. Long-flowing swings you can find here: John Daly, Vicki Goetze, and Phil Mickelson. If you want to look at people who change the shapes of their swings in mid-swing, look at Bruce Lietzke and Jim Furyk, but not for too long — you might go blind!

Some players, like Nancy Lopez, cross the line at the tops of their swings (the club points to the right of the target). Other players, like Ernie Els, have the club laid-off at the top of the swing (pointing to the left of the target at the top of the swing). If you like rhythm and balance, watch Patty Sheehan, and check out pictures of Sam Snead's swing.

Maybe swing speed is your demon. Are you trying too hard to copy some-one you admire, or are you making sure that the pace you use is as natural for you as Tour golfers' swings are for them? Ben Crenshaw, Nancy Lopez, Scott Simpson, and Jay Haas have slow-paced swings. Larry Mize's swing is extremely slow. Steve Elkington, Davis Love III, Jack Nicklaus, Sam Snead,

Annika Sorenstam, and Lee Janzen have medium-paced swings. Fast swings belong to Ben Hogan, Lanny Wadkins, Tom Watson, and Dan Pohl. Nick Price's is very fast. And all these players are very good.

Hand size can affect grip; grip can affect your swing. Watch how these players use their hands. Billy Casper and Dave Stockton use their wrists to create momentum in the clubhead with their putting strokes. Canadian Dave Barr uses the ten-finger grip. Fred Couples uses the cross-handed grip for putting. Jack Nicklaus uses the interlocking grip for his golf swing. Tom Kite uses the interlocking grip for full swings and the cross-handed grip for putting.

Maybe you want to keep tabs on golfers who have modified their games to see how a pro adapts his or her game, either to combat the yips, as did Bernhard Langer, who invented his own grip, and Sam Snead, who putted sidesaddle, or to accommodate a new tool, like Bruce Lietzke's and Orville Moody's long, long putters.

Or maybe your goals are larger than that — you don't care about all these little tricks and habits; you just want to win. Or you're only looking for a few hours of fresh air and fun. Notice how the attitudes of famous players affect not only how they play but also how much they enjoy the game. Nancy Lopez's amiability and ability to keep her cool make her one of the most popular personalities on the LPGA Tour. Fred Couples and Ben Crenshaw are also amiable golfers. Mark O'Meara is one of the rare pro golfers who truly enjoys Pro-Am tournaments.

Seve Ballesteros is a gutsy player who plays with great imagination and creativity. Arnold Palmer is a master of special shots and also a bold golfer. Other daring players include John Daly and Laura Davies, who are as fun and exciting to watch as expressive golfers Lee Trevino and Fuzzy Zoeller. Meg Mallon is always trying something new and winds up having great fun with the game.

On the other end of the attitude spectrum, you'll find Jackie Burke, who created intense drills for himself so that he knew all about pressure: His motivation was to win. Lee Janzen is a fierce competitor, not unlike Ben Hogan, who was himself a steely competitor and a perfectionist, and who surrendered finally not to any other player but to the yips. (See Chapter 9 for more on the yips.) Betsy King's tenacity earned her 20 tournaments in the span of five years. Greg Norman plays to win and is willing to take risks to do it. Other hard-working perfectionists include Tom Kite, Jack Nicklaus, Tom Watson, and Annika Sorenstam.

A conservative style of play is the trademark of Tom Kite and of Mike Reid. Nick Faldo is an analytic golfer.

Finally, there are some players you just can't go wrong watching — they've done so well that they must be doing some things right!

- Bobby Jones was the winner of the 1930 Grand Slams.

- Gary Player is the winner of nine major championships, including all four majors.

- Steve Elkington was the 1995 PGA champion.

- Tommy Armour won a U.S. Open, a British Open, and a PGA championship.

- Lee Trevino won the U.S. Open, the British Open, and the PGA championship twice and has become one of the top players on the Senior Tour.

- Bernhard Langer and Larry Mize have both won the Masters.

- Mark Calcavecchia and Nick Price were British Open champions. Price was the best golfer in the field from 1992 to 1994.

- Walter Hagen was a five-time PGA champion, winner of the British Open four times and the U.S. Open twice.

- Harry Vardon holds the record for the most British Open wins — six in all.

- Sam Snead won 81 tournaments on the PGA Tour.

- Annika Sorenstam won the Women's Open in 1995 and 1996. She also played the Solheim Cup.

- Laura Davies won 17 times through 1998.

- Babe Zaharias, an award-winning athlete, won 31 events and ten major titles in her eight years on the LPGA Tour.

- Nancy Lopez has won 48 on the times LPGA Tour.

- Mickey Wright has won 82 times during her LPGA career.

- Kathy Whitworth has won more times than anybody: 88 times, including six major championships. She was named player of the year seven times.

- Hall of Famer Betsy King won 20 tournaments between 1984 and 1989.

- Hall of Famer JoAnne Carner has won 42 events.

- Hall of Famer Pat Bradley was the first LPGA player to pass the $4 million milestone.

Chapter 9

Putting: The Art of Rolling the Ball

*T*his chapter is an important part of this book. Statistically, putting is 68 percent of the game of golf, so you may want to take notes. You can't score well if you can't putt — it's that simple. If you want proof, look at the top professionals on tour who average about 29 putts per round. In other words, these professionals are one-putting at least 7 of the 18 greens in a round of golf. The average score on tour isn't 7 under par, so even these folks are missing their fair share of greens. And where are they retrieving their mistakes? That's right: with their short game and putting.

Because most women can't physically drive the ball hundreds of yards, they can focus on refining their short game skills, such as chipping, pitching, and putting. Remember, a solid putt counts the same on the scorecard as a 200-yard drive.

No other part of golf induces as much heartache and conversation as putting. Many fine strikers of the ball have literally been driven from the sport because they couldn't finish holes as well as they started them. Why? Because putting messes with your internal organs. Every putt has only two possibilities: You either miss it or hole it. Accept that and you won't have nightmares about the ones that "should" have gone in.

You Gotta Be You

Putting is the most individual part of this individual game. You can putt — and putt successfully — in a myriad of ways. You can break all the rules with a putter in your hands as long as the ball goes in the hole. Believe me, you can get the job done by using any number of methods. You can make long, flowing strokes like Phil Mickelson, Ben Crenshaw, and Vicki Goetze. Or shorter, firmer, "pop" strokes like Corey Pavin and Gary Player. Or you can create the necessary momentum in the clubhead with your wrists — Dave Stockton and Billy Casper are living proof of how well that can work. Or if none of these styles appeals to you, you can go to a long, "witch's broom-handle" putter. Both Orville Moody and Bruce Lietzke did and have enjoyed a lot of success. Putt variety has to do with stroke length. Even on the longest putts, the "swing" required is still less than that for a short chip shot from just off the green.

Putting is more about those ghostly intangibles — feel, touch, and nerve — than about mechanics. My feeling is that getting too involved with putting mechanics is a mistake. You can have the most technically perfect stroke in the world and still be like an orangutan putting a football on the greens — if you don't have the touch, that is. Even more than the rhythm and tempo of your full swing, your putting stroke and demeanor on the greens should reflect your own personality. Your hands probably shouldn't be "behind" the ball at impact, but other than that, your style is up to you.

Be aware that if any aspect of this often-infuriating game was ever designed to drive you to distraction, it's putting. Putting may look simple — and sometimes it is — but some days you just know there's no way that little ball at your feet is going to make its way into that hole. You know it, your playing partners know it, your financial consultant knows it, everyone knows it. Putting is mystical; it comes and goes like the tide.

It's All in Your Head

In putting, visualization is everything. You can visualize in two ways: Either you see the hole as very small, or so big that any fool can drop the ball in. The former, of course, is infinitely more damaging to your psyche than the latter. When you imagine that the hole shrinks, the ball doesn't seem to fit. You can tell yourself that the ball is 1.68 inches in diameter and the hole 4.25 inches across all you want, but the fact remains that the ball is too big. I know; I've been there. It won't fit. It just won't fit no matter what I do. About this time, I usually seek psychiatric care and surround myself with pastel colors.

And on other days, happily, the hole is so big that putting is like stroking a marble into a wine barrel. Simply hit the ball, and boom, it goes in. When this happens to you, savor every moment. Drink in the feeling and bathe in it so that you don't forget it — because you may not take another bath for a long time.

The crazy thing is that these two scenarios can occur on consecutive days, sometimes even in consecutive rounds. I've even experienced both feelings on consecutive holes. Why? I've no idea. Figuring out why is way beyond my feeble intellect. Try not to think too deeply about putting.

Building Your Stroke

As I've already said, you can achieve good putting by using any number of methods or clubs. But I'm going to ignore that when talking about putting basics. At this stage, you should putt in as orthodox a manner as possible. That way, when something goes wrong — which it will — the fault is easier to fix because you know where to look. That's the trouble with unorthodoxy. It's hard to find order in chaos.

The putting grip

The putting grip isn't like the full-swing grip. The full-swing grip is more in the fingers, which encourages the hinging and unhinging of your wrists. Your putting grip's goal is to achieve exactly the opposite effect. You grip the putter more in the palm of your hands to reduce the amount of movement your hands must make. Although you may putt well despite a lot of wrist action in your stroke, I prefer that you take the wrists out of play as much as possible. Unless you have incredible touch, your wrists are not very reliable when you need to hit the ball short distances consistently. You're far better off relying on the rocking of your shoulders to create momentum in the putterhead.

Not all putting grips are the same — not even those grips where you place your right hand below the left in conventional fashion. But what all putting grips do have in common is that the palms of both hands face each other, so your hands can work together in the stroke. The last thing you want is your hands fighting one another. Too much right hand, and your ball has a bad experience. If your left hand dominates, your right hand sues for nonsupport. Both hands need to work together for a good experience and no legal hassles.

Your hands can join together in one of two ways, shown in Figure 9-1. (I describe a more advanced method of gripping the club in the following section, "Left hand low.") Go with the grip that you find most comfortable.

Place your palms on opposing sides of the grip.

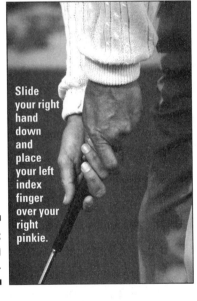

Slide your right hand down and place your left index finger over your right pinkie.

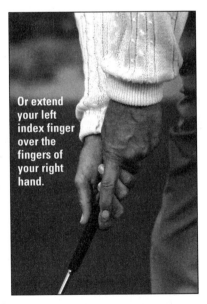

Or extend your left index finger over the fingers of your right hand.

Figure 9-1:
A gripping
start.

✔ Place the palms of your hands on either side of the club's grip. Slide your right hand down a little so that you can place both hands on the club. You should feel like you are going to adopt the ten-finger grip (see Chapter 7).

✔ Place your left index finger over the little finger of your right hand. Known as the "reverse overlap," this is probably the most-used putting grip on the PGA and LPGA Tours.

✔ Extend your left index finger down the outside of the fingers of your right hand until the tip touches your right index finger. I call this grip the "extended reverse overlap." The left index finger, when extended, provides stability to the putting stroke.

Left hand low

This method is commonly referred to as *cross-handed.* The left hand hangs below the right with the putter (or vice versa if you're a lefty). This method is used by many players today because it helps keep the lead hand (the left, in this case) from bending at the wrist as you hit the ball. (See Figure 9-2.)

A left-hand-below-right putting grip helps stop left-wrist breakdown.

Figure 9-2: Keep that left wrist firm.

One of the biggest causes of missed putts is the breaking down of the left wrist through impact. The left wrist bends through impact, causing the putter blade to twist. This twisting causes the ball to wobble off-line. The bend that your left wrist has at the address position should be maintained throughout the stroke.

The cross-handed grip is said to make maintaining your wrist position easier. Many great players such as Fred Couples and Tom Kite have gone to this type of grip.

The few times I have tried the cross-handed grip, pulling with the left wrist seemed to be easier. It seems that pulling with the lead hand makes it harder to break down with the wrist.

Another reason you see many of today's pros using a cross-handed grip is that with the left arm lower on the shaft, you pull the left shoulder more square to your target line. Pulling your left shoulder happens automatically with this grip. I tend to open my shoulders (aim to the left) with my putter. As soon as I use this type of grip, my left shoulder moves toward the target line, and I'm more square to my line.

I think the best asset that this stroke has to offer is that you swing the left arm back and forth during the stroke. The trailing hand (right) is along for the ride, which is a very good way to stroke your golf ball. I suggest that you try this grip.

Long putters

The difference with using long putters is that the length of the club dictates where you place your hands on the club. The long putter is the final refuge for the neurologically impaired. If you watch any Senior PGA Tour event on television, you see more than a few long putters.

Long putters differ greatly and range from 46 to 52 inches in length. Long putters remove all wrist movement from your putting stroke because your left hand anchors the club to your chest. Your left hand holds the club at the end of the shaft, and your fingers wrap around the grip so that the back of your hand faces the ball. That grip is the fulcrum around which the club swings. Your right hand is basically along for the ride. In fact, your right hand should barely touch the club. Your right hand's only role is to pull the club back and follow the club through.

Long putters are easy on the nerves, which is why these clubs enjoy such popularity on the Senior Tour. Although, to be fair, Senior Tour players are not alone. No fewer than three members of the European Ryder Cup team in 1995 used long putters. And all three members won their singles matches on the final afternoon, perhaps the most pressure-filled day in all of golf. So long putters definitely have something. You've got nothing to lose by trying one.

My first introduction into the advantages of the long putter came, as a lot of my golf knowledge did, from Mac O'Grady. We were playing a practice round at Riveria Country Club for the L.A. Open. Mac was not putting with much distinction at this point and decided to have two neurosurgeons from UCLA's neurological department follow us as we golfed. Mac was writing and financing a study about the yips (discussed later in this chapter) for publication, and these two doctors were helping with the study. The doctors had no background in golf and followed us for nine holes while Mac putted with a 52-inch-long putter and I used my regular 35-inch putter. The doctors had no idea that few golfers use a long putter.

Mac asked the doctors to take notes as we went about our business, and then we got together after the round and discussed the merits of both putting techniques. We first asked the doctors to explain the workings of my stroke with the short putter. One doctor said, "Gary uses bimanual manipulation of the implement that requires a left-right brain synergy because both hands and shoulder movement are constantly monitored by the brain as they are acting together." I ordered a beer.

I swallowed hard and then asked what they thought of Mac's stroke with the long putter. "Mac has isolated the left shoulder and has a fixed fulcrum with the left hand. The right shoulder joint is doing the swinging without the deployment of the right wrist. You have effectively isolated only one side of the brain (the left hemisphere controls the right side and vice versa) because there is no conspiracy going on with only one side controlling the movement. You can deter focal dystonia much longer with this movement." I ordered a Jack Daniels.

The doctors asked the last question of the day: "Why would anyone use that little short putter that Gary uses? It is obviously inferior, as he has to put two hands on it to control the movement. The long putter and its technique are superior for gradient ramp movement." I ordered two aspirins.

Putting posture

After you establish where your eyes should be as you crouch over the ball to putt, you need to be in the correct posture position. You should have a slight knee flex in your putting stance. If your knees are locked in a straight position, you're straining your back too much. Don't bend your knees too much, though, because you may start to look like a golf geek!

You should bend over from your waist so that your arms hang straight down. This stance allows the arms to swing in a pendulum motion, back and forth from a fixed point. Hold your arms straight out from your body as you are standing straight and tall. Now bend down with those arms outstretched from the waist until your arms are pointing to the ground. Then flex your knees a little bit, and you're in the correct putting posture.

Putting: Stand and deliver

You can break a lot of rules in how you stand to hit a putt. (See Figure 9-3.) Ben Crenshaw stands open to the target line, his left foot drawn back. Gary Player does the opposite: He sets up closed, his right foot farther from the target line than his left. But that's their style; I keep things simple with a square stance so that I don't need to make many in-stroke adjustments to compensate for an unorthodox stance.

Toeing the line

As in a full swing, your toe stance line is the key. Regardless of which stance you choose, your toe stance line should always be parallel to your target line (refer to Figure 9-3). Be aware that the target line isn't always a straight line from the ball to the hole — if only putting were that simple. Unfortunately, greens are rarely flat, so putts break or bend either from right to left or from left to right. (See "Reading the break," later in this chapter.) So sometimes you're going to be aiming, say, 5 inches to the right of the hole, and other times maybe a foot to the left. (See Figure 9-4.) Whatever you decide, your toe stance line must always be parallel your target line.

Being parallel to your target line is important. In effect, you make every putt straight. Applying a curve to your putts is way too complicated and affects your stroke. Imagine how you have to adjust if you aim at the hole and then try to push the ball out to the right because of a slope on the green. You have no way to be consistent. Keep putting simple. Remember, on curved putts, aim your feet parallel to the line you have chosen, not to the hole (see Figure 9-5).

Standing just right

Okay, now what about width of stance? Again, you have margin for error, but your heels need to be about shoulder-width apart at address, as shown in Figure 9-6.

You have to bend over to put the putter behind the ball. How far should you bend? Far enough so that your eye line (a much-neglected part of putting) is directly above the ball. To find out how that position feels, place a ball on your forehead between your eyes, bend over, and let the ball drop, as shown in Figure 9-7. Where the ball hits the ground is where the ball should be in relation to your body. The ball shouldn't be to the inside, the outside, behind, or in front of that point. The ball should be right there, dead center. This alignment places your eyes not just over the ball but also over the line that you want the ball to travel.

Figure 9-3:
Putting
stances are
optional.

Figure 9-4:
Playing the break.

Sometimes your target isn't the hole.

Sometimes you have to allow for the ball to bend on a sloping green.

Figure 9-5:
Feet are parallel to your putting line.

For putting, your heels should be shoulder-width apart.

Figure 9-6:
Heels and
shoulders
are the
same width.

Drop the ball from a point between your eyes.

Where the ball lands is where it should be positioned in your stance.

Figure 9-7:
Align your
eyes over
the ball.

Let the shape of your stroke dictate which putter you use

Okay, you've got an idea of how to hold onto your putter and how to stand to hit a putt. The next step is deciding what putter to use. Although you have a lot of putters to choose from, you can eliminate many by knowing the type of putter you are. In other words, the shape of your stroke is the determining factor in the type of putter that you use. Figure 9-8 shows two types of putters.

My good friend and noted teaching professional Peter Kostis explains: Most putting strokes fall into one of two groups, at least in terms of their shapes. They either move "straight back and straight through" with the blade staying square, or "inside to inside," the blade doing a mini-version of the rotation found in a full swing. Conveniently, most putters are suited to a specific stroke shape. There are two main types: face-balanced, center-shafted putters and those that are not face-balanced, such as heel-shafted blades.

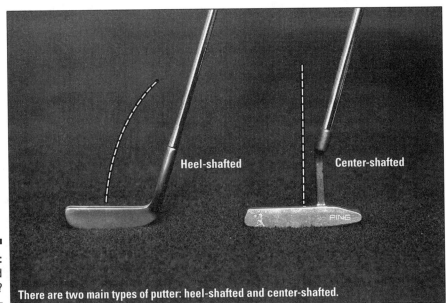

Heel-shafted

Center-shafted

Figure 9-8:
Which kind
of putter?

There are two main types of putter: heel-shafted and center-shafted.

The key to success is to match your putter to your stroke. If keeping the blade square in your stroke is important to you, get a face-balanced, center-shafted model. You can test to see whether a putter is face-balanced by resting the shaft on your finger. If the putterface stays parallel to the ground, it is face-balanced.

The inside-to-inside stroke is easier to make on a consistent basis with a heel-shafted putter. It will hang toe-down while resting on your finger.

Be warned, though. Some putters hang at an angle of 45 degrees. They are equally good — or bad! — for either stroke.

Getting up to speed

In the two decades-plus that I played on the PGA Tour, I saw a lot of putters and a lot of different putting methods. The good putters came in all shapes and sizes, too. Some good putters putted in what could be termed mysterious ways, and other good putters were very conventional. So analyzing different putting methods is no help. The best way to look at putting is to break it down to its simplest level. The hole. The ball. The ball fits into the hole. Now get the ball into the hole in the fewest possible strokes.

You have to hit each putt so that the ball rolls at the right speed. If you don't have the speed, you don't know where to aim. The right speed means hitting a putt so that the ball that misses the cup finishes 14 to 18 inches past the hole, as shown in Figure 9-9. This distance is true no matter the length of the putt. Two feet or 40 feet, your aim must be to hit the ball at a pace that will see it finish 14 to 18 inches beyond the hole.

You're probably wondering why your ball needs the right speed. Well, the right speed gives the ball the greatest chance of going into the hole. Think about it: If the ball rolls toward the middle of the cup, it won't be going so hard that it rolls right over the hole. If the ball touches either side of the cup, it may drop in. The plan is to give the ball every chance to drop in, from any angle — front, back, or side. I don't know about you, but I want that hole to seem as big as possible.

The only putts I know that certainly don't drop are those putts left short of the hole. If you've played golf for any length of time, you've heard the phrase "never up, never in" when you've left a putt 6 inches short of the cup. The phrase is annoying but true. As the Irish say, "99 percent of all putts that come up short don't go in, and the other 1 percent never get there." Remember that saying. Also remember that you should try to make every putt that lands 10 feet from the hole and closer. I hope to make every putt from 10 to 20 feet, and I try to get every putt close from 20 feet and beyond.

Figure 9-9:
How hard to
hit your
putts.

Aim to hit every putt so that if it misses, it rolls
14 to 18 inches past the hole.

Reading the break

After you have the distance control that a consistent pace brings, you can
work on the second half of the putting equation: reading the break. The
break is the amount a putt moves from right to left or left to right on a green.
Slope, topographical features such as water and mountains, the grain of the
grass, and, perhaps most important, how hard you hit the ball dictate the
break. For example, if I am an aggressive player who routinely hits putts 5
feet past the cup, I'm not going to play as much break as you. (You, remember, hit your putts only 14 to 18 inches past the cup.)

The firmer you hit a putt, the less the ball bends or breaks on even the
steepest gradient. So don't be fooled into thinking that there's only one way
a putt can be holed. On, say, a 20 footer, you probably have about five
possibilities. How hard you hit the ball is one factor.

The key, of course, is consistency, the genesis of putting. Being a bold putter
is not a bad thing (if you're willing to put up with the occasional return
5-footer) — as long as you putt that way all the time and are still in your teens.

Anyway, the first thing I do when I arrive at a golf course is to find the natural slope of the terrain. If mountains are in the area, finding the natural slope is easy. Say the mountains are off to your right on the first hole. Any slope is going to be from right to left on that hole. In fact, the slope on every green is going to be "from" the mountain (unless, of course, a particularly humorless architect has decided to bank some holes toward the mountain). So I take that into account on every putt I hit.

If the course is relatively flat, go to the pro or course superintendent. Ask about nearby reservoirs or, failing that, the area's lowest point. This point can be 5 miles away or 20 — it doesn't matter. Find out where that point is and take advantage of gravity. Gravity is a wonderful concept. Every putt breaks down a hill — high point to low point — unless you're in a zero-gravity environment. But that's another book.

After you know the lowest point, look at each green in detail. If you're on an older course, the greens probably slope from back to front because of drainage. Greens nowadays have more humps and undulations than ever and are surrounded by more bunkers. And the sand is the key. The drainage should be designed so that water runs past a bunker and not into the sand. Take that insight into account when you line up a putt. And don't forget the barometric pressure and dew point — just kidding! (For fun and entertaining information about sand traps, see Chapter 11.)

Going against the grain

Golf is played on different grasses (hopefully not on the same course), and climate usually determines the kind of grass on a course. Grasses in hot, tropical areas have to be more resilient, so they typically have thick blades. *Bermuda grass* is the most common. Its blades tend to follow the sun from morning to afternoon — in other words, from east to west. Because the blade is so strong, Bermuda grass can carry a golf ball according to the direction in which it is lying. Putts "downgrain" are faster than putts "into" the grain. All that, of course, has an effect on where you have to aim a putt.

Look at the cup to find out which way the grass is growing. Especially in the afternoon, you see a ragged half and a smooth, or sharp, half — the direction in which the grass is growing. The ragged look is caused by the grass's tendency to grow and fray. If you can't tell either way, go to the fringe (the edge of the green). The grass on the fringe is longer, so you can usually see the direction of the grain right away.

Another common type of grass is *bent grass*. You see bent grass primarily in the northern and northeastern United States. Bent grass has a thinner blade than Bermuda grass, but it doesn't stand up to excessive heat as well.

Bent grass is used by many golf course builders because you can get the greens moving real fast, and the recent trend for greens is to combine slope with speed. Try getting on the roof of your car, putting a ball down to the hood ornament, and making it stop. That's the speed of most of the greens on tour with bent grass.

I don't concern myself much with grain on bent greens. I just worry about the slope and the 47 things on my checklist before I putt. Putting could be so much fun if I didn't have a brain.

If you get the chance to play golf in Japan, you'll play on grass called *korai*. This wiry grass can be a menace on the greens because it's stronger than Astroturf and can really affect the way the ball rolls on the green. If the blades of grass are growing toward you, you have to hit the ball with a violent pop.

Isao Aoki, a great Japanese player, uses a unique putting stroke in which he has the toe of the putter way off the ground and then gives the ball a pop with his wrist to get it going — an effective way of dealing with the korai grass he grew up on.

When dealing with grasses, an architect tries to use the thinnest possible blade, given the climate, and then tries to get that grass to grow straight up to eliminate grain. Bent is better than Bermuda when it comes to growing straight, so grain is rarely a factor on bent greens.

Bobbing for plumbs

Plumb-bobbing is all about determining where vertical is. It lets you determine how much break is present. Plumb-bobbing is one reason — along with polyester pants and plaid jackets — that nongolfers laugh at serious golfers. When a plumb-bobbing golfer pops up on TV, all the nongolfer sees is a guy, one eye closed, standing with a club dangling in front of his face. Actually, if you think about this scenario, the whole thing does look more than a little goofy. I can't honestly say that I am a devotee of the method, although plumb-bobbing works for some people. I use plumb-bobbing only when I'm totally bored on the green or if I think that one of the condos on the course was built on a slant. But if Ben Crenshaw thinks that plumb-bobbing helps, who am I to argue?

The first step in plumb-bobbing is to find your dominant eye. You close the other eye when plumb-bobbing. Here's how to find yours.

Make a circle with the thumb and index finger of your right hand a couple of inches in front of your face, as shown in Figure 9-10. Look through the circle at a distant object. Keep both eyes open at this stage. Now close your right eye. Where is the object now? If the object is still in the circle, your left eye is dominant. If, of course, you can still see the object in the circle with your left eye closed, then your right eye is dominant.

Figure 9-10:
Find your
dominant
eye.

Okay, now you're ready to plumb-bob. Put some dancing shoes on and stand as close to the ball as possible. First, keeping your dominant eye open, hold your putter up in front of your face and perpendicular to the ground so that the shaft runs through the ball. Now look to see where the hole is in relation to the shaft. If the hole appears to the right of the club, the ball will break from the shaft to the hole — from left to right. If the hole is on the left, the opposite will be true. (See Figure 9-11.) What plumb-bobbing basically shows is the general slope of the green from your ball to the hole.

Remember that this is about as exact as weather forecasting, but it gives you the vicinity.

Plumb-bobbing is not an exact science. But plumb-bobbing is very cool. People who see you plumb-bobbing will think that you know something they don't. So, if nothing else, fake plumb-bobbing. People will be impressed.

Dominant eye open, hold the shaft up perpendicular to the ground and in front of your face.

Figure 9-11:
Plumbing
the depths.

Where the hole is in relation
to the shaft indicates how
much a putt will bend.

Short Putts

One of the greatest short putters of all time is former PGA champion Jackie Burke, who today helps Tour player Steve Elkington with his game. I was talking to Jackie one day about putting and asked him how he developed his ability to make short putts. His reply made short putts seem astonishingly simple. All Jackie did was analyze his game to identify his strengths and weaknesses. He concluded that his short game — his pitching and chipping — was where he could pick up strokes on his competitors. (See Chapter 10 for information about the short game.) Jackie knew that to score really well, he had to be able to make a lot of putts in the 3- to 4-foot range. He felt that most of his chips and pitches would finish 3 to 4 feet from the cup.

So every day, Jackie went to the practice putting green with 100 balls. He stuck his putterhead in the cup, and where the butt end of the club hit the ground, he put a ball. Then he went over to the caddie shed and grabbed a caddie. Jackie handed the guy a $100 bill and told him to sit down behind the cup. If Jackie made all 100 putts, Jackie kept the money. If he missed even one, the caddie pocketed the cash.

Jackie did this routine every day. All of a sudden, every short putt he hit meant something. All short putts counted. And when he got to the golf course and was faced with a short putt, he knew that he had already made 100 of them under a lot of pressure. (A hundred dollar bill in those days was backed by real gold.)

The word *pressure* is the key. You have to create a situation in which missing hurts you. Missing doesn't have to hurt you financially. Any kind of suffering is fine. You have to care about the result of every putt. If all you have to do after missing is pull another ball over and try again, you're never going to get better. You don't care enough.

So put yourself under pressure, even if you only make yourself stay on the green until you can make 25 putts in a row. You'll be amazed at how difficult the last putt is after you've made 24 in a row. The last putt is the same putt in physical terms. But mentally, you're feeling nervous, knowing that missing means that you've wasted your time over the previous 24 shots. In other words, you'll have created tournament conditions on the practice green. Now that's pressure; suck some air.

Because you don't want the ball to travel far, the stroke has to be equally short, which doesn't give the putterhead much of an arc to swing on. But the lack of arc is okay. On a short putt, you don't want the putterhead to move inside or outside the target line (on the way back). So think straight back and straight through. If you can keep the putterface looking directly at the hole throughout the stroke and you are set up squarely, you're going to make more short putts than you miss.

My instructions sound easy, but as with everything else in golf, knowing how short putting feels helps. Lay a 2 x 4 piece of wood on the ground. Place the toe of your putter against the board. Hit some putts, keeping the toe against the board until after impact, as shown in Figure 9-12. Always keep the putterhead at 90 degrees to the board so that the putter moves on the straight-back-and-straight-through path that you want. Practice this drill until you can repeat the sensation on real putts. And remember one of my *Golf For Dummies* secrets: Never allow the wrist on your lead hand to bend when putting. If you do, you'll end up in putting hell.

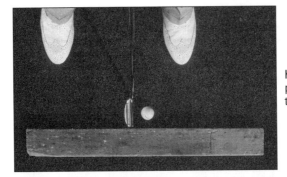

Keep the toe of your putter touching the board...

when you move the putter back...

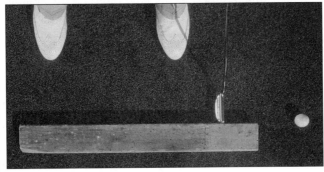

and through.

Figure 9-12: Wood that it could be this easy.

Long Putts

If short putts are a test of precision and technique, long putts are a test of your feel for pace. Nothing more. The last thing I want you thinking about over, say, a 40-foot putt is how far back you want to take the putter or what path the putter will follow. Instead, focus on smoothness, rhythm, and timing — all the things that foster control over the distance a ball travels. Or, as Chevy Chase said in the cult golf movie *Caddyshack,* "Be the ball."

The following is how I practice my long putting. First, I don't aim for a hole. I'm thinking distance, not direction. I figure that hitting a putt 10 feet short is a lot more likely than hitting it 10 feet wide, so distance is the key. I throw a bunch of balls down on the practice green and putt to the far fringe (see Figure 9-13). I want to see how close I can get to the edge without going over. I don't care about where I hit the putt, just how far. After a while, you'll be amazed at how adept you become, to the point where, after impact, you can predict with accuracy how far the ball will roll.

To get a feel for distance, putt a few balls to the far side of the practice putting green.

Figure 9-13:
Find the
pace.

One of the basic rules for a beginning golfer is to match the length of your golf swing to your putting stroke. That is, if you have a short golf swing (your left arm, if you're right-handed, doesn't get too far up in the air on your backswing), you should make sure that your putting stroke is a short one. If your golf swing is long, make sure that your putting stroke is long also. Don't fight the forces of contradiction.

Look at two of the greatest putters in the world today, Ben Crenshaw and Phil Mickelson. Both players have long and slow swings, and their putting strokes are the same. On the other hand, you have Nick Price and Lanny Wadkins, who have quick swings and quick putting strokes. They all keep a balance between golf swing and putting stroke.

Your swing tells a lot about your personality. If your golf swing is long and slow, usually you are a very easygoing individual. If your swing is short and fast, you're usually the kind of person who walks around with his hair on fire. So don't mix the two types of swings because that can lead to a contrast in styles within your game.

Making a contradiction in the two, I believe, leads to problems. Sam Snead had a great long putting stroke that went with his beautiful swing, but as the years came on the golf course, the swing stayed long and the stroke got much shorter. The yips took over (see "The Yips," later in this chapter). Johnny Miller had a big swing with his golf clubs and a putting stroke that was so fast you could hardly see it. There was a contradiction, and he had to go to the TV tower because he couldn't roll 'em in anymore. The change wasn't all bad; Johnny adds great insight to the game from his position in the announcing booth.

So keep your two swings — the golf swing and the putting stroke — the same. Keep your mind quiet and create no contradictions between the two swings.

I call my routine "being the ball." Another exercise to foster your feel for distance is what I call the "ladder" drill. Place a ball on the green about 10 feet from the green's edge. From at least 30 feet away, try to putt another ball between the first ball and the fringe. Then try to get a third ball between the second ball and the fringe and so on. See how many balls you can putt before you run out of room or putting gets too difficult. Obviously, the closer you get each ball to the preceding one, the more successful you are.

The Yips

"I've got the yips" is perhaps the most feared phrase in golf. Any professional golfer with the yips may as well be on the green setting fire to dollar bills. Make that hundred dollar bills. Simply put, *yips* is a nervous condition that prevents the afflicted unfortunates from making any kind of smooth putting stroke. Instead, they are reduced to jerky little snatches at the ball, the putterhead seemingly possessing a mind all its own.

Some of the greatest players in the history of golf have had their careers — at least at the top level — cut short by the yips. Ben Hogan, perhaps the steeliest competitor ever, is one such player. His great rival, Sam Snead, is another. Arnold Palmer has a mild case. Bobby Jones, winner of the Grand Slam in 1930, had the yips. So did Tommy Armour, a brave man who lost an eye fighting in the trenches during World War I and then later won a British Open and a PGA Championship, but whose playing career was finished by his inability to hole short putts. Peter Alliss, a commentator on ABC Television, found that he couldn't even move the putter away from the ball toward the end of his career.

Perhaps the most famous recent example of someone getting the yips is two-time Masters winner Bernhard Langer, who has had the yips not once, not twice, but three times. To Langer's eternal credit, he has overcome the yips each time, hence his rather unique, homemade style where he seems to be taking his own pulse while over a putt.

Langer, who overcame the yips and is still considered one of the best putters in Europe, is the exception rather than the rule. As Henry Longhurst, the late, great writer and commentator, said about the yips, "Once you've had 'em, you've got 'em."

Longhurst, himself a yipper, once wrote a highly entertaining column on the yips, which opened with the following sentence: "There can be no more ludicrous sight than that of a grown man, a captain of industry, perhaps, and a pillar of his own community, convulsively jerking a piece of ironmongery to and fro in his efforts to hole a 3-foot putt." Longhurst is right, too. Pray that you don't get the yips.

So what causes this involuntary muscle-twitching over short putts? Mostly, I think it's fear of missing. Fear of embarrassment. Fear of who knows what. Whatever, it starts in the head. It can't be physical. After all, we're only talking about hitting the ball a short distance. What could be easier than that?

The yips spread insidiously through your body like a virus. When the yips reach your hands and arms, you're doomed. Your only recourse is a complete revamping of your method. Sam Snead started putting sidesaddle, facing the hole, holding his putter with a sort of split-handed grip, the ball to the right of his feet. Langer invented his own grip, as I've said. Other players have tried placing their left hand below the right on the putter. The long putter (described earlier in this chapter) has saved other players.

When Mac O'Grady did his study on the yips, he mailed 1,500 questionnaires to golfers everywhere. When the doctors at UCLA's Department of Neurology looked over the results, they told us that the only way to "fool" the yips is to stay ahead of them. When you do something long enough, like bending over to putt a certain way, your body is in what the doctors call a "length tension curve." This posture is recognized by the brain, and after you have missed putts for a long period of time, the subconscious takes over and starts to help by directing muscles to help get the ball into the hole. Your conscious and subconscious are fighting, and you're going to lose. So, without you knowing it, your right hand twitches, or your left forearm has spasms trying to help you get the ball into the hole. You're in full focal dystonia (involuntary spasms) right now, and that's not fun.

The remedy the doctors suggested was to change the length tension curve, or simply change the way you stand over a putt. The long putter surely makes you stand up to the ball differently, and maybe that's why those players always putt better immediately without the constraints of having the involuntary muscle movements known as the yips.

So if you get the yips, which usually comes with age, simply change something drastic in the way you set up the ball, make your grip totally different, or go bowling.

The real key, however, is getting over the notion that using any of those methods immediately identifies you as a yipper and in some way psychologically impaired. That, to my mind, is socially harsh. Don't be afraid to look different if you get the yips. Do whatever works.

The Art of Aiming the Ball

The golf swing is an assortment of trajectories flung around in time and space, with the golf club as the servant of the brain ill-equipped to do the directing in spatial darkness. Manifestations of your binocular acuity are the key to your pilgrimage. Are you in alignment with the parallel universe of focal obedience?
—Gary McCord, circa 1998, just after eating a lungfish tart

Golf is played with an assortment of physical skills and techniques. It is also played with the mind, which makes the final decisions and tells your motor system where and when things will happen, hopefully in some sort of dignified occurrence.

Some of the skills demanded by golf, and especially by putting, relate to peripheral vision, depth perception, binocularity (your eyes working as a team), eye-hand coordination, aiming accuracy, and visualization. These skills may well be more basic than grip, stance, and swing mechanics. I label this area *optics.*

The problem in golf is that what you perceive optically can be crystal clear yet inaccurate. And almost everything you *do* begins with what you *see* or *perceive.* Having to set up to the side of the ball and the target instead of behind them, as in other sports, really wreaks havoc with your optics. Trusting your optics in golf is like being in a house of mirrors, and you can be fooled easily. If your optical perception doesn't match reality, you see an illusion. (Me dating Cindy Crawford is an example.) And when your optics are tricked, you look at things like Mr. Magoo trying to read an eye chart — a little out of whack.

But you can be "re-educated" in optics. And right now, when you're first taking up the game, is a great time to start. A few simple exercises can make a world of difference as you start off on your quest to perfect putting.

Putting doesn't involve a lot of mechanics, but it does require a whole bunch of perception.

Optics and alignment

Some say that the basis for a lot of what goes wrong out on the course is poor alignment, which often results from faulty optics. (I'll have to put this on my list of new excuses, right after solar flares.) When you miss a putt, you might blame your stroke, when really you may have missed because of improper alignment — a misperception of the target's location, the clubface as related to "square," or the green's characteristics.

Nothing is more optically dependent than alignment. As I said earlier, the difficulty is that you have to deal with the surreal situation of being beside the target line rather than behind it — or do you?

You use two optical areas in determining your alignment: the address perspective and aim. The address perspective is your perspective when you stand next to the ball and assume your stance (see Figure 9-14). This is the more confusing area for most golfers. You use aim when you stare at the trash can, getting ready to throw a wadded-up piece of paper. You also use aim when you stand behind the ball and pick a line to putt on.

Figure 9-14: Make a practice stroke while standing at a right angle to the line with both eyes in normal position instead of parallel to the line (abnormal).

Some golfers use a spot a few feet in front of the ball when aiming. When they place their putters down behind the ball, they aim the face of the putter or the lines on the putter at that spot. Aligning to a spot a foot or so in front of the ball is easier than aligning to the hole, which may be several feet away.

Bowlers use this same kind of alignment strategy. If you've ever bowled, you know about the spots that are a few feet in front of you on the lane. You look at the spots and then pick a line to roll the ball over. After I discovered this technique in my bowling league, the Gutter Dwellers, my average rocketed to 87. (Check out my bowling technique in Figure 9-15.)

Figure 9-15:
Do like bowlers do and aim at a spot a few feet in front of you.

You can use a couple of other stategies to help with your alignment problems. The first one is to take the logo of the golf ball and set it along the line that you want the putt to follow. This can help you get a better visual reference to the line. Other players, like Tiger Woods, take a Sharpie pen and make a line about 1 inch in length on the ball (see Figure 9-16). You can use this method in the same way as the logo tip — to achieve a better visual reference for directing the ball down the intended path. When you stand over the putt, the ball is already aimed. That easy.

Figure 9-16:
Aim the logo of the ball down the intended line of the putt.

Or make a line on the ball with a Sharpie pen.

The eyes like lines

Players say that they putt better when they "see the line" of the putt. Some days when I play, the line is so visible that I can't miss. Unfortunately, this happens about once every presidential election year. Most of the time, I have to really concentrate to "see" the line. Another set of lines that can help improve your optics are the lines of your feet, knees, and shoulders. By keeping them square (at a right angle) to the target line, you aid your eyes in their appreciation of what is straight — and this helps keep your stroke on line.

To help you appreciate a clubface that's square to your target line, use tape or a yardstick on the floor. Aim the tape at a distant target, such as your baby grand piano at the far end of your ballroom. Now set up at the end of the tape as if you were going to hit an imaginary ball straight down the tape line. You're practicing your visual alignment (which is a lot easier than practicing a 3-wood out of a fairway bunker with a large lip for three hours in a mild hailstorm). Give this drill a chance; it can really help you with your perception of straight lines.

When I'm having problems aligning my clubface, I take some of the gum that I've been chewing for the last three days and attach a tee to the putter with the fat end flush to the face, as shown in Figure 9-17. Then I aim that tee at the hole from about 3 feet away. (It's amazing how strong gum is after a three-day chew; in fact, I used it as mortar on my new brick mobile home.)

Figure 9-17:
Attach a tee
to the face
of your
putter to
help align to
your target.

Your job is to stand there and visually appreciate what a square clubface looks like as you look down the attached tee to the hole. Spend a couple of minutes appreciating this perspective. If it looks okay to you on your first try, you're in line for your Bachelor of Alignment diploma. If not, repeat this drill daily until it looks okay the first time you place the club down. Use this drill to educate your eyes to a straight-line perspective and a square clubface.

Instant "preplay"

A rule of optics: When you have a mental picture of what you want to do, it often happens the way you picture it. How often have you dumped a shot into the water or a bunker and said, "I knew I was going to do that!" This is because you mentally perceived doom, and in your own clairvoyance you acted out the morbid scene. Stupid game.

To help overcome this problem in putting, I recommend watching others putt. Doing so trains you to optically appreciate the speed of the greens. Make a game of it. Guess how many seconds it will take for the ball to roll from the impact of the putter to its stopping point. Then time it — count one-thousand-one, one-thousand-two . . . , or use a stop watch or the second hand on your watch. Stay in the game, and always be aware of what's going on around you. Using these situations will help you play the game better.

GARY SAYS

The longest putt ever?

I remember in one particular tournament commenting on a putt that was caught on camera: "That putt must have taken 11 seconds." It was a long putt that went over a hill and then down a severe slope to the hole. The player had to perceive the roll in order to hit it with the proper speed; he had to visually rehearse the roll of the ball over the terrain until it looked like an instant replay of the putt he was about to roll.

As you observe others putting, notice that the ball goes through speed phases: the first being the fastest (acceleration), the second being sort of a glide, and the last being the slow-down-to-stop phase. Another reason to watch others putt is that, at first, you don't see the first several feet of the ball's roll because you're still fixated on the spot where the ball was.

Often, golfers tend to do this kind of optical preview when they stand aside the line, watching the ball roll off the putter. You say, "Pull a hamstring!" or "Grow hair!" if you hit a putt too hard and it is obviously going to zoom by the hole. You make the same type of comment — "Turn up the volume!" or "Get some enthusiasm!" — when the putt isn't going to get there. You make these comments (other than because you may be a little deranged) because you made an optical decision before you hit the ball. When the speed doesn't match the speed you imagined was necessary, you start spewing insults to the golf ball. (The funnier the insults, the more the ball tends to listen.)

After you get used to seeing what other players' putts look like, use this technique for your own putts. Look at the distance from the ball to the hole as if your eyes were walking the distance. Perhaps a 30-foot putt would take your eyes four seconds to look along the ground at a meaningful pace, while a 10-foot putt would take two seconds, and a 50-foot putt would take six seconds. Then take a practice stroke and imagine yourself hitting the ball at that speed, as shown in Figure 9-18.

GARY SAYS

I find this exercise very helpful when playing professionally. I spend some time on the practice putting green and get a feel for the speed of the greens. Then I incorporate "instant preplay," tracing the line with my eyes at the exact speed at which I think the ball will roll. Watch Phil Mickelson on television the next time he has a long putt. He assumes his address position and then traces the line with his eyes, tracking the line by using the "instant preplay" technique.

Figure 9-18:
Make a
practice
stroke and
follow the
intended
line with
your eyes at
the speed
you think
the ball will
travel.

Speed kills

Almost every putt is what I call a "depth charge" launch. That means that it should have the speed to lurk around the hole and just maybe hit the hole and fall in. If you get it close, you might perform a burial with your balata. One of the best ways to develop a touch for the speed at which a putt should roll is to imagine things happening before they really do.

You must optically preview the putt's roll from its stationary point to a resting place near the hole — a tap-in is really nice. This optical preview activates the motor system to respond with the right amount of energy to hit the putt. You would use the same skill if I told you to throw a ball over a certain bush and make it land no more than 5 feet beyond the bush. All your actions use optics to determine at what arc and speed to toss the ball, and this information is relayed to the muscles.

Distance optics

Optical inaccuracy can cause an unwanted golf incident: the morbid three-putt. If there's any way to cut down on strokes, it is by eliminating extra putts. Statistics say that the average player has three to four three-putts per round — and for beginners, it's more like seven or eight. That's because you're often optically challenged when faced with long putts.

Most people perceive distances to be shorter than they actually are because of how the eyes triangulate (see Figure 9-19). You can gain this triangular perspective by holding one end of a string to your nose while the other end of the string is attached to a lazy uncle who has taken up residence on your couch for the last month.

Figure 9-19:
How the
eyes
typically
triangulate
— kind of
like a range
finder.

The two eyes act as a team, pointing their visual axis at a target (your prone uncle). The angle of difference in convergence between the two eyes depends on how far away the target is — being more of an angle for a book 16 inches away and less of an angle for the wallowing blob on your couch. The lesser the angle, the farther away you perceive things to be. Unfortunately, even though you may think that your eyes are focused on the target, they may be focused on a point in front of the target, making you perceive the target to be closer than it really is.

This view is called "eyeballing" the distance. You look at the hole and expect to optically interpret the distance accurately. Wrong! But you can combat the optical distortion of a long putt in several ways:

✔ Use the "instant preplay" technique discussed earlier in this chapter.

✔ Stand beside the line like you're going to hit the putt. This is how your eyes are accustomed to viewing the landscape, and you can better judge the speed of the ball/greens in this position than if you stand directly behind the line.

The more you improve the accuracy of the information your eyes and brain feed to your motor system, the more you can expect good results in the form of a putt that gets the ball close. This is a very good drill, and if I were you, I wouldn't go telling my friends about it.

✔ Look softly as you look at the hole from behind the ball, trying to expand your view to the sides of the hole. Doing so often improves your distance appreciation. (If you don't believe me, go back to the string exercise and instead of fixating on the end, open up your view.) Most often, expanding your peripheral vision helps you judge space.

✔ View the putt from a point off to the side and midway between the ball and the hole, as shown in Figure 9-20, rather than from behind the ball. Doing so may give you a better appreciation of the distance. Some players believe that, from this position, they can better visualize the speed necessary for the putt.

Figure 9-20: Viewing the putt from the low side may help you better judge the distance and speed.

Optics and reading greens

Poor green reading is the number-one culprit for golfers; they just don't do it as well as they could or should. One reason is that greens are the most diabolically devilish form of fun that a course architect has.

Greens cause the balls to curve right, left, and sometimes both ways — a dual existence of fun and frolic. Even the pros know that reading greens is visual mayhem and that if they can minimize their misreads, they will make more putts and experience the sweet nectar of cash flow.

Optics are important in green reading, and here's why: It's all in the eyes of the beholder. Those demonic course designers are very sure of the ways they can create visual chaos. For example, it's common to make snap judgments as you approach a green. When your eyes look at all greens from several yards in front, they look like they slope from back to front. Many of the old, pre-1950 courses have this design, which drains the greens so that water doesn't collect on the putting surfaces and rot the grass.

If the green does slope from back to front, to keep things simple, all putts break toward the fairway. A putt that is hit from the left side of the green to the center or the right generally breaks toward the fairway. The same goes for a putt hit from the right side of the green to the center or the left side.

How much break is the key here. The only way to tell is to look from the best optical perspective — to assess the green from the side. For a putt going from back to front or vice versa, this is the best position from which to optically assess the slope — uphill, downhill, or level. Don't worry if at first it's hard to tell how much higher the back of the green is than the front. Keep looking for these subtleties. Your optics will improve as you become more observant.

Looking behind the ball or behind the hole is the best way to tell optically whether the putt is straight or breaks right or left. One of the smartest things you can do is to arrange a green-reading tour with your local golf course professional. Look at this as a field trip to an outdoor library, and take some sunscreen.

A good general rule: Don't change your mind about your stroke strategy while over a putt. First, things look different from here than from the side! Second, the ground you stand on may not be sloped the same as it is up by the hole. And because of the speed of the putt, unless it is all downhill, the ball will travel too fast over the slope near it and break only near the middle to the last third of the putt. (Another reason to stand to the side of the putt — it's easier to assess the last third of the putt from this position.)

The best putters I have seen wield the wand

- ✔ George Archer

- ✔ Jerry Barber

- ✔ Billy Casper

- ✔ Ben Crenshaw

- ✔ Bob Charles

- ✔ Brad Faxon

- ✔ Bobby Locke

- ✔ Phil Mickelson

- ✔ Jack Nicklaus

- ✔ Norm "Sweet Jesus" Numby (He could roll a pear better than I could a golf ball.)

- ✔ Dave Stockton

Some things you may want to write down in your reminder book:

- ✔ Fast greens break more, so don't hit the ball too hard. But keep in mind that hitting the ball more softly means that the slope will affect it more.

- ✔ Downhill putts act like fast greens, as the roll of the ball to the hole is affected by the slope for more than the last few feet.

- ✔ Slow greens break less, so you must hit the ball harder. That initial burst of speed prevents the ball from breaking as much.

- ✔ Uphill putts act like slow greens. Your challenge is to figure out how much uphill slope you're dealing with, and then adjust your putt accordingly — the more slope, the more power it takes, or the farther back you imagine the hole from where it really is.

Points of the roll

I gave you a lot on information on some complicated stuff relating to optics and alignment, so here's a summary of the points that were made:

- ✔ Keep your alignment parallel to the target line.

  - • Feet

  - • Knees

  - • Shoulders

  - • Eye line

- ✔ Know what your putter blade looks like square to the line.

- ✔ Follow the line of your intended putt with your eyes at the speed that you think the ball will roll.

- ✔ Stare at the line of your putt longer than you look at the golf ball.

- ✔ Use the logo line or a line that you have marked on the golf ball to help you align your putts.

You start off not housebroken in relation to putting. You have to be trained. It takes practice. The boys at the club practice putting less than anything else, and putting can take up more than half the strokes you play in this silly game. Create some games on the putting green to enhance your desire to go there.

GARY SAYS

It's just a putt . . .

Nothing can be as tame as a 3-foot putt, right? Try making a putt on Friday on your last hole to make the cut. This electrochemical-induced movement suddenly becomes the hardest thing you've ever done. Let me illustrate this bizarre mental Ping-Pong match, and you'll never think that it's easy again.

I was in Arizona for the Phoenix Open. It was late afternoon on Friday, and I was choking my guts out trying to make the cut: 142, or even par. I was in the penultimate group. My 7-iron shot had landed in the middle of the green, with the pin tucked right. No time for bravery, just two putts and get out of here and enjoy making the cut. If you make the cut, you play on the weekend and get paid. That's much different from not making it and taking it out on your rental car.

The first putt screamed to a halt 3 feet short of the hole. My brain and my body were not in agreement. How seemingly innocent this putt looked as I stalk in from behind. My brain had an itch, and I couldn't scratch it. Quiet the mind, you idiot, you're taking this way too seriously! I'm now in a squat behind the ball looking over 3 feet of straight putt. Or is it? I can't hit this putt easy and play it outside the hole; my nerves can't take that. I'll have to put the speed freak on it and tattoo it on the back of the hole. I don't want to hit it too hard; it might catch an edge and spin out. I must put my goose-down stroke on it and let it use all of the hole.

I approach the setup and am startled by the odd-looking putter that I am gazing upon. Where did that head come from? I thought I had a blade putter. This thing looks like an old wheel rim from a Desoto with a crooked shaft attached to it. I am now flirting with a nervous breakdown. I just remembered that I went to that putter seven years ago. Must be the first time I've paid attention to its profile. As I put my hands on the grip, I can't help but smell the sweat as it pours over the suddenly crooked grip. My hands feel like two crabs trying to mate. How in the world did I get like this?

I notice now that my shoes are in desperate need of a shine. The wandering through the desert had taken its toll, and the jumping cholla needles have made my shoes look like they've been acupunctured. I must call Foot-Joy and get some of those new saddle models that Davis Love has on today . . . . What am I thinking about? I've got to make this stupid putt for my own sanity.

The strength to hit a 3-foot putt is about the same as required to brush your teeth, but for some reason I can't seem to get this putter back from the ball. My mind is willing, but my body is as stubborn as a rented mule. It's very simple; all you do is concentrate on a small piece of grass at the very back of the hole, taking the putter back slowly and square to the line. Smooth transition, and stroke it with an accelerating putter. There's nothing left but to hit the stupid ball and let the golf gods take over. The putter lurches forward and the never-ending battle between good and evil prevails. It slops in!

Somehow, I recovered from the trauma of that putt, made the cut, and ended up playing very well over the weekend, finishing in ninth place.

Chapter 10

Chipping and Pitching

Five-time PGA champion Walter Hagen had the right attitude. He stood on the first tee knowing that he would probably hit at least six terrible shots that day. So when he did hit terrible shots, he didn't get upset. Hagen simply relied on his superior short game (every shot within 80 yards of the hole) to get him out of trouble. That combination of attitude and dexterity made him a fearsome match player. His apparent nonchalance — "Always take time to smell the flowers," he used to say — and his ability to get up and down "from the garbage" put a lot of pressure on his opponents. His opponents became depressed or annoyed and eventually downhearted. More often than not, Hagen won his matches without having hit his full shots too solidly. Golf is more than hitting the ball well. Golf is a game of managing your misses.

Say you have a strong long game relative to your short game prowess. What's probably going to happen is that your range of scores isn't going to be that large. Your high scores will probably be only about six shots higher than your low ones. Now, you probably think that's pretty good, and it is. But it's a two-sided coin. While your long game may give you consistency, your short game takes away your ability to capitalize on it in the form of some really low scores.

Golf Has Its Ups and Downs

As I mentioned earlier, the short game is every shot hit within 80 yards of the hole. That includes sand play (which I cover in Chapter 11) and putting (which I cover in Chapter 9). But they have chapters of their own. So what's left? Chipping and pitching — two versions of short shots to the green, pitching being the higher flier.

Hang around golfers for only a short while, and you inevitably hear one say something along the lines of, "I missed the third green to the right but got up and down for my par." At this stage, you're probably wondering what in the world "up and down" means. Well, the "up" part is the subject of this chapter — chipping or pitching the ball to the hole. The "down" half of the equation, of course, is holing the putt after your chip or pitch (see Chapter 9). Thus a golfer with a good short game is one who gets "up and down" a high percentage of the time (anywhere above 50 percent).

The weird thing is that, although a good short game is where you can retrieve your mistakes and keep a good score going, a lot of amateurs tend to look down on those blessed with a delicate touch around the greens. They hate to lose to someone who beats them with good chipping and putting. Somehow a strong short game isn't perceived as "macho golf" — at least not in the same way as smashing drives 300 yards and hitting low, raking iron shots to greens is macho. Good ball strikers tend to look down on those players with better short games. This attitude is a snobbery thing. It's also a missing-the-point thing.

In golf, you want to get the ball around the course while achieving the lowest score you can. How you get that job done is up to you. No rule says that you have to look pretty when you play golf. Your round isn't going to be hung in an art gallery. As someone once said, "Three of them and one of those makes four." Remember that saying. You can rescue a lot of bad play with one good putt.

You don't hear today's professionals downplaying the importance of a good short game. Professionals know that the short game is where they make their money. Here's proof: If you put a scratch (zero) handicap amateur and a tournament pro on the tee with drivers in their hands, the two shots don't look that much different. Sure, you can tell who is the better player, but the amateur at least looks competitive.

The gap in quality grows on the approach shots, again on wedge play, and then again on the short game. In fact, the closer the players get to the green, the more obvious the difference in level of play. On the green is where a mediocre score gets turned into a good score and where a good score gets turned into a great score. (Take a look at the sample scorecard in Figure 10-1. It probably wouldn't hurt to keep this kind of record for yourself once in a while.)

Okay, I've convinced you of the importance of the short game in the overall scheme of things. Before you go any further, you need to know the difference between a chip and a pitch. In the United States, this question is easy to answer. A *chip* is a short shot that's mostly on the ground. A *pitch*, in contrast, is generally a longer shot that's mostly in the air.

Blue Tees	White Tees	Par	Hcp	JOHN				HOLE	HIT FAIRWAY	HIT GREEN			NO. PUTTS		Hcp	Par	Red Tees
Men's Course Rating/Slope: Blue 73.1/137 — White 71.0/130														Women's Course Rating/Slope: Red 73.7/128			
377	361	4	11	4				1	✓	✓			2		13	4	310
514	467	5	13	8				2	✓	0			3		3	5	428
446	423	4	1	7				3	0	0			2		1	4	389
376	356	4	5	6				4	0	0			2		11	4	325
362	344	4	7	5				5	0	✓			3		7	4	316
376	360	4	9	6				6	✓	0			2		9	4	335
166	130	3	17	4				7	0	✓			3		17	3	108
429	407	4	3	5				8	✓	✓			3		5	4	368
161	145	3	15	5				9	0	0			2		15	3	122
3207	2993	35		50				Out	4	4			22			35	2701
Initial														Initial			
366	348	4	18	5				10	0	0			2		14	4	320
570	537	5	10	7				11	✓	0			3		2	5	504
438	420	4	2	5				12	✓	0			2		6	4	389
197	182	3	12	4				13	0	0			2		16	3	145
507	475	5	14	5				14	✓	✓			2		4	5	425
398	380	4	4	5				15	0	✓			3		8	4	350
380	366	4	6	5				16	✓	0			2		10	4	339
165	151	3	16	4				17	0	0			2		18	3	133
397	375	4	8	5				18	0	0			2		12	4	341
3418	3234	36		45				In	3	2			20			36	2946
6625	6227	71		95				Tot	7	6			42			71	5647

Handicap / Net Score / Adjust (Men's) — Handicap / Net Score / Adjust (Women's)

Scorer — Attested — Date

Figure 10-1: A scorecard with putts and chips highlighted.

Golf gets a bit more complicated in a country like Scotland. In Scotland, the game of golf is played with the ball more on the ground. The climate is generally colder and windier and the turf firmer, so hitting low shots makes more sense and is more effective, given the conditions. As a result, the contrast between a chip and a pitch is a little more blurred. In Scotland, golfers hit what they call *pitch and runs,* where the ball spends a fair amount of time in the air and then the same amount of time on the ground. Especially in the summer, when the ground is hard, Scottish players cannot land shots directly on the putting surface. So the bounce and roll of the ball becomes a bigger part of the shot.

Having made that qualification, thinking of chipping and pitching in the "American" way is a lot simpler.

A Chip Off the Old Block

Chips are short shots played around the greens with anything from a 5-iron to a sand wedge. The basic idea is to get the ball on the green and rolling as fast as you can. If you get the ball running like a putt, judging how far it will go is a lot easier.

Points of reference

Your first point of reference is the spot where you want the ball to land. If at all possible, you want that spot to be on the putting surface. The putting surface's turf is generally flatter and better prepared and makes the all-important first bounce more predictable. You want to avoid landing chips on rough, uneven, or sloping ground.

Pick a spot about 2 feet onto the green (see Figure 10-2). From that spot, I visualize the ball running along the ground toward the hole. Visualization is a big part of chipping. Try to see the shot in your mind's eye before you hit the ball. Then be as exact as you can with your target. You can't be too precise.

Which club to use

You determine which club to use by the amount of room you have between your landing point and the hole. If you only have 15 feet, you need to use a more lofted club (one with a face that is severely angled back from vertical), like a sand wedge so that the ball doesn't run too far.

If you've ever watched golf on TV, you've probably seen Phil Mickelson use a full swing to hit the ball straight up in the air and cover only a short distance on the ground. Phil can do another thing that is really astounding. You stand about 6 feet away from Phil and turn your back to him. You then cup your hands and hold them out from your chest. Phil takes a full swing with his sand wedge and lofts the ball over your head and into your sweaty, waiting hands — all from only 6 feet away. Now that's a lob wedge!

Figure 10-2:
Pick your
spot.

If that gap is a lot bigger — say, 60 feet — then a straighter-faced club, like a 7-iron, is more practical. Figure 10-3 illustrates this concept.

From address...

think where you want the ball to land...

then try to hit it...

so that the ball runs to the hole.

Figure 10-3: Get the ball rolling.

The problem of lie

Then you have the problem of how the ball is lying on the ground. When the ball is in longer grass, you need to use a more lofted club and make a longer swing (longer grass means a longer swing), no matter where the hole is. You need to get the ball high enough to escape the longer rough. If the ball is lying "down" in a depression and you can't get the ball out with the straight-faced club, which the situation normally calls for, you have to go to more loft and move the ball back in your stance (closer to your right foot) a little to make the shot work; see Chapter 12 for more information about low shots. So this part of the game does require flexibility.

Use the philosophy that I've outlined as a starting point, not as a holy writ that must be followed to the letter. Let your own creativity take over. Go with your instincts when you need to choose the right club or shot. The more you practice this part of your game, the better your instincts become.

Practice, and only practice, makes you better. Try all sorts of clubs for these shots. Sooner or later, you'll develop a feel for the shots. I stress that you should use as many clubs as possible when practicing. Using different clubs helps you work on the technique and not the shot.

How to hit a chip

Short game guru Phil Rodgers taught me my chipping technique, which is basically the same one that I employ for putting. I use a putting stroke, but with a lofted club. And I want you to do the same. Take your putting grip and stroke — and go hit chip shots.

The key to chipping is the setup. Creating the right positions at address is essential.

You want your stance to be narrow, about 12 inches from heel to heel, and open — pull your left foot back from the target line. Your shoulders should be open to the target as well. Then place about 80 percent of your weight on your left side. By moving your hands ahead of the ball, you encourage the downward strike that you need to make solid contact with the ball. Place the ball on a line about 2 inches to the left of your right big toe, as shown in Figure 10-4.

During your stroke, focus on the back of your left wrist. Your left wrist must stay flat and firm, as in putting (see Figure 10-5). To keep your wrist flat, tape a Popsicle stick to the back of your wrist (between your wrist and your watch works almost as well). You feel any breakdowns right away. Now go hit some putts and chips.

When I play a tour event, one of the first things I do is go to the putting green and hit some putts/chips to get an idea of the speed of the greens. I get a flat spot in the green and take some golf balls off the green by 5 feet. I then put a coin down on the green 2 feet from the fringe (the *fringe* is a collar of grass, which is longer than the grass on the green but shorter than the grass on the fairway, that surrounds the green). Then I take an 8, 9, and wedge from the spot off the green and chip balls onto the green, trying to bounce each ball off the coin and letting it then run to the hole. I get a real good idea of how fast the greens are that week. You can also develop a touch for those shots — and when you miss as many greens as I do, the practice comes in real handy.

Narrow your stance...

and keep your left wrist flat...

through impact...

and beyond.

Figure 10-4:
Chipping.

Figure 10-5:
No wrist
break.

Put a pen inside
your watchband.

That'll firm up
your wrist.

Make Your Pitch

Pitch shots, which you play only with your wedges and 9-iron, are generally longer than chip shots, so, as you'd expect, you need to make a longer swing, which introduces wrist action into the equation. Which introduces the problem of how long your swing should be and how fast. In other words, pitch shots need some serious feel.

Even the best players try to avoid pitch shots. They are "in-between" shots. You can't just make your normal, everyday full swing — that would send the ball way too far. You're stuck making a half-type swing. A half-type swing is never easy, especially when you're under pressure.

Anyway, here's how to build your pitching swing.

First, adopt the same stance that you did for the chip shot: same width, same posture, same ball position. The only difference is in the alignment of your shoulders, which should be parallel to your toe line, open to the target line, as shown in Figure 10-6.

When you pitch, your shoulders and feet must be aligned to the left of where you want the ball to go.

Figure 10-6:
Set up to
pitch.

Now make a mini-swing (which I describe in Chapter 7). Without moving the butt end of the club too far in your backswing, hinge your wrists so that the shaft is horizontal. Then swing through the shot. Watch how far the ball goes. That distance is your point of reference. You want to hit the next pitch 10 yards farther? Make your swing a little longer (see Figure 10-7). Shorter? Your swing follows suit. That way, your rhythm never changes. You want the clubhead accelerating smoothly through the ball. And that acceleration is best achieved if the momentum is built up gradually from address.

Poor pitchers of the ball do one of two things: Either they start their swings way too slowly and then have to speed up too much at impact, or they jerk the club away from the ball and have to decelerate later. Both swings lead to what golf columnist Peter Dobereiner christened "sickening knee-high fizzers" — low, thin shots that hurtle uncontrollably over the green, or complete duffs that travel only a few feet. Not a pretty sight. The cause of both is often tension. Relax. Imagine that you're swinging with a potato chip between your teeth. Focus on not biting down on it. That'll keep you relaxed.

Here's a game we play at the back of the range at our facility at Grayhawk Golf Course in Scottsdale, Arizona. We get five empty buckets and place them in a straight line at 20, 40, 60, 80, and 100 feet. We then have one hour to hit one ball in each bucket, starting at 20 feet. The winner gets the title to the other guy's car. We're still driving our own cars; we usually get frustrated and quit before the one hour time limit expires or we go to lunch, but we get some good practice pitching the ball.

From address...

swing the club with
hands/arms only...

Figure 10-7:
Think
"tempo."

accelerate
through impact
to a relaxed finish.

Remember, in golf, you get better by doing; you don't get better by doing nothing.

Last pitching thought: Although pitch shots fly higher than chips, apply the same philosophy to your pitching. Get the ball on the ground as soon as possible. Pick out your landing area and let the ball roll. See the shot in your mind's eye before you hit the ball, and remember your *Golf For Dummies* secret: Hit down; don't lift the ball.

Chapter 11

It's Your Sandbox: Sand Play

I have read countless articles and books on sand play, and they all say the same thing: Because you don't even have to hit the ball, playing from the sand is the easiest part of golf. Bull trap! If sand play were the easiest aspect of the game, all those articles and books would have no reason to be written in the first place. Everyone would be blasting the ball onto the putting surface with nary a care in the world. And that, take it from me, is certainly not the case.

Bunkers: Don't Call 'Em Sand Traps!

Bunkers, or sand traps (as I am told not to call them on television), provoke an extraordinary amount of "sand angst" among golfers. But sometimes, *aiming* for a bunker actually makes sense — on a long, difficult approach shot, for example. The pros know that the "up and down" from sand (see Chapter 9) can actually be easier than from the surrounding (usually long and thick) grass.

Bunkers began life as holes in the ground on the windswept Scottish linksland. Because the holes were sheltered from the cold breezes, sheep would take refuge in them. Thus the holes expanded. When the land came to be used for golf, the locals took advantage of what God and the sheep left and fashioned sand-filled bunkers from the holes. (No word on what the sheep thought of all this.)

On these old courses, the greens were sited so as to maximize the bunker's threat to golfers' shots, which is why they came to be named "hazards" in the rules of golf. Later, course architects would place these insidious "traps" so as to penalize wayward shots. That's why you generally don't see bunkers in the middle of fairways — they're mostly to the sides.

As for how much sand you find in a typical bunker, that varies. I prefer a depth of about 2 inches. That stops balls from burying too much on landing but still provides a decent cushion for the escape shot.

I don't know too many amateurs who have ever aimed at a bunker. Mired in a bunker is the last place they want to finish. Typifying the way in which amateur golfers look at bunkers is the experience the late Tip O'Neill had a few years ago during the first few days of the Bob Hope Chrysler Classic, which is a Pro-Am tournament. The former Speaker of the House, admittedly not the strongest golfer (even among celebrities), found himself in a very deep bunker. He then spent the next few hours (okay, the time just seemed that long) trying to extricate first the ball, and then himself, from the trap — all on national television. You could almost hear the millions of viewers saying to themselves, "Yeah, been there, done that."

Well, they haven't really done that from this bunker. The bunker that poor Tip O'Neill was trying to extricate himself from is the deepest pit I've seen since my financial situation in the 1980s. This greenside bunker is located on the 16th hole at PGA West Stadium Golf Course in LaQuinta, California. The bunker is so deep that you can't walk straight up out of it; a path goes diagonally up the hill, and the famous Himalayan mountain guides, the Sherpas, lead the way. I did a video on this course back in the late '80s. We used a helicopter, which started on the bunker floor and rose up to the green as my ball was blasted from this insidious hole with the cameras rolling. Gosh, I love show business.

Why is that, though? Why is it that most amateurs are scared to death every time their shots end up in a greenside bunker? Just what is it about sand play that they find so tough? Well, after much research, some of it in a laboratory, I've come to the conclusion the problem is simple. (If it weren't simple, I would never have discovered it.) It all comes down to lack of technique and/or a lack of understanding.

Faced with a bunker shot, many golfers are beaten before they start. You can tell by their constipated looks, sweaty foreheads, and hesitant body language. Their reaction when they fail is also interesting. After a couple of shots finish up back in the bunker, most people don't focus on their technique. They merely try to hit the shot harder, making more and more violent swings. Not good. Hitting the ball harder only makes them angrier than before because the ball sure isn't going to come out. Still, they finish with a nice big hole, which is perfect if they want to bury a small pet but not much good for anything else.

Practice only helps

Getting the ball out of a bunker can be very easy after you practice enough and get a feel for it. I knew at an early age that my scoring depended on getting up and down out of the bunkers with a certain regularity, so I practiced bunkers with a vengeance. As a result, I can get a ball out of a bunker with everything from a sand wedge to a putter.

One day I was playing in the Kemper Open in Charlotte, North Carolina, when I saw a notoriously bad bunker player who was on the tour practicing hard on his sand play. After a few moments of idle conversation and general harassing, a bet transpired. He would hit ten balls

with his sand wedge; I would hit five balls with a putter. If I got my ball closer than his ball, he would have to go in the locker room and announce to everyone that I beat him with a putter out of a bunker. If he won, I would take him to dinner and then not bother him for the rest of the year.

The laughter from the locker room echoed throughout the clubhouse, and his reputation as the worst bunker player on tour remained intact. I cannot divulge his name because he is playing the senior tour now and is doing very well. He got much better getting out of the sand after some needed practice.

Part of the reason for this all-too-human reaction is that long stretches of failure resign you to your fate. In your mind, you've tried everything, and you still can't get the damn thing out. So you trudge into the bunker expecting the worst, and you usually get it.

The Problem with Sand Play

A huge majority of golfers stand to the ball in a way that makes it all but impossible for them to create the correct angles in their golf swing. Golf, and especially bunker play, is only the creation of the proper angle that the clubhead must take into the ball. Sometimes, the root of the many duffs, hacks, slashes, and any other sort of poor shot is ball position. If you have the ball positioned way back toward your right foot, as so many people seem to do, you won't ever get the ball out of the trap. You can't hit the ball high enough, for one thing. For another, the clubhead enters the sand at too steep an angle. In other words, the clubhead digs into the sand instead of sliding through it. When that happens, the ball usually remains in the bunker sucking sand.

And that's what I mean by a lack of understanding. Poor bunker players get into the sand and start "digging" as if they are having a day out at a quarantined beach. Sometimes I feel like throwing poor bunker players a bucket and shovel so that they can dig for clams. Then at least they'd have something to show for all their efforts.

To Be — Or Not to Be — Handy from Sand

To be a competent sand player, you must take advantage of the way your sand wedge is designed. The bottom of the club can have a different width (see Figure 11-1). The bounce is the bottom of the clubhead — the part that, when you hold the club in front of your face, hangs below the leading edge. Believe me, if you can make the best use of the bounce, bunker play will be taken off your endangered species list.

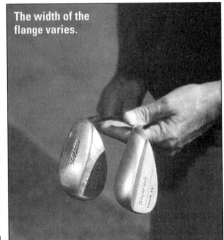

The width of the flange varies.

Figure 11-1: Sand wedges are different.

The bounce is the part of the clubhead that should contact the sand first. Doing so encourages the sliding motion that's so crucial to good bunker play. Think about it. The sand is going to slow the club as you swing down and through, which is okay. But you want to keep the slowdown to a minimum. If the club digs in too much, it will also slow down too much. If that happens, the ball probably won't get out of the bunker. So *slide* the clubhead; don't use it to "dig." Take note, however, that not every sand wedge is equipped with the same amount of bounce. The width of the sole and the amount that it hangs below the leading edge varies. This, of course, begs another question: How do you know how much bounce your sand wedge needs? The determining factor is the type of sand you play from. The bigger the bounce or the wider the sole on your sand wedge, the less it will dig into the sand.

If the sand at your home club is typically pretty firm underfoot, to be most effective, you need to use a sand wedge with very little bounce. A club with a lot of bounce does just that — bounce. And hard (or wet) sand only accentuates that tendency. So using that club is only going to see you hitting a lot of shots thin, the clubhead skidding off the sand and contacting the ball's equator. Either you hit the ball into the face of the bunker and don't get out at all, or the ball misses the face and finishes way over the green. Neither result is socially acceptable.

At the other end of the scale is really soft, deep sand. For that sort of stuff, you need a lot of bounce. In fact, because the clubhead digs so easily when the sand is soft, you can't have enough bounce.

Anyway, enough of this preamble. Take a look at how a sound sand technique is properly — and easily — achieved.

GARY SAYS

"Hoe-ly cow!"

Once, while in Vail, Colorado, I received an urgent phone call from director Ron Shelton while he was shooting the movie *Tin Cup*. He said, "Gary, we forgot to ask you this, but how do you hit a gardening hoe out of a bunker?" "Gee, Ron," I said, "I haven't done that in a while; let me think. What do you mean, how do you hit a gardening hoe out of a bunker?" Ron told me that a scene had to be taken the next day with Kevin Costner hitting a shot out of a bunker, with a hoe, and that the ball had to land no more than 3 feet from the hole. Sure. Right.

I went to the practice green at Singletree Golf Course with my shag bag full of balls and a hoe. It was pouring down rain. It took me at least 40 minutes to get a single ball out of the bunker, and I *bladed* (hit the center of the ball with the leading edge) that one to get it out. I finally decided that the bottom edge of the hoe was too sharp and I needed some bounce to make it perform better in the sand. So I bent the hoe on the bottom and immediately started to get the ball up and out.

I called the movie set and gave directions on the technique of how to bend the hoe. I saw the film three days later, and Kevin Costner hit the first ball 3 feet out of the bunker, with the hoe, to 2 feet. That's a take; wrap it up, as they say. So if the bounce can work to get a ball out of a bunker with a hoe, think what it can do for your sand wedge.

The Splash

Okay, you're in a greenside bunker. You want to get the ball out and onto the putting surface in fewer than two shots. Here's what to do: Open your stance by pulling your left foot back. Pull your foot back until you start to feel vaguely ridiculous. Your left foot's position must feel funny to you. If it doesn't, pull your foot back more. Next, open (turn to the right) your sand wedge to the point where the face is almost looking straight up at the sky, as shown in Figure 11-2. The ball should be positioned forward in your stance toward your left heel. (Do this even more if you're unlucky enough to finish very close to the face of the bunker.) You should feel like you'll go right under the ball when you swing at it. This position should feel just as weird as your stance. Again, if it doesn't, turn your sand wedge to the right even more.

Most amateurs I play with don't do either of those things. They stand too square and don't open the clubface nearly enough (see Figure 11-3). In effect, they don't take advantage of their sand wedges. This club is most efficient when the face is wide open (turned clockwise). Sand wedges are designed that way. The open face sends the ball up when you hit the sand.

Here's one other thing that you should be aware of. When I go home to play, I notice that nobody practices bunker shots, not even my pal "sand wedge Sam." (He got his nickname after demonstrating an uncommon prowess in the much underestimated and neglected art of sand wedge tossing.) Don't fall into that trap (I love bad puns); get into a bunker and *practice*. Besides, you never know, you may like bunkers.

Finally, remember that your club must not touch the sand before you hit the ball.

Okay, you're over the shot, now what? You want to know where to hit the sand, right?

Aim to hit the sand about a credit card length behind the ball. Swing at about 80 percent of full speed. Think of it as a sliding motion. Don't hit down. Let the clubhead throw a "scoop" of sand onto the green, as shown in Figure 11-4. Focusing on a full, uninhibited follow-through will help you (see Figure 11-5). Forget the ball. All you're trying to do is throw sand out of the bunker. (The more sand you throw, the shorter the shot will be. So if you need to hit the shot a fair distance, hit maybe only 2 inches behind the ball.) If you can throw sand, the ball will be carried along for the ride. And that's why better players say that bunker play is easy — the clubhead never actually contacts the ball. Now go get some sunblock and spend some time practicing in the sand.

Your hands should be "behind" the ball.

At address, pull your left foot back.

Turn the clubface clockwise until it looks skyward.

Figure 11-2:
'Til you feel
silly . . .

Figure 11-3:
The ball is too far back in my stance.

Figure 11-4:
No digging allowed.

Make a full follow-through. Recock your wrist right after impact.

Figure 11-5:
Keep going!

Buried Alive!

Unfortunately, not every lie (where the ball is sitting) in a bunker is perfect. Sometimes the ball *plugs* — embeds itself in the sand so that only part of it is visible. You'll hear other golfers describe this sort of lie as a *fried egg.* When that happens to your ball, and after you're through cursing your bad luck, you need to employ a different technique.

Or at least a different alignment of the clubface. You still need your open stance, but this time don't open the clubface. Keep it a little *hooded.* In other words, align the clubface to the left of your ultimate target. Now, shift nearly all your weight to your left side, which puts you "ahead" of the shot (see Figure 11-6). Also, the ball should be played back in your stance. This is the one time that you want the leading edge of the club to *dig.* The ball, after all, is below the surface.

Okay, you're ready. Swing the club up and down, and I mean up and down like you're chopping wood with a dull ax. Hit straight down on the sand a couple of inches behind the ball (see Figure 11-7). A follow-through isn't needed. Just hit down. Hard. The ball should pop up and then run to the hole. Because no backspin is on the golf ball, the ball will run like it just stole something. So allow for it.

Put the ball back in your stance...

but don't change your posture.

Close the clubface at address.

Figure 11-6:
Now you can dig!

Just how hard you should hit down is hard for me to say because it depends on the texture and depth of the sand and on how deep the ball is buried. That old standby, practice, tells you all that you need to know.

"Bury" the club in the sand...

which shortens your follow-through.

Figure 11-7:
Hit down
hard!

Second-to-last point: Experiment with different lofted clubs, and then use whatever works. Many times I use my pitching wedge (which has little bounce and a sharper leading edge and, therefore, digs more) with this technique.

Last point: Always smooth out your footprints when leaving a bunker. If a rake isn't lying nearby, use your feet.

Or if you're like my buddy Steamroller Ron, just roll around in the bunker until it's real smooth. Groups used to gather to watch Ron smooth out the sand. We had very few rakes at the Muni, and the Steamroller was the nearest thing we had to one. I miss Steamroller; he sold his gravel business and moved to Saudi Arabia.

Part III
Special Shots, Conditions, and Considerations

The 5th Wave   By Rich Tennant

"The book said I should place the ball opposite my left armpit. So I put it in my right armpit."

In this part . . .

*I*f you ever want to play in bad weather or learn how to hit the ball from uneven lies, this part of the book will keep you reading by the fireplace.

This part also covers common faults — and how to fix them. Have you ever had one of those days when nothing goes right? You're hitting the ball fat, or thin, or when you do hit the thing it slices off the premises? I'll supply you with some remedies for your ailments. You didn't know that we provided health care for golf, did you?

Chapter 12

How Tough It Is: The Weird and Wonderful Shots

*I*f you break golf down into its primal form, the sport is simple. All you have to do is hit a ball from a flat piece of ground (you even get to tee the ball up) to, say, a 40-yard-wide fairway, find the ball, and then hit the ball onto a prepared putting surface. Then the golf gods allow you to hit not one, but two putts. And even after all that stuff, you still get to call your score par.

However — you knew a catch had to exist, didn't you? — golf isn't often so straightforward. For one thing, you're going to make mistakes. We all do. Usually the same ones over and over. That won't change, by the way. Even the best players in the world have little glitches in their swings that give them problems. Everyone has a bad shot that they tend to hit when things go wrong in their methods. You may not hit that fairway with your drive or that green with your approach shot, or you may miss both. You may take three putts to get the ball into the hole now and again. And golf doesn't often take place on a level playing field. Not every shot is played from a perfectly flat piece of ground. Very seldom is the ball lying enticingly atop the grass. (Unless you're the guy at home we call "The Foot." He never has a bad lie.) Often wind or rain is in your face or at your back.

Every shot is unique. No two shots are ever exactly the same, particularly when you stray from the straight and narrow. When you start making friends with trees, rough, and all the other flora and fauna out there, your ball is going to land in places a lawn mower has never been. And you have to know how to escape from those and many other awkward spots (see Figure 12-1).

If you get into trouble on the course, you'll often be faced with a choice of escape routes.

Figure 12-1:
Under or
around?

Remember to Eat Your Roughage!

Well, Mom, if you knew that I was going to end up playing the PGA Tour and Senior PGA Tour with a crooked driver, you probably wouldn't have left me with those words of wisdom. I have eaten a lot of rough getting from tee to green, but I think it's made me a better person.

Rough is the grass on the golf course that looks like it should be mowed. It's usually 2 to 3 inches in length and lurks everywhere but the tees, fairways, and greens. I grew up on a municipal golf course where the grass was short everywhere because the only thing they watered down was the whiskey.

When you try to hit a ball out of long grass, the grass gets between the clubface and the ball. The ball then has no backspin and goes off like a Scud missile, and direction can be a concern. But the real problem is that with no backspin, the ball can take a longer voyage than you expected. No backspin is on the ball, therefore less drag occurs while the ball is in the air. The ball not coming out of the sky has never been a problem with the driver off the tee, but it's a concern when you're trying to hit the ball a certain distance.

If you understand the reasons for irregular flight and shot length, is there anything you can do about them? My philosophy is that if the lie is bad enough, just get the ball back into the fairway. If you can hit the ball, the technique for this shot is much the same as the shot out of a divot: Play the ball back in your stance and put your hands forward. A chopping down motion allows the club to come up in the backswing and avoid the long grass; then you can hit down on the ball. Swing hard because if you swing easy, the grass will wrap around the club and turn it, giving the ball an unpredictable pitch.

Again, the more you play this game, the more you hit these shots, and the more you understand how to play them. Keep your sense of humor and a firm grip on the club and keep eating roughage — your mother was right!

Dancing with the Trees

A walk into the woods can be a serene, soul-enhancing, mystical journey, blending one's spirit and body in front of nature and all her beauty. But when I'm walking into the trees to find my golf ball, I feel like I'm in a house of mirrors with branches and leaves. The trees seem to be laughing at my predicament, and I end up talking to them in less than flattering dialogue. You've got the picture by now.

The trees are playing games with me, so to extract my ball from this boundless maze of bark, I play a game with the trees. Usually, one lone tree is in my way as I try to exit this forest. All I do is take dead aim at that tree and try to knock it over with the ball. The key here is to not be too close to the tree in case you score a direct hit. You don't want to wear that Titleist 3 as a permanent smile.

My reasoning is that I got into these trees with something less than a straight shot. So if I now try to hit something that is 30 yards away from me and only 12 inches in diameter, what's the chance that I hit it? If I do hit it, what a great shot it was, and I turn a negative into a positive. I'm still in the trees, but I'm happy about my shot. Now you probably know why I'm in television and not on the regular tour anymore.

Special Shots

Arnold Palmer was the master of special shots. At the peak of his powers, Arnold was an awesome sight. He'd stand on the tee and simply hit the ball as hard as he could. Where the ball went didn't matter. He'd find an exciting and inventive way to get the ball back in play, onto the green, and into the hole. That ability is one reason Arnold is so popular. How can you not love a guy who plays with such daring? Much as I admire guys like Tom Kite and Mike Reid, watching their conservative style of play puts me into a semi-coma after a while. Give me "hair on fire" players like Arnie, Seve Ballesteros, Laura Davies, or John Daly. A fire extinguisher may not be handy, but these players are fun to watch.

More important, watching these players is also educational. How they conjure up these "special" shots is worth paying attention to. Although you may not be able to reproduce their results, the principles remain the same no matter what your level of play.

Because golf is a game of mistake management, you're going to get into trouble at least a few times in every round. How you cope with those moments and shots determines your score for the day and, ultimately, your ability to play golf. Never forget that even the greatest rounds have moments of crisis. Stay calm when your heart tries to eject through the top of your head.

These special shots have diversity, too. Trouble is everywhere on a golf course. You have to know how to hit long shots, short shots, and, perhaps most important, in-between shots. All sorts of shots exist. You may be faced with a shot from 200 yards where a clump of trees blocks your path to the hole. Or you may be only 50 yards from the hole and have to keep the ball under branches and yet still get it over a bunker. Whatever the situation, the key is applying the magic word — time out for drumroll — *imagination*.

A vivid imagination is a great asset on the golf course. If you can picture the way a shot has to curve in the air in order to land safely, you're halfway to success. All you have to do is hit the ball. And the best way to accomplish both things is through practice — practice on the course, that is. You can't re-create on the range most shots that you encounter out on the course. The range is flat; the course isn't. The wind constantly blows the same way on the range. On the course, the only constant about the wind is that it changes direction. That's golf — a wheel of bad fortune spin.

The best way to practice these weird and wonderful shots is to challenge yourself. See how low you can hit a shot. Or how high. Practice hitting from bad lies and see how the ball reacts. Play from slopes, long grass, and all the rest. Or play games with your friends. The first player to hit over that tree, for example, gets $5. The trick is to make practice competitive and fun and also beat your friends out of $5.

The more advanced you get in this game, the more rampant your imagination becomes, simply because you have more shots at your command.

Wait a minute, though. Hang on. We're getting a little ahead of ourselves. I have to tell you that many of the trouble shots hit by the likes of Arnie and Seve are not only very low-percentage plays but also way, way out of most people's reach. Even the pros miss the tough shots now and again. And when they do miss, the consequence means triple bogey (a score of 3 over par for one hole — for example, a 7 on a par-4) or worse. So admire them. But never, ever try to copy them, at least not yet.

The good news is, at this stage of your development, all you need is a couple of basic shots. Leave the really fancy stuff for another time, another book. All you need to know to score well is how to hit the ball low or high back onto the fairway. That's enough to cover 99 percent of the situations that you encounter. Better to give up one shot rather than risk three more on a shot that you couldn't play successfully more than once in 20 tries.

Adjusting your heights

Because golf isn't played in a controlled environment, you're going to come across situations where a higher or lower shot is required. For example, when you have a strong wind in your face, a lower shot is going to go farther and hold its line better. The great thing is that you make all your adjustments before you begin. After you start the club away from the ball, you can make your regular swing. You don't have to worry about adding anything else to your swing. Figure 12-2 illustrates the following shots.

Hitting the ball lower

Hitting the ball lower is easy. All you have to do is subtract from the effective loft of the club. And the best way to do that is to adjust your address position. Play the ball back in your stance toward your right foot. Move your hands targetward until they are over your left leg.

Now you swing, focusing on re-creating the positional relationship between your hands and the clubface as the ball is struck. In other words, your hands should be "ahead" of the clubface at impact, thus ensuring that the ball flies lower than normal.

This sort of technique is commonly employed when playing in Florida, Texas, and Hawaii, where golf swings get a little shorter and the divots get a little longer. When you play the ball back in your stance with your hands ahead, you come down into the ground with a more abrupt angle that takes more turf.

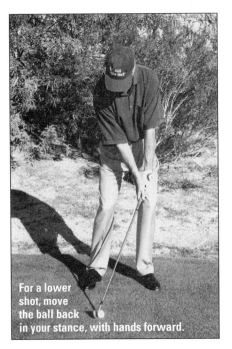

For a lower shot, move the ball back in your stance, with hands forward.

Then return your hands, at impact, to your address position. Hands ahead of ball at impact.

For a higher shot, move the ball forward in your stance.

Your head should be behind the clubhead when the ball is struck.

Figure 12-2:
Downs and ups of golf.

I remember one good story about a low shot. It happened at Pebble Beach years ago during the Bing Crosby tournament on the 7th hole (which is a downhill par-3 of 110 yards). From an elevated tee, you can just about throw the ball to the green. On this particular day, the wind was howling from the coast (the green sits on the ocean), and the 7th hole was impossible. Water was erupting from the rocks; wind was blowing water everywhere; seals were hiding; and seagulls were walking. Definitely a bad day for windblown golf balls.

Billy Casper arrived on the tee and surveyed the situation. Many players were using long irons (irons that go 200 yards) because the wind was so fierce. Billy went to his bag and got his putter! He putted the ball down a cart path into the front bunker. From there he got the ball down in two for his par 3. Now that's keeping it low into the wind and using your imagination!

Hitting the ball higher

As you'd expect, hitting the ball higher than normal involves making the opposite types of adjustments at address. Adjust your stance so that the ball is forward in your stance, toward your left foot. Then move your hands back, away from the target. Again, hitting the ball is that simple. All you have to do is reproduce that look at impact, and the ball takes off on a steeper trajectory.

Gyroscope golf: Sidehill lies

Not many golf courses are flat. Every now and again, you need to hit a shot off a slope. The ball may be below or above your feet. Both positions are sidehill lies. Or you may be halfway up or down a slope.

When you're faced with any or all of these situations, you need to make an adjustment. And again, if you can make most of your changes before starting your swing, things are a lot easier. The common factor in all these shots is the relationship between your shoulders and the slope. On a flat lie, you're bent over the ball in a certain posture. You should stand about 90 degrees to the ground.

In other words, if the ball is above your feet, you have to lean a little into the hill to keep your balance. If you stood at your normal posture to the upslope of the hill, you would fall backward. You're close to the ball because of the lean, and you need to choke up on the club.

The reverse is also true. When the ball is below your feet, lean back more to retain your balance on the downslope. Because you're leaning back, you're a little farther away from the ball; grip the club all the way to the end and use the whole length of the shaft.

The main idea for side hill lies is to stay on balance. I don't want you falling down the hills.

For uphill and downhill lies, it's a little different. Imagine that your ball is halfway up a staircase, and you have to hit the next shot to the top. Because your left leg is higher than your right, your weight naturally shifts to your right leg. Let that weight shift happen so that your shoulders are parallel to the banister. On a downslope, your weight shifts in the opposite direction, onto your left leg. Again, let that weight shift happen. Keep your shoulders and the banister parallel, as shown in Figure 12-3.

On an upslope, leave your weight on your right side.

On a downslope, shift your weight to your left side.

Figure 12-3:
Keep shoulders and slope parallel.

Finally, follow these three rules:

- ✔ **Adjust your aim when you're on a slope.** Off a downslope or when the ball is below your feet, aim to the left of where you want the ball to finish. Off an upslope or when the ball is above your feet, aim right.

- ✔ **As far as ball position is concerned, play the ball back toward the middle of your stance when on a downhill lie, or forward, off your left big toe, when on an uphill lie.**

✔ **Take more club (a club that has less loft) on an uphill lie because the ball tends to fly higher.** Use less club (a club that has more loft) on a downhill lie because the ball has a lower trajectory from this situation. For example, if the shot calls for a 7-iron, take your 8-iron and hit it. Remember, from these lies, swing about 75 percent of your normal swing speed to keep your balance.

Small graves and divots

Unfortunately for your golfing life, your ball occasionally finishes in a hole made by someone who previously hit a shot from the same spot and did not replace the grass. These holes are known as *divots*. This may cause quiet muttering beneath your breath, but don't panic. To get the ball out, first move the ball back in your stance to encourage a steeper attack at impact. Push your hands forward a little, too. You need to feel as if you're really hitting down on this shot. A quicker cocking of the wrists on the backswing helps, too. I like to swing a little more upright on the backswing with the club (take the arms away from the body going back). This allows a steeper path down to the ball. (See Figure 12-4.)

Depending on the severity and depth of the divot, take a club with more loft than you would normally use. You need extra loft to counteract the ball being below ground level. Don't worry — the ball comes out lower because your hands are ahead of the ball. That makes up for the distance lost by using less club.

When you're feeling fairly uncomfortable over the ball as it sits in that divot, remember that the ball will come out a lot lower and run along the ground more than a normal shot. So aim your shot accordingly.

On the downswing of your shot out of a divot, there will be no follow-through. Because the ball is back in your stance and your hands are forward (hopefully), your blow should be a descending blow. When is the last time you had a follow-through when chopping wood?

The one thought I've had in this situation is to not swing too hard at this shot. When you swing too hard, you move your head and don't hit the ball squarely. And when the ball is lying below the ground, you need to hit it squarely.

Figure 12-4:
Digging
holes.

Toupee Alert: Strong Winds Reported

When conditions are rough because of wind or rain, scores (including yours) are going to go up. You have to be ready for that occurrence. Adjust your goals. Don't panic if you start off badly or have a couple of poor holes. Be patient and realize that sometimes conditions make it difficult to play golf. And remember that bad weather conditions are equally tough on all the other players.

I've played the tour for some 25-odd years, and I've played in some very bad conditions. Because I'm not a patient person, my scores in bad weather have been high. If I got a few strokes over par early in my round, I would take too many chances during the rest of the round trying to make some birdies. I'd then boil as I watched my score rise with my blood pressure. A calm head and good management skills are just as important as hitting the ball solidly when you're trying to get through tough days in the wind and rain.

I remember playing the TPC Championship at Sawgrass in the late 1980s on one of the windiest days we'd ever seen. J. C. Snead hit a beautiful downwind approach to an elevated green. Somehow the ball stopped on the green with the wind blowing upwards of 50 mph. J. C. started walking toward the green when his Panama hat blew off and started to tumble toward the green. After minutes of scurrying along the ground, the hat blew onto the green and hit his golf ball! That's a 2-shot penalty, and a really bad case of luck. (I don't know if this involves better management skills, but it's a good story.)

The average score that day at Sawgrass was about 84, and those were the best players in the world! If conditions get this bad, my advice is to sit at home and watch the Weather Channel. But if the wind is blowing just hard enough to be a nuisance, the following may help you deal with wind conditions:

- ✔ **Widen your stance to lower your center of gravity.** This automatically makes your swing shorter (for control) because it's harder to turn your body when your feet are set wider apart. (See Figure 12-5.)

- ✔ **Swing easier.** I always take a less lofted club than normal and swing easier. This way, I have a better chance of hitting the ball squarely. By hitting the ball squarely, you can rely on a consistent distance the ball will travel with every club, even in bad conditions.

- ✔ **Use the wind — don't abuse the wind.** Let the ball go where the wind wants it to go. Don't try to fight it, or it will be a long day. If the wind is blowing left to right at 30 mph, aim your ball left and let the wind bring it back. Don't aim right and try to hook it back into the wind. Leave that up to the pilots and the guys on the tour!

A wide stance helps you keep your balance in a breeze.

Figure 12-5:
Windy
means
wider.

✔ **Choke down more on the club.** Choking down on the club means that you don't have to have your left hand (for right-handed golfers) all the way at the end of the grip. This gives you more control. I like to put my left hand about 1 inch from the top of the grip. I have more control over the club, but the ball doesn't go as far because I don't use the full length of the shaft.

✔ **Allow for more run downwind and for shorter flight against the wind.** This part of the game has to be experienced to be understood. The more you play in windy conditions, the more comfortable you become in them.

Waterworld: Days When You Can't Find Dry Land

I'm from southern California. I never saw too much rain, let alone played in it all the time. The rain that would make us Californians stay inside and play Yahtzee would be nothing for my buddies from the Northwest. Not even an inconvenience. They learned how to play in the rain and expected to play in the rain.

The right equipment: Smooth sailing or choppy seas

The best advice I can give you for playing in the rain is to be prepared to play in it. Have all the necessary equipment to handle the wetness (see Figure 12-6):

The right clothing and equipment is a must when playing golf in wet conditions.

Figure 12-6: Swinging in the rain.

✔ **An umbrella:** Have one of those big golf umbrellas. And never open it downwind, or you'll end up like Mary Poppins and the umbrella will end up looking like modern art.

✔ **Good rain gear:** That means jackets, pants, and headwear created to be worn in the rain. You can spend as much as you want on these items. If you play in wet weather all the time, get yourself some good stuff that will last a long time. I don't mean a garbage bag with holes cut out for your head and arms. I mean the good stuff that you buy from a pro shop or see in a magazine ad. Good rain gear costs between $100 and $600. Gore-Tex, a fabric that repels water, is a very popular fabric for rain gear.

✔ **Dry gloves:** If you wear gloves, have a few in plastic bags in your golf bag. This will protect them in case you leave a pocket open and the rain comes pouring in.

✔ **Dry towels:** Keep some dry towels in your bag, because the one you have outside will get wet sooner or later. On the tour, I keep a dry towel hanging from the rib on the underside of the umbrella and another dry one inside my side pocket. When it gets really wet, I wipe my club off on the closest dry caddie.

✔ **Dry grips:** This is one of the most important things to have in wet-weather golf. I once had a club slip out of my hands on the driving range and go through the snack shop window. I blamed it on an alien spacecraft.

✔ **Waterproof shoes:** And keep an extra pair of socks in your bag in case the advertiser lied.

Rainy golf course conditions

It's important to remember that a golf course changes significantly in the rain. You need to adjust your game accordingly and keep the following in mind:

✔ On a rainy day, the greens will be slow when you putt. Hit the putts harder and the ball won't curve as much.

✔ If you hit a ball in the bunker, the sand will be firmer, and you don't have to swing as hard to get the ball out.

✔ The golf course will play longer because it's so soft. The good news is that the fairways and greens get softer and more receptive. The fairways and greens become, in effect, wider and bigger respectively because your shots don't bounce into trouble as much. If you're like me, you're in favor of your bad shots getting a favorable break.

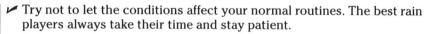

✔ Try not to let the conditions affect your normal routines. The best rain players always take their time and stay patient.

✔ Playing in the rain is one thing. Playing in lightning is another thing altogether. When lightning strikes, your club (along with the fact that you tend to be the highest point at the golf course, unless there's a tree around) can make you a target. Don't take chances. Drop your club and take cover.

All washed up

Sometimes people do things for the wrong reasons. You simply can't put yourself through torture and ridicule for money. If you put yourself through torture and ridicule, ethics should have something to do with it.

I learned this when I did a commercial for the lovely people at Foot-Joy, advertising their Dry-Joy line of shoes. I had done a commercial for them, and we bonded. Happiness and the smell of money was in the air — or should I say under the water?

My agent told me that I would be doing an underwater commercial (not too far underwater) in a pool at Universal Studios in Orlando, Florida, with Davis Love III. The money was good, the friendship abounded, and the shoot would last only one day.

I showed up in the wee hours of the morning for makeup — heavy-duty underwater makeup. Keeping my handlebar mustache up throughout the underwater shoot was the only problem. The makeup lady was talented, and spirit gum was our choice. On with the clothes and out to the pool.

The director informed me that two speakers were underwater so that he could talk to me while I wallowed on the bottom. I would just follow his instructions and not swallow any water. He then introduced me to my assistant, the diver who would be giving me air as I waited breathlessly on the bottom. Deep Dive

Dan was his name, and his only purpose in life was to keep me from drowning.

As I jumped into the shallow end of the pool, Deep Dive Dan wanted to know how many times I had been scuba diving. I told him I used to watch *Sea Hunt* — did that count?

"You don't know how to use this equipment?" he asked.

"No, I don't," I said. "Do I have enough time to learn before I die?"

We started on our 15-minute survival program. The first thing we noticed was that I was way too light to stay in the water, so I kept floating to the top. Two lead flak jackets and two 10-pound weights duct-taped to the insides of the my knees did the trick.

I was now ready to be submerged. Deep Dive Dan informed me that I had to close my eyes going down and that I couldn't wear a mask because it would leave a ring around my face.

"We'll go to the bottom when the director says, 'Action,'" Deep Dive Dan said. "When we get there, wait until I pull the air hose out of your mouth, count to three, and go on with your lines."

"How far down are we going?" I asked.

"We'll be down about 15 feet standing on the bottom," he said.

(continued)

(continued)

I told him my agent said that I would have to be under only 2 feet of water. He told me to get a new agent.

In the scene, I was supposed to turn to the camera and say something like, "These are the best shoes in the world for wet weather." I would turn to Davis Love, who was behind me, and he would mumble something about what I had just said. Then I would turn back to the camera and say, "That means yes." End of shoot.

I thought, "This has got to be the easiest way in the world to make a living."

I grabbed onto Deep Dive Dan and away we went. Down, down, and farther down. We hit, my eyes were closed, and I started hyperventilating. Air bubbles were flying everywhere. Suddenly, someone pulled my air hose out of my mouth — I suspected Deep Dive.

In my agitated state, with air bubbles burbling past my ears, I could not hear the director. The action was starting, but I wasn't. I opened my eyes and found the camera halfway through the dialogue. I ran out of air and motioned to Deep Dive that I had not long to live. The air hose came at me like a snake with its tail caught in a blender. I sucked the air, got some water and some skin from Deep Dive's fingers, and motioned him to take me to the top. We arrived with me wondering how I was going to thank my agent.

To make a long story very wet, I was on the bottom of the pool for seven hours doing this commercial. I now know what diver's panic is. I never got comfortable on the bottom with my eyes closed and enough weight to sink a Russian freighter. The slightest panic and I wanted to swim toward the top. The problem was that I weighed too much and I couldn't go anywhere. So I stayed and counted the minutes when I could rejoin the living out of the pool. My last thought was that my agent would not be long among the living — or at least, the employed.

Four-Season Golf: Weathering the Elements

If you live in a place like Florida, California, or Arizona, you only notice the change of seasons when 40 bazillion golfers from colder climes flood the area trying to get the seven starting times that are still available. For those of you who live in all-season climates and prefer to enjoy the changing weather without giving up your golf game, this section will help.

Northern exposure: Tips for wintertime golf

For those of you who choose to get away from the fireplace, golf in the winter can be tolerable. For much of the country, anyone can play in winter on a reasonable day with a light wind — especially when you don't have to mow the grass until April.

Prepare yourself for brisk weather

If you're brave enough to venture onto the frozen tundra, I have three musts for you:

- ✔ **In a large thermos, take something warm to drink for the whole day.** You may think that bourbon chasers will make the day much more fun, but the golf deteriorates and you'll actually feel colder.

- ✔ **Dress warm.** I've used silk long johns on cold days, and they work well. Women's seamless long johns work best, but if you're a guy, the salesperson looks at you funny when you ask for a women's size 14. That kind of request may lead to the wrong conclusions.

  - **Wear waterproof golf shoes and thick socks.** Some hunting socks have little heaters in them. I also wear wool pants over the silk long johns and then use my rain pants as the top layer when it's really cold. A turtleneck with a light, tightly knit sweater does well under a rain or wind jacket made of Gore-Tex or one of those miracle-fiber, space-age fabrics. A knit ski cap tops off this cozy ensemble.

  - **Among the great inventions of all time are those little hand warmers that come in plastic pouches.** You shake those things, and they stay warm for eight hours. I put them everywhere on cold days. Let your imagination run wild. Hand warmers can keep you toasty on a cold winter's day when you're three down to your worst enemy.

  - **Keep your hands warm by using cart gloves.** These oversize fingerless gloves have a soft, warm lining and fit right over your hand, even if you're already wearing a glove. I put a hand warmer in each one.

- ✔ **Your attitude is the best weapon for a harsh winter day.** Remember, you're out on the course for the exercise — walk instead of taking a cart. Besides, you really feel cold when your fresh face collides with winter's arctic blast. If you must take a cart, make sure that it has a windshield. Some clubs have enclosed carts with heaters in them. (Beware of clubs that have these carts, though; you may not be able to afford the greens fee.)

Adjust your golf swing for a cold day

When you swing a club with all these clothes on, you probably won't have as long a swing as normal. The clothes restrict your motion. I usually take my jacket off to swing the club and then put it right back on. Because of the restriction of the clothes, I make my swing a little slower than normal, which helps put my swing into a slow rhythm on a cold day. Don't get fast and furious to get done.

Keep in mind a couple of points when you're golfing in cold weather:

- ✔ **Lower your expectations as the weather worsens.** When you're dressed for the Iditarod (Alaska's premier dogsled race), don't think that you can pull off the same shots that you normally do. Good short game skills and game management are the most important aspects of winter golf.

- ✔ **Get counseling if you play much in these extreme conditions.** Golf may be too much of a priority in your life.

Indoor golf: What you can do at home

Winter is the time to practice fixing all those faults that you accumulated during the preceding year. Here's how:

1. **Place a large mirror behind you.**

2. **Pretend that you're hitting away from the mirror, checking your swing when your shaft is parallel to the ground in your backswing.**

   Is your shaft on a line that's parallel to the line made by your toes? If it is, that's good.

3. **Continue to swing and go to the top.**

   Is your shaft on a line that's parallel to the line made by your heels? If it is, that's good.

These two positions are important to the golf swing. Repeat these exercises until you can do them in your sleep.

Winter is a good time to become one with your swing (say, what?). Have someone make a videotape of your golf swing. Play your golf swing over and over on your VCR until you have a really good picture of what it looks like. Feel your own swing. Then work on those areas that you need to attend to — an instructor can help determine those areas. Make your changes and do another tape of your swing. Not only should you be able to see the changes, but you should feel the changes as well. Videotaping helps you understand your movements and helps the body and brain get on the same page. Golf can be Zenlike.

If you really can't get golf off your mind (and it's too cold to go ice fishing!), stay safe and warm indoors and check out the online golf options that I discuss in Chapter 18.

Spring cleaning: Time to thaw out and get to work

The golfing populace anticipates spring like no other season. You have been indoors for most of the winter and have read every book pertaining to your golf game. You have watched endless hours of golf on TV and ingested everything the announcers have told you not to do. It's time to bloom!

One of the first things you need to do is decide your goals for the upcoming year. Is your goal to be a better putter? Or do you want to become a longer driver? Or do you simply want to get the ball off the ground with more regularity?

You must establish what you want to do with your game and then set out to accomplish that feat. Set simple and attainable goals and work to achieve them.

Goals are much easier to obtain with instruction. Get with a teacher you trust and share your goals with him or her. Your teacher can help you decide how you can best achieve those goals and can watch your progress in case you run into a hazard along the way.

My other springtime advice includes the following tips:

✔ **Practice all phases of your game.** Don't neglect weak areas of your game, but stay on top of your strengths as well. Spring is a time of blossoming; let your game do the same.

✔ **Map out an exercise program.** You probably neglected exercise during the winter. Spring is a good time to map out a game plan for your personal needs. Are you strong enough in your legs? Does your rotator cuff need strength? Does your cardiovascular system short out later in the round? Address these problems and get on a treadmill or hit the weight room. Chapter 4 talks about developing a golf-specific fitness program.

✔ **Dress correctly for the weather.** Spring is the hardest time of year to figure out what to wear. It can be hot. It can be cold. It can rain. It can be blowing 40 mph. It can be doing all these things in the first three holes. If you're carrying your bag, it can get heavy with all the extra gear in it. Take along your rain gear. Take along a light jacket. Bring hand warmers and your umbrella. Put an extra towel in your bag. Take along some antihistamines; it's spring and the pollen is everywhere.

> ✔ **Learn about yourself and your golf game.** Remember, spring is the time of year to be enlightened.
>
> *To be surprised, to wonder, is to begin to understand.* —Spanish philosopher Jose Ortega y Gasset

Summer fun: Making the most of sunny weather

Summer is the time of year to go play the game. I hope that you've been practicing hard on your game, working toward those goals you set forth in the spring. But there's a big difference between practicing and playing the game. The more you practice, the easier you should find it to play the game well. Summer is the time to find out whether your game has improved. The following suggestions help you make the most of your play:

✔ **Work on your course management.** How can you best play this particular golf course? Sometimes, for one reason or another, you cannot play a certain hole. Figure out how you can best avoid the trouble you're having on that hole, or course, and devise a plan. Everyone has strengths and weaknesses. Do you have the discipline to carry out your plan? That's why summer is great for playing the game and understanding yourself. You can go out after work and play 18 holes before it gets dark. Summer is the time to stop thinking about your golf swing and become the ball.

✔ **Maintain your equipment.** During the summer, I get new grips on my clubs. The grips are called *half cord* because they have some cord blended into the underside of the grip. The new grips give me a better hold on the club during sweaty summers. I also use a driver that has a little more loft to take advantage of the drier air (which causes the ball to fly farther).

✔ **Practice competing by playing in organized leagues.** You play a different game when your score counts and is published in the paper.

✔ **Dress for fun in the sun.** Take along sunblock of at least 15 SPF, and put it on twice a day. Not everyone wants to look like George Hamilton. And wear a hat that covers your ears. Mine burn off in the summer.

✔ **Play in the mornings.** The afternoons are usually too darned hot.

✔ **Drink plenty of fluids during those hot days.** You don't want to dehydrate and shrivel up like a prune, so keep your liquid intake constant. I try to drink water on every tee during the heat of summer. One hint: Alcoholic beverages will knock you on your rear end if you drink them outdoors on a hot day. Stick with water and save the adult beverages for later in the coolness of the clubhouse.

If you see me at all, it will be in the fall

Without a doubt, fall is the best time of the year to play golf. The golf courses are in good shape. The leaves are changing, and the scenery is amazing. The weather is delightful, and all sorts of sports are on TV. Both you and your game should be in good shape.

If you have the time and the money, make travel plans to the Northeast and play golf. The colors are astounding. I live in Vail, Colorado, which is also breathtaking in the fall. Many vacation plans are affordable and very enjoyable. Get a bunch of friends you enjoy and start planning a trip now. My house is out. It's way too small.

Play as much golf as you can in the fall so that you'll be really tired of the game and won't miss it going into winter — you can take a legitimate golf break. (If you still can't get golf off your mind, check out the wintertime tips earlier in this section to help you stay on your game.)

Things you should keep in mind about the fall include the following:

- ✔ **Dress for the fall much like you do for the spring.** Take a lot of stuff because the weather can do anything.

- ✔ **Assess everything you did with your golf game.** Did your techniques work? If not, were your goals unrealistic? Was your teacher helpful? Take a long, hard look and start to devise a game plan for next spring.

- ✔ **Look at new equipment as your game progresses.** Fall is a good time to buy equipment because all the new stuff comes out in the spring and prices are lower for last year's clubs. I love a good buy, although I haven't had to buy clubs since I bought a putter eight years ago in San Diego.

- ✔ **Start stacking all those wooden clubs for the fireplace; it could be a long, hard, cold winter.**

Chapter 13

Common Faults and How to Fix Them

*1*f you're like everyone else who has ever played the game, playing golf is a constant battle against annoying faults in your full swing or putting stroke. Even the best golfers have some little hitch in their methods that they have to watch for, especially under pressure. A few years ago, Greg Norman displayed a tendency to hit the ball well to the right of the target on the closing holes of big tournaments. That tendency was Greg's particular nemesis, but pressure manifests itself in many ways. Watch your playing companions when they get a little nervous; you can see all sorts of things happen. Putts are left short. Even simple shots take longer to play. Conversation all but stops. And best of all, from your point of view, any faults in their swings are cruelly exposed.

You're going to develop faults in your swing and game. Faults are a given, no matter how far you progress. The trick is catching your faults before they spoil your outlook on your game. Faults left unattended turn into major problems and ruin your game.

The root cause of most faults is your head position. Your cranium's position relative to the ball as you strike it dictates where the bottom of your swing is. The bottom of your swing is always a spot on the ground relative to where your head is positioned. Test that assertion. Shift your weight and your head toward the target onto your left side. Leave the ball in its regular position. Then make your normal swing with, say, a 6-iron. The hole made by the club will be more in front of the ball. The bottom of your swing moves targetward with your head.

The opposite is also true. Shift your weight and head to the right, and the bottom of your swing moves in the same direction.

The bottom line? If your head moves too much during the swing, you have little chance to correct things before impact, and the result is usually some form of poor shot.

Don't get the idea that excessive head movement is responsible for absolutely every bad shot. Other poor plays can stem from improper use of your hands, arms, or body. But try to keep your head as steady as possible.

Anyway, that's the big picture. I'll get more specific now. What follows is a discussion of the most common faults you are likely to develop, with cures for each fault. After you know what your tendencies are, you can refer to this section regularly to work on fixing them.

Skying Your Tee Shots (Fountain Ball)

One of the most common sights I see on the first tee of a Pro-Am or member-guest tournament is the skyed tee shot, which is when a ball goes higher than it goes forward. It is usually hit on the top part of the driver, causing an ugly mark to appear, which is one reason why a tour player never lets an amateur use his wooden club. If the amateur hits a fountain ball (as my wife likes to call it, because she says that a skyed tee shot has the same trajectory as one of those fountains in Italy) with a wooden club, an acne-like mark is left on the wood, and then the club needs to be refinished. Take a look at your friends' drivers. They probably have disgusting marks all over the tops of their wooden clubs.

At the municipal course where I nurtured my game, we had few rules, but one of them was that if you could catch your drive off the tee, you could play it over again with no penalty. We had so many guys wearing tennis shoes for speed that it looked like a track meet.

If you're hitting the ball on the top side of your driver, you're swinging the club on too much of a downward arc at impact. What's that mean, you ask? That means that your head is too far in front of the ball (toward the target side of the ball) and your left shoulder is too low at impact — bad news for the complexion of your driver.

Here's what you do. Go find an upslope. Your left foot (if you're right-handed) will be higher than your right. Tee the ball up and hit drivers or 3-woods until you get the feeling of staying back and under the shot. The uphill lie promotes this feeling. I'll tell you a secret about this teaching trick. People who hit down on their drivers want to kill the stupid ball in front of their buddies. These golfers have a tremendous shift of their weight to the left side on the downswing. If you hit balls from an upslope, you can't get your weight to the left side as quickly. Consequently, you keep your head behind the ball, and your left shoulder goes up at impact. Practice on an upslope until you get a feel and then proceed to level ground. The next time I see you in the sky, it will be on Delta Airlines.

Slicing and Hooking

Most golfers *slice,* which means that the ball starts to the left of the target and finishes well to the right. I think slicing stems from the fact that most players tend to aim to the right of their target. When they do so, their swings have to compensate so that the resulting shots can finish close to the target.

In most cases, that compensation starts when your brain realizes that if you swing along your aim, the ball will fly way to the right. The resulting flurry of arms and legs isn't pretty — and invariably, neither is the shot. Soon this weak, left-to-right ball flight makes your life a slicing hell. Slices don't go very far. They are horrible, weak shots that affect your DNA for generations to come.

In general, slicers use too much body action and not enough hand action in their swings. Golfers who hook have the opposite tendency — too much hand action, not enough body.

Attitude is key

Golf is a good walk spoiled. — Mark Twain

Golf is played in a hostile environment with inferior equipment for the task at hand. You have to use every facet of your being to conquer the forces that are working against you. Success and failure walk hand in hand down the fairways, and your attitude toward the game has a direct effect on how you handle both. Golf teases you with brilliant moments of shot-making, and then, in the next moment, it wilts your knees with swift failure. Hopefully, you can reflect on the brilliant moments and use the swift failure for experience.

I've had few moments of brilliance while playing the PGA Tour, but in those moments, I have been locked into trances that allow me to play my best. I don't know what brings on that mystical state where mind and body meld to a very efficient unison called the *zone.* If I knew, I would have a lot more real estate by now. A quote by Janwillem Van De Weterin says, "Not only has one to do one's best, one must, while doing one's best, remain detached from whatever one is trying to achieve." That's the zone. Sounds easy, but it's hard to do!

Play the game for whatever reason you play the game, and nobody else's reason. Golf is a journey without a destination and a song with no ending. Enjoy the companionship and the solitude, experience the brilliance and the failure, and do your best to enjoy all the seasons.

Fear not, hapless hackers: Two variations of the same drill offer solutions.

If you're a slicer, you need to get your hands working in the swing. Address a ball as you normally do. Turn your whole body until your butt is to the target and your feet are perpendicular to the target line. Twist your upper body to the left so that you can again place the clubhead behind the ball. Don't move your feet, however. From this position, you have, in effect, made it impossible for your body to turn to your left on the through-swing (see Figure 13-1). Try it. Should I call a chiropractor yet? The only way you can swing the club through the ball is by using your hands and arms. Hit a few balls. Focus on letting the toe of the clubhead pass your heel through impact. Quite a change in your ball flight, eh? Because your hands and arms are doing so much of the rotating work in your new swing, the clubhead is doing the same. The clubhead is now closing as it swings through the impact area. The spin imparted on the ball now causes a slight right-to-left flight — something I bet you thought that you'd never see.

If you slice, try this drill: Stand with your back to the target. Then turn your whole body until your butt is to the target and twist your upper body to address the ball.

Swing back...

and then swing your hands and arms through...

to finish. The ball should fly from right to left.

Figure 13-1: More hand action kills the slice.

After you have hit about 20 shots using this drill, switch to your normal stance and try to reproduce the feel you had standing in that strange but correct way. You'll soon be hitting hard, raking *draws* (slight hooks) far up the fairway.

Those golfers prone to *hooks* (shots that start right and finish left) have the opposite problem as slicers — too much hand action and not enough body. After adopting your regular stance, turn your whole body until you are looking directly at the target. Now twist your upper body to the right — don't move your feet — until you can set the clubhead behind the ball. Hit some shots. (See Figure 13-2.) You'll find solid contact easiest to achieve when you turn your body hard to the left, which prevents your hands from becoming overactive. Your ball flight will soon be a gentle *fade* (slight slice).

After about 20 shots, hit some balls from your normal stance practicing the technique I just described. Reproduce the feel of the drill, and you're on your way.

If you hit hooks, try this drill: Stand with both feet facing the target. Then turn your upper body until you are facing the target.

Swing back...

and then turn your body in concert with the club...

to finish. The ball should fly from left to right.

Figure 13-2: More body action will straighten your hook.

Topping Shots

Topping isn't much fun. Plus, it's a lot of effort for very little return. *Topping* is when you make a full-blooded, nostrils-flaring swipe at the ball, only to tick the top and send the ball a few feeble yards.

Topping occurs because your head is moving up and down during your swing. A rising head during your downswing pulls your shoulders, arms, hands, and the clubhead up with it. Whoops! Airball!

In order not to top the ball, you have to stop your head from lifting. And the best way to stop your head from lifting is to establish a reference for your eyes before you start the club back. Stick the shaft of a golf club in the ground just outside the top of the golf ball. Focus your eyes on the top of the grip throughout your swing, as shown in Figure 13-3. As long as your eyes are focused on the grip, your head and upper torso cannot lift, which ends topped shots.

Duffing and Thinning Chip Shots

Duffing and thinning chip shots are exact opposites, yet, like the slice and the hook, they have their roots in the same fault (see Figure 13-4).

When you *duff* a chip (also called a *chili-dip* or, as I like to say, *Hormel*), your swing is bottoming out behind the ball. You are hitting too much ground and not enough ball (also called hitting it *fat*), which means that the shot falls painfully short of the target and your playing partners laugh outrageously. Duffing a chip is the one shot in golf that can get you so mad that you can't spell your mother's name.

One shot, which is rare to actually witness, is the *double chip,* where you hit the chip fat, causing the clubhead to hit the ball twice, once while it's in the air. You could never do this if you tried, but sometime, somewhere, you'll see it performed and will stand in amazement.

I was playing a tournament in Palm Springs, California, when one of the amateurs, standing near the condos surrounding the course, hit a chip shot. He had to loft the ball gently over a bunker and then have it land like a Nerf ball on a mattress on the green. He hit the shot a little fat, the ball went up in the air slowly, and his club accelerated and hit the ball again about eye level. The ball went over his head, out of bounds, and into the swimming pool. The rule says that you may have only four penalty strokes per swing maximum, but I think he beat that by a bunch with that double-hit chip shot. When I saw him last, he was still trying to retrieve that ball with the guy's pool net.

Stare hard at the top of the grip...

from address...

to impact.

Figure 13-3:
Keep your
head steady
to avoid
topped
shots.

Neutral position, head over the ball.

If you tend to hit it thin, place your head behind the ball to fix the problem.

If you tend to hit it fat, place your head ahead of the ball to fix the problem.

Figure 13-4:
The cure for chipper nightmares.

Thinned chips (skulls, as they call it on tour, or *Vin Scullys,* as I call them after the famous Dodgers baseball announcer) are the opposite of the Hormels (duffs). You aren't hitting enough ground. In fact, you don't hit the ground at all. The club strikes the ball right above the equator, sending the shot speeding on its merry way, past the hole into all sorts of evil places. You need to hit the ground slightly so that the ball hits the clubface and not the front end of the club.

Again, stick your golf club shaft in the ground outside the top of the ball.

If you continually hit Hormels (duffs), get your nose to the left of the shaft, which moves the bottom of your swing forward. Doing so allows you to hit down on the ball from the right position. Make sure that your head stays forward in this shot. Most people I play with who hit an occasional Hormel move their heads backward as they start their downswings, which means that they hit behind the ball.

If you're prone to hit an occasional Vin Scully (a thin shot), set up with your nose behind or to the right of the ball, which moves the bottom of your swing back. When you find the right spot, you hit the ball and the ground at the same time, which is good. I have found that most people who hit their shots thin have a tendency to raise their entire bodies up immediately before impact. Concentrate on keeping your upper torso bent in the same position throughout the swing. Hopefully, the next time you hear the name Vin Scully, it will be on a televised Dodgers game.

Can't Make a Putt?

Some people argue that putting is more mental than physical. But before you resort to a series of seances with your local fortune-teller, check your alignment. You often can trace missed putts to poor aim.

I like to use a device you can make easily at home. Get two metal rods, each about a foot in length. Then get some string to tie to each end of the rods. The rods should be about 1/8 inch in diameter, and the string should be about 10 feet long.

Go to the putting green and find a putt that is 6 feet long, fairly straight, and level. Stick the first rod about 6 to 8 inches behind the center of the hole. Then stick the other rod on the line of the straight putt until there is tension in the string. The string is tied on the top of the rod so that it's about 10 inches off the ground.

Place a golf ball directly under the string so that it appears to cut the ball in half when you look down. Put your putter behind the ball and take a stroke; if the putter goes straight back and straight through with the stroke, the string should be in the middle of the putter blade as it goes back and forth. If it is not, you will notice the putter blade's position will vary relative to the line of the string. Practice until the putter stays in the same line as the string during your stroke. Because you can see a line to the hole, you can easily solve alignment problems with this handy and easy-to-use homemade device.

Another important lesson to be learned with this device is the line that you see to the hole. The string easily allows you to envision the path of the putt. Keep this mental image when you proceed to the golf course. Putting takes a lot of imagination, and if you can see the line, it's much easier to stroke the ball along the intended path to the hole. After you use this device enough, you start to "see" the line on the golf course as you lurk over those 6-foot putts. This is one cheap yet effective way to learn how to putt!

Shanking

GARY SAYS

Bet the man who has the shanks, and your plate will be full.
— Gary McCord, 1996

It must have started centuries ago. Alone with his sheep in a quiet moment of reflection, he swung his carved shepherd's crook at a rather round multi-colored rock, toward a faraway half-dead, low-growing vine. The rock peeled off the old crook, and instead of lurching forward toward the vine, it careened off at an angle 90 degrees to the right of the target. "What was that?!" cried the surprised shepherd. "That was a shank, you idiot!" cried one of the sheep. "Now release the toe of that stick or this game will never get off the ground."

This story has been fabricated to help with the tension of this despicable disease. The *shanks* are a virus that attack the very soul of a golfer. They can come unannounced and invade the decorum of a well-played round. They leave with equal haste and lurk in the mind of the golfer, dwelling until the brain reaches critical mass. Then you have meltdown. This sounds like one of those diseases that they're making movies about. And to a golfer, no other word strikes terror and dread like the word *shank*.

I remember as a kid getting the shanks once in a while, but because of my innocence they were not a part of my daily life. As a junior golfer, I was visiting the Tournament of Champions in 1970 when a bunch of the guys were watching the tournament winners hit balls on the driving range. I was completely mesmerized by Frank Beard as he hit shank after shank on the practice tee. These were the years when the rough was so high at LaCosta that you could lose your golf cart in it if you weren't careful. My buddies wanted to go watch Nicklaus, but being somewhat of a masochist, I told them that I would follow "Frank the Shank" around and meet them afterward. I witnessed one of the greatest rounds I have ever seen. He shot a 64 and never missed a shot. How could a man who was so severely stricken by this disease on the practice tee rally and unleash a round of golf like he played? That is the mystery of this affliction. Can it be controlled? Yes!

Shanking occurs when the ball is hit with the hosel of the club and goes 90 degrees to right of your intended target. (The *hosel* is the part of the club that attaches to the clubhead.) A shank is sometimes called a *pitch out*, a *Chinese hook, El Hosel,* a *scud,* or a *snake killer* — you get the idea. Shanking is caused when the heel of the club (the *heel* is the closest part of the clubhead to you; the *toe* is the farthest) continues toward the target and then ends up right of the target. This forces the hosel upon the ball, and a shank occurs. The idea is to have the toe of the club go toward the target and then end up left of the target.

Here's an easy exercise that helps get rid of the shanks. (See Figure 13-5.) Get a 2-x-4 board and align it along your target line, put the ball 2 inches away from the inside of the board, and try to hit the ball. If you have the shanks, your club will want to hit the board. If you're doing it properly, the club will come from the inside and hit the ball. Then the toe of the club will go left of the target, the ball will go straight, and your woes will be over.

In a world full of new, emerging viruses, we have the technology to lash back at this golfing disease and eliminate it altogether from our DNA. Stay calm and get a 2-x-4 board, practice the drill, and never have the shanks again.

Release the toe and don't hit the board.

Figure 13-5:
Shank and
push fix.

The Push

The *push* is a shot that starts right of the target and continues to go in that direction. This shot is not like a slice, which starts left and then curves to the right; it just goes right. This shot is caused when the body does not rotate through to the left on the downswing, and the arms hopelessly swing to the right, which produces the push.

Hitting a push is like standing at home plate, aiming at the pitcher, and then swinging your arms at the first baseman. If this sounds like you, listen up. I'll show you how to fix this problem.

Place a wooden 2-x-4 parallel to the target line and about 2 inches above the golf ball. You push the ball because your body stops rotating left on the downswing, and your arms go off to the right. If your arms go off to the right with that old 2-x-4 sitting there, splinters are going to fly. Naturally, you don't want to hit the board, so you will — hopefully — swing your hips left on the downswing, which will pull your arms left and avoid the push.

The Pull

The *pull* is a shot that starts left and stays left, unlike a hook, which starts right of the target and curves left. The pull is caused when the club comes from outside the target line on the downswing and you pull across your body, causing the ball to start and stay left.

Hitting a pull is like standing at home plate and aiming at the pitcher, but swinging the club toward the third baseman, which is where the ball would go. This swing malady is a little more complicated, and it's more difficult to pick out one exercise to cure it, so bear with me.

Pulls are caused when your shoulders "open" too fast in the downswing. For the proper sequence, your shoulders should remain as close to parallel to the target line as possible at impact. Here are some hints to help you cure your pull:

> ✔ **Check your alignment.** If you're aimed too far to the right, your body will slow down on the downswing and allow your shoulders to open at impact to bring the club back to the target.

✔ **Check your weight shift.** If you do not have a weight shift to your left side on the downswing, you will spin your hips out of the way too fast, causing your shoulders to open up too quickly and hit a putrid pull. So shift those hips toward the target on the downswing until your weight is all on your left side after impact.

✔ **Feel your grip pressure.** Too tight a grip on the club will cause you to tense up on the downswing and come over the top for a pull.

Not Enough Distance

Everyone in the world would like more distance. John Daly and Laura Davies would like more distance. I would like more distance, and I'm sure you would also. Here are some simple thoughts to help you get some needed yardage:

✔ **Turn your shoulders on the backswing.** The more you turn your shoulders on the backswing, the better chance you have to hit the ball longer. So stretch that torso on the backswing, and try to put your left shoulder over your right foot at the top of your swing.

If you're having difficulty moving your shoulders enough on the backswing, try turning your left knee clockwise until it's pointing behind the ball during your backswing. This frees up your hips to turn, and subsequently your shoulders. A big turn starts from the ground up.

✔ **Get the tension out of your grip.** Grip the club loosely; remember, you should grip it with the pressure of holding a spotted owl's egg. If there's too much tension in your hands, your forearms and chest will "tighten up," and you'll lose that valuable flexibility that helps with the speed of your arms and hands.

Turning your hips to the left on the downswing and extending your right arm on the through-swing are trademarks of the longer hitters. Here's a drill that you can use to accomplish this feat of daring.

Tee up your driver in the normal position. Place the ball off your left heel and/or opposite your left armpit. Now reach down, not moving your stance, and move the ball toward the target the length of the grip. Tee the ball up right there; it should be about 1 foot closer to the hole. Address the ball where the normal position was and swing at the ball that is now teed up. To hit that ball, you will have to move your hips to the left so that your arms can "reach the ball," thereby causing you to extend your right arm. Practice this drill 20 times and then put the ball back in the normal position. You should feel faster with the hips and a tremendous extension with the right arm.

Too Low

Does your ball fly too low when you hit it? Does it look like a duck trying to take off with a bad wing? Do your friends call you "Stealth"? If you're having this problem with your driver, make sure that your head is behind the ball at address and at impact. Moving your head laterally back and forth with your driver can cause too low a shot. Also, drivers come in different lofts. If you're hitting the ball too low, try a driver that has 11 to 12 degrees of loft.

If you're having a problem with low iron shots, you're probably trying to lift those golf balls into the air instead of hitting down. Remember, with irons, you have to hit down to get the ball up.

Poor Direction

If your golf ball takes off in more directions than the compass has to offer, check your alignment and ball position for the problem. Choose the direction you're going and then put your feet, knees, and shoulders on a parallel line to the target line. Be very specific with your alignment.

Ball position can play a major role in poor direction. If the ball is too far forward, it's easy to push the ball to the right. If the ball is too far back in your stance, it's easy to hit pushes and pulls. The driver is played opposite your left armpit. (As the club gets shorter, the ball should move back toward the middle of your stance.)

If nobody is around and you want to check your ball position, here's what you can do. Get into your stance — with the driver, for example — and then undo your laces. Step out of your shoes, leaving them right where they were at address. Now take a look: Is the ball where it's supposed to be in your stance? Two suggestions: If it's wet out, don't do this. And if your socks have holes in them, make sure that nobody is watching.

Hitting from the Top

When you start cocking the wrist in your golf swing, the thumb of your right hand (if you're a right-handed golfer) points at your right shoulder on the backswing. That's good! When you start the downswing, you should try to point your thumb at your right shoulder for as long as you can, thus maintaining the *angle*. That's golfspeak for keeping the shaft of the club as close to the left arm on the downswing as possible. If your right thumb starts pointing away from your right shoulder on the downswing, not good! That is known as *hitting from the top*. In essence, you're uncocking the wrist on the downswing.

To stop hitting from the top, you must reduce your grip pressure on the club. Too much tension in your hands will make you throw the clubhead toward the ball, causing you to hit from the top. After you have relaxed your grip pressure, get an old 2-x-4 and place it on the side of the ball away from you, parallel to the target line. The ball should be about 2 inches away from the board. You will find that if you keep pointing your right thumb at your right shoulder on the downswing, you won't hit the board with your club. If you point your thumb away from your shoulder on the downswing, your chances of creating sparks are very good. (See Figure 13-6.)

Reverse Pivots

A *reverse pivot* is when you put all your weight on your left foot on the backswing (shown in Figure 13-7) and all your weight on your right foot during the downswing. That is the opposite of what you want to do! Picture a baseball pitcher. Pitchers have all their weight on the right foot at the top of the windup, the left foot is in the air (for a right hander), and on the through motion, all the weight goes to the left foot. (The right foot is in the air.) That's the weight transfer you need. Here's how you can accomplish it.

Start your backswing, and when you get to the top of your swing, lift your left foot off the ground. Now you can't put any weight on that foot! You'll feel your whole body resist placing your weight over your right foot. Take your time and let your weight transfer there. Start the downswing by placing your left foot back where it was and then transfer all your weight over during the swing. When you have made contact with the ball (hopefully), put all your weight on your left foot and lift your right foot off the ground. Try to stand there for a short time to feel the balance. This rocking-chair transfer drill lets you feel the proper weight shift in the golf swing. Take it easy at first. Practice short shots until you get the feel and then work your way up to your driver.

On the downswing, try to point your right thumb at your right shoulder (if you're right-handed).

Keep trying!

So this is how John Daly does it!

Figure 13-6:
Hitting from
the top.

Figure 13-7:
Reverse
pivots.

Sway Off the Ball

In a *sway,* your hips and shoulders don't turn on the backswing, but simply slide back in a straight line, as shown in Figure 13-8. Here is a good drill to help you prevent the sway.

Find a bare wall. Using a 5-iron, lay the club on the ground with the clubhead touching the wall and the shaft extending straight into the room. Place your right foot against the end of the shaft with the little toe of your right shoe hitting the end of the club so that you're standing exactly one club length from the wall. Put your left foot in the normal address position for the 5-iron and, without moving your feet, bend over and pick up the club. Take a backswing. If you sway with your hips 1 inch to the right on your backswing, you'll notice that you hit the wall immediately with the club. Practice this until you don't hit the wall. I put so many marks and holes in the motel room, I eventually could see the guy in the next room!

I suggest that you practice this drill in your garage at first to save the walls at home. You might want to use an old club, too.

Figure 13-8:
Don't sway
off the ball.

Belly Button Twist

A common fault is to slide too far toward the target with the hips at the start of the downswing. How far should they slide until they turn left? They must slide until your left hip and left knee are over your left foot. Then those hips turn left in a hurry!

Here's the best way to improve your hip position at the downswing. Get a broken club that has just a shaft and a grip on it. You can find broken clubs in lost-and-found barrels, or just ask somebody at a driving range. (Or your golf pro can help you find one.) Stick the broken club into the ground just outside your left foot; the top of the grip should be no higher than your hip. Now hit a few shots. When you swing, your left hip should not hit the club stuck in the ground. It should turn to the left of the shaft. The key here is to straighten the left leg in your follow-through.

Your Swing Is Too Long

If your swing is too long and sloppy (past parallel to the ground at the top of the swing), here are two positions to work on. The first is the right arm in the backswing (for a right-handed golfer); it must not bend more than 90 degrees. It must stay at a right angle, as shown in Figure 13-5. Combined with the right elbow, it must not get more than a dollar bill's length (6 inches) away from your rib cage at the top of the backswing (see Figure 13-9). If you can maintain these two simple positions at the top of your swing, you won't overswing.

Figure 13-9: The right arm position in the backswing.

Your right arm should form a right angle at the elbow.

Your Swing Is Too Short

In most cases, a short swing comes from not enough shoulder turn. Turn your left shoulder over your right foot at the top of your backswing. If you can't, lift your left heel off the ground until you can. Many players I see with a short swing also have their right elbow against their rib cage at the top of their swing. The right elbow should be away from the rib cage (6 inches) to allow some freedom in the swing and get the needed length to your swing arc.

You Want More Backspin

How can you back up the ball like the pros on the tour do? People ask this question all the time. The answer is, the more you hit down on the ball, the more spin you put on it. When people who play this game for a living hit those short irons, they have a very steep angle of descent into the ball, which causes a lot of spin. We also play golf balls that are made out of *balata,* a cover that spins more and is softer than the two-piece surlyn ball most people play. (Chapter 3 explains the different types of golf balls in detail.) We also play on grass that's manicured and very short so that we can get a clean hit with the club off these fairways. All this helps a bunch when you're trying to spin the ball. Many things help us spin the ball.

The bottom line is that we're trying to control the distance a ball goes. I don't care if the ball backs up to get to that distance or rolls forward to get there. Consistency is knowing how far you can hit each club in your bag. Don't worry about how much spin you put on it; worry about how far each club travels.

Most of the faults you'll develop in your game are pretty standard; they can all be cured. The pointers in this chapter will help you cure them. I've supplied the operation; you supply the therapy.

Part IV
Taking Your Game Public

In this part . . .

You're finally out there among the flora and fauna chasing your golf ball around the golf course. In this part, I show you how to play "smart golf" and impress your new friends. And in case the idea of betting strikes your fancy, Chapter 16 gives you the odds.

Chapter 14

Ready, Set, Play!

In This Chapter

▶ Warming up your mind and body

▶ Arriving early to work on your swing

▶ Developing your plan of attack

▶ Getting used to golfing in front of an audience

*O*kay, you're ready to hit the links. The first thing you need to be sure of is that you are at the right course. The second thing is that you know where each hole goes. Both may seem obvious and easy to achieve, but things can go wrong. I know. I've been there. Listen to this tale of woe from a few years ago.

I was trying to qualify for the U.S. Open. The sectional qualifying course I was assigned to was Carlton Oaks in southern California. No problem. I'd played there many times and knew the course well. I'd have a good shot at qualifying on this course. Or so I thought.

I got to the 13th hole and still had a chance of making the U.S. Open. But I needed a good finish. The 13th is a dogleg to the left, par-4, some 400-plus yards: a good, testing hole. But I needed a birdie, so I decided to hit my drive down the 12th fairway, the hole I had just played. That would leave me a better angle for my second shot to the 13th green and cut more than 50 yards from the hole. The only slight snag was that my ball would have to fly over some trees.

I drove the ball perfectly and then hit a long iron to the green over the trees, a good one, too. The only thing I recall thinking is that the hole was longer than I remembered; I had to hit a 4-iron to the green when I expected a 7-iron to be enough. Still, I hit it solidly, so all was well.

When I got to the green, I was alone. So I waited for the rest of my group. And waited. And waited. Eventually I lost patience, putted out, and then started to look for the others. I soon found them. They were waving to me from a green about 100 yards away. I had played to the wrong green! There was only one thing left to do. Two, actually. I fired my caddie and walked to the clubhouse. Luckily, I found the right clubhouse.

Creating a Positive Attitude

Firing my caddie may seem petty, but one's caddie is actually an important part of being a professional golfer. Even if you aren't a pro, no matter what goes wrong on the course, it is never — repeat, *never* — your fault. You must always find someone or something else to blame for any misfortune. In other words, you must be creative in the excuse department.

There have been some great excuses over the years. My own particular favorite came from Greg Norman. A few years ago, he blamed a miscued shot on a worm popping up out of the ground next to his ball as he swung. Poor Greg was so distracted that he couldn't hit the shot properly! Then there was Jack Nicklaus at the 1995 British Open at St. Andrew's. In the first round, Jack hit his second shot on the 14th hole, a long par-5, into what is known as Hell Bunker. It's well named, being basically a large, deep, sand-filled hole in the ground. Anyway, that his ball came to rest there came as a bit of a surprise to Jack. He apparently felt that his shot should have flown comfortably over said bunker. And his excuse? His ball must have been deflected by seedheads!

These two examples are extreme, of course. But you should apply the same principle to your game. You can often tell a good player from his reaction to misfortune. He'll blame his equipment, the wind, a bad yardage, or whatever is there. On the other hand, less-secure golfers take all responsibility for bad shots. Whatever they do is awful. In fact, they really stink at this stupid game. That's what they tell themselves — usually to the point that it affects their next shot. And the next. And the next. Soon, they're playing badly. Whatever they perceive themselves to be, they become.

Again, that's the extreme example. Just be sure that you err toward the former rather than the latter. What the heck, be a little unrealistic. Try to fool yourself!

Warming Up Your Body

After you've warmed up your mind, you need to do the same for your body. Warm-ups are important. Not only do a few simple warm-up exercises loosen your muscles and help your swing, but they help you psychologically as well. I like to step onto the first tee knowing that I'm as ready as I can be. Feeling loose rather than tight is reassuring. Besides, golfers, along with the rest of the world, are a lot more aware of physical fitness and diet today than in days gone by. Lee Trevino, a two-time U.S. Open, British Open, and PGA champion and now one of the top players on the senior tour, calls the

PGA Tour players "flat-bellies." Which they are, compared to some of the more rotund "round-bellies" on the senior tour. I think this improvement is called progress!

Johnny Bench, the great Cincinnati Reds catcher, showed me the following stretches. He used them when he played baseball, and he's in the Hall of Fame — so who am I to argue?

Holding a club by the head, place the grip end in your armpit so that the shaft runs the length of your arm (use a club that is the same length as your arm for this one, as shown in Figure 14-1). That action in itself stretches your arm and shoulders. Now bend forward until your arm is horizontal. The forward movement stretches your lower back, one of the most important areas in your body when it comes to playing golf. If your back is stiff, making a full turn on the backswing is tough. Hold this position for a few seconds; then switch arms and repeat. Keep doing this stretch until you feel "ready" to swing.

Holding the club like this, bend forward.

Then switch arms and do it again.

Figure 14-1:
Stretch those muscles!

This second method of loosening up is more traditional. Instead of practicing your swing with one club in your hands, double the load (see Figure 14-2). Swing two clubs. Go slowly, trying to make as full a back-and-through swing as you can. The extra weight soon stretches away any tightness.

This next exercise is one that you'll see many players use on the first tee. Jack Nicklaus has always done it. All you have to do is place a club across your back and hold it in place with your hands or elbows. Then turn back and through as if making a golf swing, as shown in Figure 14-3. Again, this action really stretches your back muscles.

Warming Up for Success

If you go to any professional golf tournament, you'll see that most players show up on the practice range about one hour before they're due to tee off. Showing up early leaves players time to tune their swings and strokes before the game starts for real.

Swing two clubs back...

and through.

Figure 14-2: Double your swing weight and swing nice and easy.

Stand as if at address, a club behind your back. Then turn back...

and through.

Figure 14-3:
Watch your
back!

I'm one of those players who likes to schedule about an hour for pre-round practice. But half that time is probably enough for you. Actually, you don't use the time for practice on your swing. You shouldn't make any last-minute changes. You're only going to hit some balls so that you can build a feel and a rhythm for the upcoming round.

Start your warm-up by hitting some short wedge shots (see Figure 14-4). Don't go straight to your driver and start blasting away. That's asking for trouble. You can easily pull a muscle if you swing too hard too quickly. Plus, it's unlikely that you'll immediately begin to hit long, straight drives if you don't warm up first. More than likely, you'll hit short, crooked shots. And those shots aren't good for the psyche.

1. **Start with the wedge.**

   Focus on making contact with the ball. Nothing else. Try to turn your shoulders a little more with each shot. Hit about 20 balls without worrying too much about where they're going. Just swing the club smoothly.

2. **Move next to your midirons.**

   I like to hit my 6-iron at this point. I'm just about warmed up, and the 6-iron has just enough loft that I don't have to work too hard at getting the ball flying forward. Again, hit about 20 balls.

Before each round, hit a few wedge shots...

and then a few 6-irons...

Figure 14-4:
Warming
up.

and then a few drivers...

and finish up with a few long putts.

3. Hit the big stick.

I recommend that you hit no more than a dozen drives. Getting carried away with this club is easy. And when you go overboard, your swing can get a little quick. Remember, you're only warming up. Focus on your rhythm and timing — not the ball.

4. Before you leave the range, hit a few more balls with your wedge.

You're not looking for distance with this club, only smoothness. That's a good thought to leave with.

5. Finally, spend about ten minutes on the practice putting green.

You need to get a feel for the pace of the greens before you start. Start with short uphill putts of 2 to 3 feet. Get your confidence and then proceed to longer putts of 20 to 30 feet. After that, practice putting to opposite fringes to get the feeling of speed. Focus on the pace rather than the direction. You're ready now — knock them all in!

Planning Your Game

The best players start every round with a plan for how they're going to approach the course. They know which holes they can attack and which holes are best to play safely. So should you.

Many people say that golf is 90 percent mental and 10 percent physical. You'll find a lot of truth in that statement. The fewer mental errors you make, the lower your score will be. And the great thing about bad thinking is that everyone at every level of play can work on eliminating it.

Think of golf as a game of chess. You have to think two or three moves ahead every time you hit the ball. Over every shot, you should be thinking, "Where do I need to put this ball in order to make my next shot as easy as possible?"

I could write a whole book on the countless number of strategic situations you can find yourself in on the course. Trouble is, I don't have the space for that in this book, and you don't need all that information yet. So what follows is a brief overview of "tactical golf." I've selected three very common situations; you'll come across each one at least once in almost every round you play. You can apply the thinking and strategy behind each one to many other problems that you'll encounter. So don't get too wrapped up in the specifics of each scenario — think "big picture."

Strategy 1: Don't be a sucker

You're playing a 170-yard par-3 hole (see Figure 14-5). As you can see, the hole is cut toward the left side of the green, behind a large bunker. If your first inclination is to fire straight at the flag, think again. Ask yourself these questions:

- What are your chances of bringing off such a difficult shot successfully?
- What happens if you miss?
- Is the shot too risky?

If the answers are (a) less than 50 percent, (b) you take five to get down from the bunker, or (c) yes, then play toward the safe part of the green.

Only if you happen to be an exceptional bunker player should you even attempt to go for the flag.

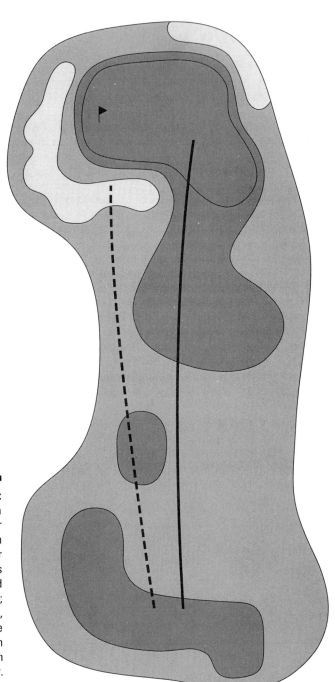

Figure 14-5:
Don't be a sucker and aim straight for the flag, as the dotted path shows; instead, take the safer path away from the bunker.

Think of it this way: Golf is a game of numbers. If you shoot at the pin here, you bring the number 2 into play. If you hit a great shot, you have a great opportunity for a deuce. That's the upside. The downside is that missing the green makes the numbers 5, 6, and maybe even 7 possibilities, especially if you aren't too strong from sand or if you're unlucky enough to find a really bad lie.

If, on the other hand, you play for the middle of the green, your numbers are reduced. Say you hit the putting surface with your first shot. In all likelihood, the most you can take for the hole is 4, and you can take that only if you three-putt. You'll get a lot of 3s from that position, and once in a while you'll hole the long putt — so a 2 isn't impossible.

Even if you miss the green on that side, the odds are that you're going to be left with a relatively simple chip or pitch. So unless you mess up terribly, 4 is again your worst possible score for the hole. I like those numbers better, don't you?

Anyway, those are the specifics of this particular situation. In the broader scheme of things, you should follow this policy more often than not. If you decide to be a "middle of the green" shooter, practice your long putting a lot. You're going to have a lot of 30- to 40-foot putts, so be ready for them. In the long run, though, you'll come out ahead.

Strategy 2: Know that your driver isn't always best

You're on a par-4 hole of just over 400 yards (see Figure 14-6). But the actual yardage isn't that important. The key to this hole is the narrowing of the fairway at the point where your drive is most likely to finish. When this situation comes up, tee off with your 3-wood, 5-wood, or whatever club you can hit safely into the wide part of the fairway. Even if you can't quite reach the green in two shots, that's the best strategy. Again, it's a question of numbers. If you risk hitting your driver and miss the fairway, you're going to waste at least one shot getting the ball back into play — maybe more than one if you get a bad lie. Then you still have a longish shot to the green. If you miss the green, you're going to take at least 6 shots. Not good.

Now follow a better scenario. You hit your 3-wood from the tee safely down the fairway. Then you hit your 5-wood, leaving the ball about 25 yards from the green. All you have left is a simple little chip or pitch. Most times, you're not going to take more than 5 from this position. Indeed, you'll nearly always have a putt for a 4. I know most of you won't do this, but it sounds like the right thing to do, doesn't it?

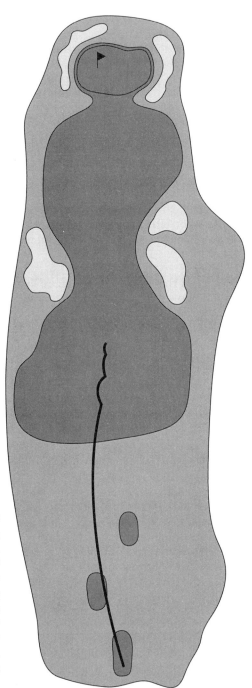

Figure 14-6:
Go for the
wide part of
the fairway
by using
less club (a
3-wood or
5-wood, for
example).

All this requires of you is that you pay attention to the layout of the hole and plan accordingly.

Strategy 3: Play three easy shots

The par-5 hole is long, just over 500 yards (see Figure 14-7). Your first inclination is again to reach for your driver. Most of the time, your driver is probably the correct play — but not always. Look at this hole. You can break this down into three relatively easy shots with the same club. Say you hit your 4-iron 170 yards. Three shots can put you on the green. To me, breaking down the shot is easier for the beginning player than trying to squeeze every possible yard out of the driver and getting into trouble. (I know you won't consider this. But I had to do this as a disclaimer.)

Remember, no law of golf says that you have to use your driver from the tee. If you don't feel comfortable with your driver, go with your 3-wood. If your 3-wood doesn't feel right, go to the 5-wood. And if you still aren't happy, try your 3-iron. Don't hit until you're confident that you can hit the ball into the fairway with the club in your hands. I'd rather be 200 yards from the tee and in the fairway than 250 yards out in the rough. If you don't believe me, try this test. Every time you miss a fairway from the tee, pick your ball up and drop it 15 yards farther back — but in the middle of the fairway. Then play from there. Bet you'll shoot anywhere from 5 to 10 shots fewer than normal for 18 holes. In other words, it's much better to be in a spot where you can hit the ball cleanly than in a tough spot — even if the clean shot puts you farther from the green.

Take advantage of your strengths and weaknesses

To really take advantage of good strategy on the golf course, you have to know where your strengths and weaknesses are. For example, on the par-4 hole described earlier in this chapter, a really accurate driver of the ball could take the chance and try to hit the ball into the narrow gap. That strategy is playing to his strength.

But how do you find out where your pluses and minuses are? Simple. All you have to do is keep a close record of your rounds over a period of time. By a close record, I don't simply mean your score on each hole. You have to break down the numbers a bit more than that.

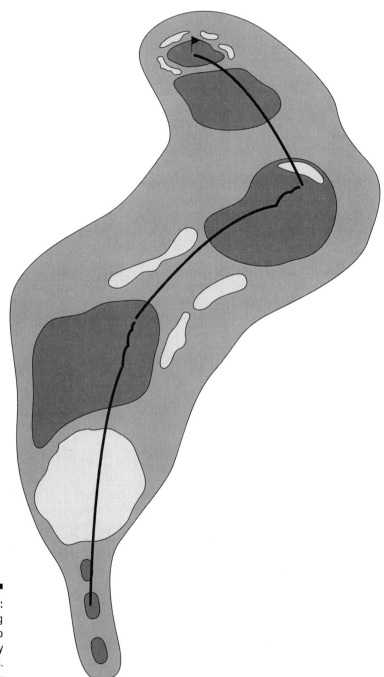

Figure 14-7:
Turn long
holes into
three easy
shots.

Look at the scorecard in Figure 14-8, on which John has marked his score in detail. You can see how many fairways he hit. How many times he hit the green. And how many putts he took on each green.

Men's Course Rating/Slope
Blue 73.1/137
White 71.0/130

Women's Course Rating/Slope
Red 73.7/128

Blue Tees	White Tees	Par	Hcp	JOHN				HOLE	HIT FAIRWAY	HIT GREEN		No. PUTTS	Hcp	Par	Red Tees
377	361	4	11	4				1	✓	✓		2	13	4	310
514	467	5	13	8				2	✓	0		3	3	5	428
446	423	4	1	7				3	0	0		2	1	4	389
376	356	4	5	6				4	0	0		2	11	4	325
362	344	4	7	5				5	0	✓		3	7	4	316
376	360	4	9	6				6	✓	0		2	9	4	335
166	130	3	17	4				7	0	✓		3	17	3	108
429	407	4	3	5				8	✓	✓		3	5	4	368
161	145	3	15	5				9	0	0		2	15	3	122
3207	2993	35		50				Out	4	4		22		35	2701
		Initial											Initial		
366	348	4	18	5				10	0	0		2	14	4	320
570	537	5	10	7				11	✓	0		3	2	5	504
438	420	4	2	5				12	✓	0		2	6	4	389
197	182	3	12	4				13	0	0		2	16	3	145
507	475	5	14	5				14	✓	✓		2	4	5	425
398	380	4	4	5				15	0	✓		3	8	4	350
380	366	4	6	5				16	✓	0		2	10	4	339
165	151	3	16	4				17	0	0		2	18	3	133
397	375	4	8	5				18	0	0		2	12	4	341
3418	3234	36		45				In	3	2		20		36	2946
6625	6227	71		95				Tot	7	6		42		71	5647
Handicap													Handicap		
Net Score													Net Score		
Adjust													Adjust		

Scorer Attested Date

Figure 14-8: Keep a close record of your rounds over a period of time to track your strengths and weaknesses.

If John tracks these things over, say, ten rounds, trends soon appear. Assume that this round is typical for John. Clearly, John isn't a very good putter. Forty-two for 18 holes is poor by any standard, especially when he isn't hitting that many greens — only one in three. If John were hitting 12 or 13 greens, you'd expect more putts because he'd probably be some distance from the hole more often. But this card tells another story. John's missing a lot of greens and taking a lot of putts. So either his chipping and pitching are very bad indeed, or his putting is letting him down. Probably the latter.

On the other hand, John isn't a bad driver, at least in terms of accuracy. He's hitting more than half the fairways. So, at least in the short term, John needs to work on his short game and putting.

Keep a record of your scores that draws a picture of your game, and you'll soon know which part (or parts) of your game need some work.

Overcoming the first-tee nerves

The opening shot of any round is often the most stressful. You're not "into" your round yet. Even the practice shots that you may have hit aren't exactly the real thing. And people are nearly always around when you hit that first shot. If you're like most people, you'll be intimidated by even the thought of striking a ball in full view of the public.

How a player reacts to "first tee nerves" is an individual thing. You just have to get out there and do it and see how you feel and what you do. But the first tee nerves do have some common factors. Blurred vision. A desire to get this over and done with as soon as possible. A loss of reason.

The most common mistake, however, is doing everything twice as fast as you normally would. By everything, I mean looking down the fairway, standing to the ball, swinging — the lot. Your increased pace is due to the misguided notion that if you get this swing over with really quickly, no one will see it. It's the "hit it and go" syndrome, and you should avoid it.

I remember when my golf swing wasn't where I wanted it to be. I had a bad grip. A bad takeaway. A bad position at the top. I was never comfortable with myself, so how could I be comfortable with others watching? I'd get up there, hit the ball as soon as I could, and get out of the way.

After I understood the mechanics of my swing, I lost that dread. All of a sudden, I stood over the ball as long as I wanted to. I thought about what I was doing, not about what others were thinking. I wanted them to watch, to revel in the positions in my golf swing, because they were good positions. I didn't mind showing off.

Look cool when you get to the course

When you show up at the course, you want to be a little late. If you've got a 9 a.m. tee time, get there at about 8:30. Then your partners are starting to panic a bit about where you are. Always change your shoes while sitting on the trunk of your car. That's cool. Always have a carry bag, never a pull cart. Pull carts aren't cool. Get one of those little bags with the prongs on to keep it upright when you set it down. Very cool.

Never tie your shoelaces until you get to the tee. On the tee, bend down to tie them while complaining about all the things that were wrong with you the night before. Bursitis in your right shoulder. That pesky tendonitis in your left knee. The sore elbow you sustained while playing racquetball. Whatever. Elicit sympathy from your companions. Get up very slowly. Adjust yourself. Grab your back. Then get into stroke negotiations. . . .

What's also very cool is having your own turn of golfing phrase. Make up your own language to an extent. Don't say stuff like "wow" or "far out." Keep your talk underground. Use stuff that no one else can understand. For example, Fairway Louie refers to the local denizens of our golf course as "herds of grazing hack" because they're always looking for balls in the rough. If you come up with some good stuff, everyone will start using your language. It's a domino effect.

At first, though, I'd recommend that you do more listening than talking. It's like when you go to a foreign country. You've got to listen. Listen to how golfers express themselves during moments of elation, anger, and solitude. After you pick up the lingo, you can add your own touches to it. In golf terminology, there's no right or wrong as long as you don't act like a geek.

Being overly concerned about your audience is really a social problem. Instead of taking refuge in your preshot routine and whatever swing thought you may be using, you're thinking about what other people may be thinking. The secret to overcoming this social problem is to immerse yourself in your routine. Forget all that outside stuff. Say, "Okay, I'm going to start behind the ball. Then I'm going to look at my line, take five steps to the ball, swing the club away to the inside and turn my shoulders." Whatever you say to yourself, just remember to focus internally rather than externally.

Playing Other Games

The best game I know of for the beginning golfer is a *scramble*. In that format, you're usually part of a team of four. Everyone tees off. Then you pick the best of the four shots. Then everyone plays another shot from where that "best shot" lies. And so on. A scramble is good because you have less pressure to hit every shot well. You can lean on your partners a bit.

Plus, you get to watch better players up close. And you get to experience some of the game's camaraderie. Scrambles are typically full of rooting, cheering, and high-fives. In short, they're a lot of fun.

You can also play in games where the format is *stableford*. In this game, the scoring is by points rather than strokes. You get one point for a *bogey* (score of one over par) on each hole; two points for a par; three for a *birdie* (one under par); and four points for an *eagle* (two under par). Thus a round in which you par every hole reaps you 36 points. The great thing is that in a stableford, you don't have to complete every hole. You can take your nines and tens without irreparably damaging your score. You simply don't get any points for a hole in which you take more than a bogey (that's with your handicap strokes deducted, of course).

After you've played for a while, however, you may find that you play most of your golf with three companions, known as a *foursome* in the United States (a *four-ball* elsewhere). The format is simple. You split into two teams of two and play what is known as a *best-ball* game. That is, the best score on each team on each hole counts as the score for that team. For example, if we're partners and you make a five on the first hole and I make a four, then our team scores a four for the hole.

Keeping Score

Don't get too wrapped up in how many shots you're taking to play a round, at least at first. For many golfers, the score doesn't mean that much anyway. Most of the guys I grew up with never kept score. I've never seen most of them count every shot. That's because they always play a match against another player or team. The only thing that matters is how they compare with their opponents. It's never "me against the course." It's always "me against you." So if I'm having a really bad hole, I simply concede it to you and then move on to the next one.

Believe me, that's a totally different game from the one that you see the pros playing on TV every week. For them, every shot is vital — the difference between making the cut or not, or finishing in or out of the big money. That's why the pro game is better left to the pros.

Practicing

It's amazing, but nearly half of high-handicap golfers don't practice. Are you one of them? You can't expect to improve your golf game if you don't put some time in. Now, I can already hear you whining, "I don't have the time!" Well, stop your griping, because I made it easy for you. I put together a sample practice schedule that you can easily work into your weekly routine. You may want to tone it down at the office — it tends to look bad if your boss walks in while you're practicing your putting — although you may be able to make use of all the time you spend on those long conference calls.

Remember, practice can be fun. You can modify the schedule to fit your goals and your playing level. Now, if you don't want to take strokes off your game, skip this part, but if you're a weekend warrior who wants to improve his or her game, follow this quick roadmap to success:

1. **Practice your swing whenever possible** — see Part II of this book. You can practice most of the suggestions in Part II in your basement, living room, or backyard. Place old clubs in various locations around your house so that it's convenient to swing when the spirit (or schedule) moves you.

2. **Make imaginary swings in front of a mirror or window** with your arms and hands in the proper position (see Part II). If you don't have a club handy, that's okay. Visualize and feel the correct position.

3. **Grip a club when you watch television** — you're not doing anything else! Try swinging a club during a commercial — unless it's one of my commercials. In that case, put your club down and turn down the volume.

4. **Build a practice area in your house or office** where you can easily work on your short game. Use those plastic practice balls. Set up a small obstacle course in your yard. (Your kids can help you with this part.)

5. **Where and when possible, hit a bucket of balls during lunch**. If it's a hot day in July, you may want to hit the showers before you head back to the office.

Sample practice schedule:

✔ **Monday**: Health club workout (1 hour); putt on rug (15 minutes)

✔ **Tuesday**: Swing a club at home in front of a mirror or window ($\frac{1}{2}$ hour)

✔ **Wednesday**: Health club workout (1 hour); read a magazine or book or watch a golf video ($\frac{1}{2}$ hour)

✔ **Thursday**: Swing a club or chip (1 hour)

✔ **Friday**: Health club workout (1 hour); practice range, including golf drills (1 hour)

✔ **Saturday**: Practice range (1 hour); play 18 holes

✔ **Sunday**: Watch golf on TV; practice range ($\frac{1}{2}$ hour); play 9 holes

Tips for seniors

Now that I'm on the Senior Tour, I get a chance to tee it up with some of the same guys who used to beat the pants off me on the PGA Tour. I still love to play, but I realize that as I age, my game will change. I can deal with it. We all have to. If you have become a senior golfer since the last edition of this book came out, or if you're taking up the game for the first time, you need to know some things to keep your game "young."

As you may be finding out already (or will find out soon enough), you just don't hit the ball as far as you used to. There are four basic reasons for this:

✔ Poor posture: Poor posture — often from wearing bifocals — stops you from turning properly. Be careful how you hold your head, and keep it off your chest. Get in the habit of good posture by standing in front of a full-length mirror and holding a club out in front of you. Continue looking in the mirror as you lower the club into the hitting position. Don't let your head tilt or move forward. Once you master this technique, you'll be able to make that turn and swing your arms.

✔ Lack of rotation on your backswing: You probably aren't turning your hips and shoulders enough on the backswing. You only need to increase your range of motion by increasing your flexibility. See Chapter 4 for stretching exercises that can help your range. Then review the elements of the swing in Chapters 5 and 6 and get out to the range and work out those kinks.

＊ Decrease in strength: As you grow older, you lose strength in your hands and forearms, which makes it harder to hold your wrists in the proper position on the downswing. This weakness causes the clubhead to be thrown from the top and reduces the speed at which the club strikes the ball. Simple drills to combat loss of strength include squeezing a tennis ball, doing forearm curls with light barbells, and Harvey Penick's drill: Swing a club back and forth like a scythe 20 or 30 times a day. I don't recommend doing this one in close quarters near the Ming vase.

✔ Lack of rotation in the follow-through: You may be so intent on hitting the ball that you're not swinging through the ball to the other side. This causes the club to stop 3 or 4 feet beyond the ball and the arms to stop somewhere around your chest, with your belt buckle pointing way to the right of your target. As you can imagine, this type of swing will not result in a pretty shot. The ball will push to the right and be, well, weak. To correct the problem, repeat this drill each day until it feels natural: While looking in a full-length mirror, go to the top of your backswing (see Chapter 6) and then mirror-image that position on the follow-through. Your belt buckle should always face to the left of your target. To make this happen, you must transfer 90 percent of your weight from your right foot to your left foot.

I can't stress this enough: If you're not on some kind of exercise program, get on one. (See Chapter 4.) Consult your local golf pro for suggestions, too. A good program coupled with a stretching routine will not only improve your flexibility and strength — and your golf game — but it will benefit your life as well.

Chapter 15
Rules, Etiquette, and Scoring

- -

In This Chapter

▶ Playing by the rules

▶ Respecting other players

▶ Keeping score

▶ Handling penalty shots

- -

Golf is not a game lacking in structure. In fact, it is rife with rules of play, rules of etiquette, and rules of scoring. You may never master all the intricacies of these rules, but you should familiarize yourself with some of the more important ones.

The Rules of Golf in 1744

The Honourable Company of Edinburgh Golfers devised the original 13 rules of golf in 1744. Over a "wee dram" (whisky) or 12, no doubt. Anyway, the rules are worth recounting in this chapter, to show you how little the playing of the game has changed.

1. You must tee your ball, within a club's length of the hole.

2. Your tee must be upon the ground.

3. You are not to change the ball which you strike off the tee.

4. You are not to remove any stones, bones, or any break club, for the sake of playing your ball. Except upon the fair green, and that's only within a club's length of your ball.

5. If your ball comes among watter, or any watery filth, you are at liberty to take out your ball and bringing it behind the hazard and teeing it, you may play it with any club and allow your adversary a stroke, for so getting out your ball.

6. If your balls be found anywhere touching one another you are to lift the first ball, till you play the last.

7. At holling, you are to play honestly for the hole, and not to play upon your adversary's ball, not lying in your way to the hole.

8. If you should lose your ball, by its being taken up, or any other way you are to go back to the spot, where you struck last, and drop another ball, and allow your adversary a stroke for the misfortune.

9. No man at holling his ball, is to be allowed, to mark his way to the hole with his club or any thing else.

10. If a ball be stopp'd by any person, horse, dog, or any thing else, the ball so stopp'd must be played where it lyes.

11. If you draw your club, in order to strike and proceed so far in the stroke, as to be bringing down your club; if then, your club shall break, in any way, it is to be counted a stroke.

12. He whose ball lyes farthest from the hole is obliged to play first.

13. Neither trench, ditch or dyke, made for the preservation of the links, nor the scholar's holes or the soldier's lines, shall be counted a hazard. But the ball is to be taken out, teed and play'd with any iron club.

As you can tell from the language and terms used in 1744, these rules were designed for match play. My particular favorite is Rule 6. It wasn't that long before the rule was redefined from "touching" to "within 6 inches" — which in turn led to the *stymie rule*. The stymie has long since passed into legend, but it was a lot of fun. Basically, *stymie* meant that whenever your opponent's ball lay between your ball and the hole, you couldn't ask him to mark his ball. You had to find some way around it. Usually, that meant chipping over his ball, which is great fun, especially if you were very close to the hole.

Another rule I particularly like is the one stating that you could leave your opponent's ball where it lay if it was near the edge of the hole. As of the late 1960s, you could use such a situation to your advantage, with the other ball acting as a backstop of sorts. Nothing could hack off your opponent more than your ball going into the hole off his! Happy days!

The Rules Today

The rules since those far-off early days have been refined countless times. Take a look at a rule book today (you can pick one up from almost any professional's shop, or order one directly from the United States Golf Association), and you'll find a seemingly endless list of clauses and subclauses — all of which make the game sound very difficult and compli-cated (see Figure 15-1). In my opinion, the rules are too complex. You can get by with about a dozen rules. In fact, common sense can help, too. I've always thought that you won't go too far wrong, if you

Sometimes the rules of golf can be a little complicated!

Figure 15-1:
Say what?

✔ Play the course as you find it.

✔ Play the ball as it lies.

✔ If you can't do either of those things, do what's fair.

To demonstrate just how crazy the rules of golf can get and how easy it is to perpetrate an infraction, look at the cases of Craig Stadler and Paul Azinger.

You may remember the Stadler case from a few years ago. Craig was playing the 14th hole at Torrey Pines in San Diego during a tour event. Because his ball was under a tree, he used a towel to kneel down as he hit the ball out because he didn't want to get his pants dirty.

That sounds harmless enough, doesn't it? Think again. Some smart guy out there in TV land was watching all this (the next day, no less) and thought he was part of a new game show: *You Make the Ruling.* He called the PGA Tour and said that Stadler was guilty of "building a stance." By kneeling on top of something, even a towel, Stadler was technically changing his shot, breaking Rule 13-3 (a player is entitled to place his feet firmly in taking his stance, but he shall not build his stance).

The officials had no option but to agree, so Craig was disqualified for signing the wrong scorecard 24 hours earlier. Technically, an event isn't over until the competitors have completed 72 holes. At the time Craig's rules infraction came to light, he had played only 54 holes. Madness! Stadler clearly had no intent to gain advantage. But it was adios, Craig.

TIP

Ten rules you need to know

By Mike Shea, PGA Tour Rules Official

1. **Rule 1:** You must play the same ball from the teeing ground into the hole. Change only when the rules allow.

2. **Rule 3-2:** You must hole out on each hole. If you don't, you don't have a score and are thus disqualified.

3. **Rule 6-5:** You are responsible for playing your own ball. Put an identification mark on it.

4. **Rule 13:** You must play the ball as it lies.

5. **Rule 13-4:** When your ball is in a hazard, whether a bunker or a water hazard, you cannot touch the ground or water in the hazard with your club before impact.

6. **Rule 16:** You cannot improve the line of a putt before your stroke by repairing marks made by the spikes on player's shoes.

7. **Rule 24:** Obstructions are anything artificial. Some are moveable so you can move them; some are not so then you have to drop within one club length of your nearest point of relief — no penalty.

8. **Rule 26:** If your ball is lost in a water hazard, you can drop another behind the hazard keeping the point where the ball last crossed the hazard between you and the hole — with a one-stroke penalty.

9. **Rule 27:** If you lose your ball anywhere else but in a hazard, return to where you hit your previous shot and hit another — with a one-stroke penalty.

10. **Rule 28:** If your ball is unplayable you have three options:

    ✔ Play from where you hit your last shot.

    ✔ Drop within two club lengths of where your ball is now, no closer to the hole.

    ✔ Keep the point where the ball is between you and the hole and drop a ball on that line. You can go back as far as you want.

    In all cases, you are assessed a one-stroke penalty.

Source: *The Rules of Golf* as approved by the United States Golf Association (USGA) and the Royal & Ancient Golf Club of St. Andrews, Scotland

The same sort of thing happened with Paul Azinger. At the Doral tournament in Florida in 1996, Azinger played a shot from inside the edge of the lake on the final hole. Just before he started his swing, he flicked a rock out of the way while taking his stance. Cue the rules police. Another phone call got Azinger thrown out for "moving loose impediments in a hazard." Common sense and the rules parted company again.

In both cases, the rules of golf were violated. The players were not cheating, however; they just didn't know the rules. And what got them thrown out of those tournaments was not the original rule infractions, but signing incorrect scorecards.

Anyway, the point is that although the rules of golf are designed to help you, they can be a minefield. Watch where you step!

Marking a scorecard

Scorecards can be a little daunting when you first look at them (see Figure 15-2). All those numbers and little boxes. But fear not, first impressions can be misleading. There isn't much to learn; keeping score is a simple process.

Say your handicap is 9 and mine is 14. That means you're going to give me 5 strokes over the course of the round. I get those strokes at the holes rated the most difficult. That's logical. And equally logical is the fact that these holes are handicapped 1 through 5. So mark those stroke holes before you begin. (I discuss scoring and handicaps later in this chapter.)

After the match has begun, keep track of the score with simple pluses or minuses in a spare row of boxes.

In stroke or medal play, you are expected to keep and score your playing companion's card. His name will be at the top, his handicap in the box at the bottom of the card. All you have to do is record his score for each hole in the box provided. You don't even have to add it up.

Finding a lost ball

At this stage of your life, you're going to hit more than your fair share of errant shots. Some of those are going to finish in spots where finding the ball is a little tricky. And on occasion, you won't find the ball at all.

	Men's Course Rating/Slope Blue 73.1/137 White 71.0/130			JOHN - 8	PAUL - 14 + 6		HOLE							Women's Course Rating/Slope Red 73.7/128		
Blue Tees	White Tees	Par	Hcp											Hcp	Par	Red Tees
377	361	4	11	4	4	E	1							13	4	310
514	467	5	13	4	5	J+1	2							3	5	428
446	423	4	(1)	4	4	E	3							1	4	389
376	356	4	(5)	5	5	P+1	4							11	4	325
362	344	4	7	4	6	E	5							7	4	316
376	360	4	9	5	5	E	6							9	4	335
166	130	3	17	2	4	J+1	7							17	3	108
429	407	4	(3)	5	5	E	8							5	4	368
161	145	3	15	4	3	P+1	9							15	3	122
3207	2993	35		37	41		Out								35	2701
		Initial												Initial		
366	348	4	18	4	5	E	10							14	4	320
570	537	5	10	5	6	J+1	11							2	5	504
438	420	4	(2)	4	4	E	12							6	4	389
197	182	3	12	3	4	J+1	13							16	3	145
507	475	5	14	5	6	J+2	14							4	5	425
398	380	4	(4)	5	5	J+1	15							8	4	350
380	366	4	(6)	4	4	E	16							10	4	339
165	151	3	16	4	3	P+1	17							18	3	133
397	375	4	8	4	3	P+2	18							12	4	341
3418	3234	36		38	40		In								36	2946
6625	6227	71		75	81		Tot								71	5647
Handicap														Handicap		
Net Score														Net Score		
Adjust														Adjust		

Scorer   Attested   Date

Figure 15-2: Marking your card.

If you can't find the ball in the five minutes you're allowed, you have to return to the tee or to the point from which you last hit the ball and play another ball. With penalty, stroke, and distance, you will be hitting three off the tee. One way to avoid having to walk all the way back to the tee after failing to find your ball is to hit a provisional ball as soon as you think that the first one may be lost. Then, if you can't find the first ball, play the second ball. Be sure, however, to announce to your playing partners that you are playing a provisional ball. If you don't, you must play the second ball even if you find the first ball.

Given that, you can keep lost balls to a minimum. First, when your wild shot is in midair, watch it. If you don't, you won't have any idea where it went. Now you're probably thinking that sounds pretty obvious, but not watching the shot is perhaps the number-one reason (after bad technique) why balls are lost. Temper gets the better of too many players. They're too busy slamming the club into the ground to watch where the ball goes. Don't make that mistake.

Pay attention when the ball lands, too. Give yourself a reference — like a tree — near the landing area. You should also put an identifying mark on your ball before you begin, to be sure that the ball you find is the ball you hit (see Figure 15-3).

Looking for a ball is a much neglected art form. I see people wandering aimlessly, going over the same spot time after time. Be systematic. Walk back and forth without retracing your steps. Your chances of finding the ball are much greater.

Give your ball an identifying mark.

Figure 15-3:
So you
know it's
yours . . .

You have five minutes to look for a lost ball from the moment you start to search. Time yourself. Even if you find the ball after five minutes have elapsed, you still have to go back to the spot you played from to hit another ball. Them's the rules.

Dropping the ball

There are going to be times when you have to pick up your ball and drop it. Every golf course has places away from which you are allowed to drop. A cart path is one. Casual water (such as a puddle) is another. If you find yourself in this position, follow this routine:

1. **Lift and clean your ball.**

2. **Find the nearest spot where you have complete relief from the problem and mark that spot with a tee.**

   You not only have to get the ball out of the obstruction, but your feet as well. So find the spot where your feet are clear of the obstruction and then determine where the clubhead would be if you hit from there. This is the spot you want to mark. The spot you choose cannot be closer to the hole.

3. **Measure one club length from that mark.**

4. **Now drop the ball.**

   Stand erect, face the green, hold the ball at shoulder height and at arm's length, as shown in Figure 15-4. Let the ball drop vertically. You aren't allowed to "spin" the ball into a more favorable spot. Where you drop depends on what rule applies — just be sure that the ball doesn't end up nearer the hole than it was when you picked it up. If it does, you have to pick the ball up and drop it again.

How you drop the ball makes no difference; however, you always have to stand upright when dropping. I once had to drop my ball in a bunker where the sand was wet. The ball was obviously going to plug when it landed (that is, get buried in the sand), so I asked whether I could lie down to drop it. The answer was negative. Oh, well. . . .

First, find the spot where your feet are clear of the obstruction.

You get one more club length from there.

Now drop your ball.

Figure 15-4:
Dropping your ball.

Teeing up

You must tee up between the markers, not in front of them, and no more than two club lengths behind them (see Figure 15-5). If you tee off outside this area, you get a two-shot penalty in stroke play, and in match play, you must replay your shot from the teeing area.

Figure 15-5:
The tee is
bigger than
you think.

You don't have to tee up your ball right between the markers; you can go back as much as two club lengths.

You don't have to stand within the teeing area; your feet can be outside of it. This is useful to know when the only piece of level ground is outside the teeing area or if the hole is a sharp dogleg. You can give yourself a better angle by teeing up wide (standing outside the teeing area).

Taking advice

Advice has two sides. First, you cannot either give advice to or receive advice from anyone other than your caddie. That means you can't ask your playing companion what club she hit. Neither can you tell her anything that may help in the playing of her next stroke.

This rule is a tough one, and even the best have been caught breaking it. In the 1971 Ryder Cup matches in St. Louis, Arnold Palmer was playing Bernard Gallacher of Scotland. Palmer hit a lovely shot onto a par-3, whereupon Gallacher's caddie said, "Great shot, Arnie, what club did you hit?" Arnold, being Arnold, told him. Gallacher was unaware of the exchange, but the referee heard it. Palmer, despite his own protestations, was awarded the hole. That was in match play; in stroke play, it's a two-shot penalty. So take care!

Second, you're going to find yourself playing with people, lots of people, who think of themselves as experts on every aspect of the golf swing. These know-it-alls usually mean well, but they are dangerous to your golfing health. Ignore them. Or, if that proves too difficult, listen, smile politely, and then go about your business as if they had never uttered a word.

Etiquette: What You Need to Know

Golf, unlike almost any of the trash-talking sports you can watch on TV nowadays, is a game where sportsmanship is paramount. Golf is an easy game to cheat at, so every player is on his honor. But there's more to it than that. Golf has its own code of etiquette, semi-official "rules" of courtesy that every player is expected to follow. Here are the main things you need to know:

✔ **Don't talk while someone is playing a stroke.** Give your partners time and silence while they are analyzing the situation, making their practice swings, and actually making their swing for real. Don't stand near them or move about, either, especially when you're on the greens. Stay out of their peripheral vision while they are putting. Don't stand near the hole or walk between your partner's ball and the hole. Even be mindful of your shadow. The line of a putt — the path it must follow to the hole — is holy ground.

The key is being aware of your companions' — and their golf balls' — whereabouts and temperament. Easygoing types may not mind that you gab away while they choose a club, but that isn't true for everyone. If in doubt, stand still and shut up. If you're a problem more than once, you'll be told about it.

✔ **Be ready to play when it's your turn — for example, when your ball lies farthest from the hole.** Make your decisions while you're walking to your ball or while waiting for someone else to play. Be ready to play. And when it is your turn to hit, do so without any undue delay. You don't have to rush; just get on with it.

✔ **The *honor* (that is, the first shot) on a given tee goes to the player with the lowest score on the previous hole.** If that hole was tied, the player with the lowest score on the hole before that is said to be up and retains the honor. In other words, you have the honor until you lose it.

✔ **Make sure everyone in your foursome is behind you when you hit.** You're not going to hit every shot where you're aimed. If in doubt, wait for your playing partners to get out of your line of play. The same is true for the group in front; wait until they are well out of range before you hit. Even if it would take a career shot for you to reach them, wait. Lawyers love golfers who ignore that rule of thumb.

✔ **Pay attention to the group behind you, too.** Are they having to wait for you on every shot? Is there a gap between you and the group ahead of you? If the answer to either or both is yes, step aside and invite the group behind you to play through. This is no reflection on your ability as golfers. All it means is that the group behind plays faster than you do.

The best and most time-efficient place to let a group behind play through is at a par-3 (it's the shortest hole and therefore the quickest way of playing through). After hitting your ball onto the green, mark it, and wave to them to play. Stand off to the side of the green as they do so. After they have all hit, replace your ball and putt out. Then let them go. Simple, isn't it?

Sadly, you're likely to see this piece of basic good manners abused time and again by players who don't know any better and have no place on a golf course. Ignore them. Do what's right. Stepping aside makes your round more enjoyable. Think about it. Who likes to ruin someone else's day? Give your ego a rest and let them through.

✔ **Help the greenskeeper out.** A busy golf course takes a bit of a pounding over a day's play. All those balls landing on greens. Feet walking through bunkers. And divots of earth flying through the air. Do your bit for the golf course. Repair any ball marks you see on the greens. (You can use your tee or a special tool called a divot fixer, which is about 50 cents in the pro's shop.)

Here's how to repair ball marks. Stick the repair tool in the green around the perimeter of the indentation. Start at the rear. Gently lift the compacted dirt. Replace any loose pieces of grass or turf in the center of the hole. Then take your putter and tap down the raised turf until it is level again (see Figure 15-6). You can repair ball marks either before or after you putt. It's a good habit to have.

When a ball lands on a soft green, it often leaves a *pitch mark.*

Lift the back edge of the hole... and then flatten it out.

Figure 15-6:
Take care
of the green.

Finally, smooth out or rake any footprints in bunkers, as shown in Figure 15-7 (but only after you play out). And replace any divots you find on the fairways and tees.

Figure 15-7:
Use your
rake.

GARY SAYS

Ten things to say when you hit a bad shot

1. I wasn't loose.

2. I looked up.

3. I just had a lesson, and the pro screwed me up.

4. I borrowed these clubs.

5. These new shoes are hurting my feet.

6. This new glove doesn't fit.

7. I had a bad lie.

8. The club slipped.

9. I can't play well when the dew point is this high.

10. The sun was in my eyes.

> ✔ **If you must play in a golf cart (take my advice and walk whenever you can), park it well away from greens, tees, and bunkers.** To speed up play, you should park on the side of the green nearest the next tee. The same is true if you are carrying your bag. Don't set it down near any of the aforementioned, but do leave it in a spot on the way to the next tee.
>
> ✔ **Leave the green as soon as everyone has finished putting.** You'll see this a lot, and after a while it'll drive you crazy. You're ready to play your approach shot to the green, and the people in front are crowding round the hole marking their cards. That's poor etiquette on two counts. One, it delays play, which is never good. And two, the last thing the greenskeeper wants is a lot of footprints around the cup. Mark your card on the way to the next tee.

The Handicap System

If you, as a beginner, are completing 18-hole rounds in less than 80 shots, you are either a cheat or the next Jack Nicklaus or Nancy Lopez. In all probability, you are neither, which makes it equally likely that your scores are considerably higher than par. Enter the handicap system.

The United States Golf Association constructed the handicap system to level the playing field for everyone. The association has an esoteric system of "course rating" and something called "slope" to help them compute exactly how many strokes everyone should get. In all my years in golf, I have yet to meet anyone who either understands or can explain how the course rating and slope are computed, so I'm not going to try. Be like everyone else — accept both and go with the flow.

The handicap system is one reason I think that golf is the best of all games. Handicapping allows any two players, whatever their standards of play, to go out and have an enjoyable — and competitive — game together. Try to compete on, say, a tennis court. I can't go out with Pete Sampras and have any fun at all. Neither can he. The disparity in our ability levels makes playing competitively impossible. Not so with golf.

Getting your handicap

If you have never played golf before, you won't have a handicap yet. Don't worry; you've got plenty of time for that. When you can consistently hit the ball at least 150 yards with a driver, you are ready to play a full 18-hole round of golf.

When you reach the stage where you can hit the ball a decent distance on the range, you're ready to do the same on a real golf course. You want to test yourself and give your progress a number. Make that two numbers: your score and your handicap.

The first thing you need to do is keep score. Get a golfer friend to accompany you in a round of 18 holes. (That's the accepted length of a golf course.) This person must keep score and sign your card at the end of the round. To be valid, a card needs two signatures — your own and the person's with whom you're playing. That way, all scores are clearly valid, and corruption is kept to a minimum.

You need to play at least ten rounds before you are eligible for a handicap. Don't ask why; those are the rules. Before you complete ten rounds, you are in a kind of black hole from which you emerge as a full-fledged handicap golfer.

At first, your handicap will probably drop quite quickly. Most new golfers improve by leaps and bounds at first. After that, improvement may continue, but at a much slower pace.

Of course, the handicap system is easy to abuse, and some people do. Interestingly, most abuse occurs when players want their handicaps to be higher. They either fabricate high scores, or they don't record their better rounds, so that their handicaps will rise. A few golfers go the other way; they want a lower handicap than they can realistically play to so that their scores look better. Find these people with vanity handicaps and wager with them for everything they own!

Don't get too cynical, though. Any abuse of the system is thankfully confined to a tiny minority of players, which is another reason why golf is such a great game. Golfers can generally be trusted. The few cheats are soon identified and ostracized.

Calculating your handicap

Okay, you're wondering how you get a handicap, right? All you have to do is hand in your scores at the course where you normally play. Then you're off and running. Your handicap at any one time is the average of the best 10 of your previous 20 scores (see Figure 15-8). Your handicap fairly accurately reflects your current form because you must record your score every time you go out. A lot of clubs and public facilities make things easy for you. They have computers into which you feed your scores. The program does all the work and updates your handicap. Golf goes high-tech.

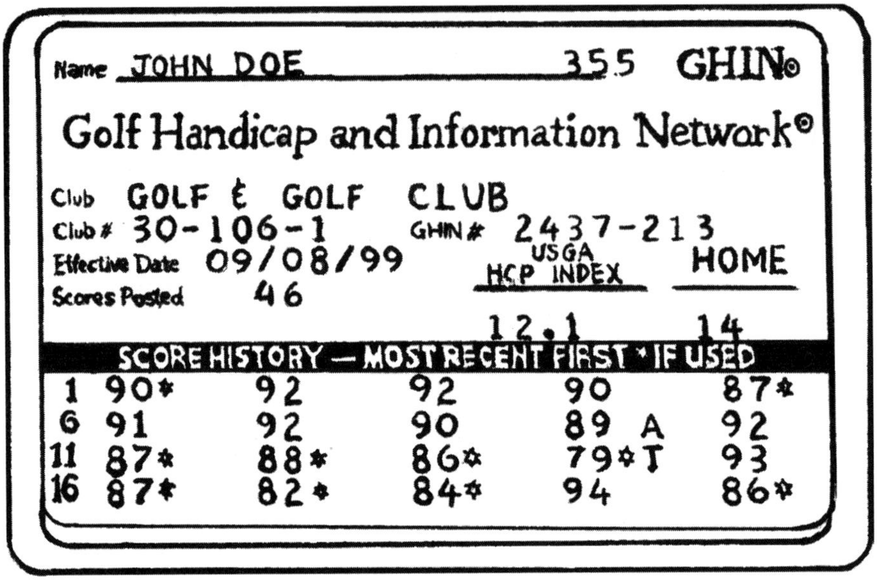

Name JOHN DOE   355 GHIN®

Golf Handicap and Information Network®

Club GOLF & GOLF CLUB
Club # 30-106-1   GHIN # 2437-213
Effective Date 09/08/99   USGA   HOME
Scores Posted   46   HCP INDEX

                                    12.1   14

SCORE HISTORY — MOST RECENT FIRST * IF USED

1	90*	92	92	90	87*
6	91	92	90	89 A	92
11	87*	88*	86*	79*T	93
16	87*	82*	84*	94	86*

Figure 15-8:
Your
handicap
card.

You don't have to be a member of a club to get a handicap. Many public facilities have their own handicap computers. For a nominal fee, you can usually get yourself an identification number and access to the software.

Suppose that your ten scores average out at exactly 100. In other words, for your first ten rounds of golf, you hit 1,000 shots. If par for the 18-hole course you played on is 72, your average score is 28 over par. That figure, 28, is your handicap.

Every time you play from then on, your handicap adjusts to account for your most recent score. Suppose that your 11th round is a 96. That's only 24 over the par of 72. So your net score — your actual score minus your handicap — is 68, 4 under that magic number of 72. That's good.

Remember: The lower your score is, the better you have played. When you feed that score into the handicap computer, you'll probably find that your handicap drops to about 23.

What your handicap means

In golf, the lower your handicap is, the better you are. Thus, if your handicap is 6 and mine is 10, you are a better player than I. On average, four strokes better, to be exact.

Assume that par for the 18-hole course we are going to play is 72. You, as someone with a handicap of 6, would be expected to play the 18 holes in a total of 78 strokes, six higher than par. I, on the other hand, being a 10 handicapper, would on a normal day hit the ball 82 times, 10 higher than par. Thus, your handicap is the number of strokes over par you should take to play an 18-hole course.

When you're just starting out, you don't want to team up with three low-handicap players. Play with someone of your own ability at first. Once you get the hang of it, start playing with people who are better than you so that you can learn the game.

How to Keep Score

Scoring is another great thing about golf. You can easily see how you're doing because your score is in black and white on the scorecard. Every course you play has a scorecard. The scorecard tells you each hole's length, its par, and its rating relative to the other holes (see Figure 15-9).

The relationship of the holes is important when you're playing a head-to-head match. Say I have to give you 11 shots over 18 holes. In other words, on 11 holes during our round, you get to subtract one shot from your score. The obvious question is, "Which holes?" The card answers that question. You get your shots on the holes rated 1 through 11. These holes, in the opinion of the club committee, are the hardest 11 holes on the course. The number 1–rated hole is the toughest, and the number 18-rated hole is the easiest.

Although you have to report your score every time you set foot on the golf course (stroke play), most of your golf will typically be matches against others (match play), which is why each hole's rating is important.

Match play and stroke play have slightly different rules. For example, in stroke play, you must count every shot you hit and then record the number on the card. In match play, you don't have to write down any score. The only thing that matters is the state of the game between you and your opponent.

The score is recorded as holes up or holes down. For example, say my score on the first hole was four, and your score was five and you received no strokes on that hole. I am now one up. Because each hole is a separate entity, you don't need to write down your actual score; you simply count the number of holes you've won or lost. In fact, if you're having a particularly bad time on a given hole, you can even pick up your ball and concede the hole. All you lose is that hole. Everything starts fresh on the next tee. Such a head-to-head match is over when one player is more holes up than the number of holes remaining. Thus, matches can be won by scores of "four and three." All that means is that one player was four holes ahead with only three left, the match finishing on the 15th green.

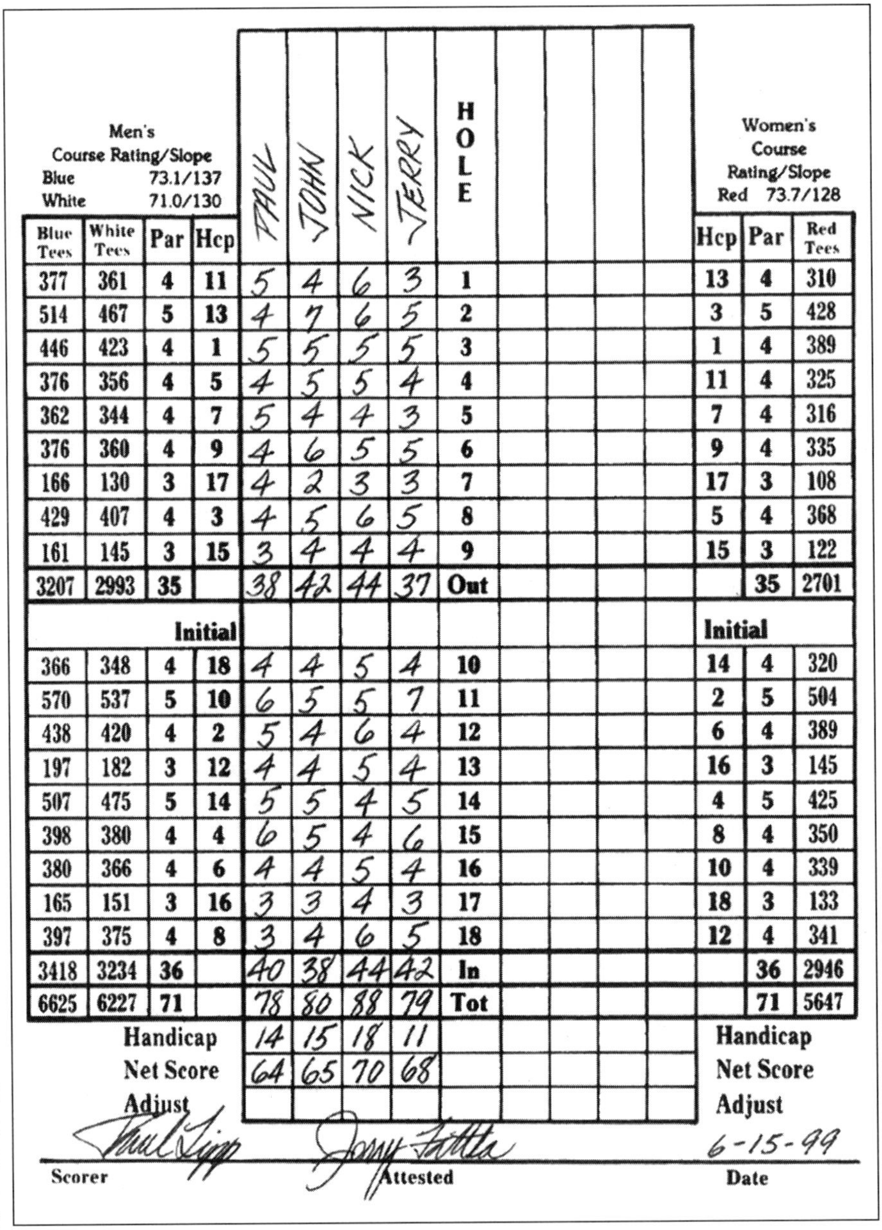

Blue Tees	White Tees	Par	Hcp	PAUL	JOHN	NICK	JERRY	HOLE					Hcp	Par	Red Tees
377	361	4	11	5	4	6	3	1					13	4	310
514	467	5	13	4	7	6	5	2					3	5	428
446	423	4	1	5	5	5	5	3					1	4	389
376	356	4	5	4	5	5	4	4					11	4	325
362	344	4	7	5	4	4	3	5					7	4	316
376	360	4	9	4	6	5	5	6					9	4	335
166	130	3	17	4	2	3	3	7					17	3	108
429	407	4	3	4	5	6	5	8					5	4	368
161	145	3	15	3	4	4	4	9					15	3	122
3207	2993	35		38	42	44	37	Out						35	2701
		Initial											**Initial**		
366	348	4	18	4	4	5	4	10					14	4	320
570	537	5	10	6	5	5	7	11					2	5	504
438	420	4	2	5	4	6	4	12					6	4	389
197	182	3	12	4	4	5	4	13					16	3	145
507	475	5	14	5	5	4	5	14					4	5	425
398	380	4	4	6	5	4	6	15					8	4	350
380	366	4	6	4	4	5	4	16					10	4	339
165	151	3	16	3	3	4	3	17					18	3	133
397	375	4	8	3	4	6	5	18					12	4	341
3418	3234	36		40	38	44	42	In						36	2946
6625	6227	71		78	80	88	79	Tot						71	5647

Men's Course Rating/Slope
Blue 73.1/137
White 71.0/130

Women's Course Rating/Slope
Red 73.7/128

Handicap	14	15	18	11		Handicap
Net Score	64	65	70	68		Net Score
Adjust						Adjust

Scorer / Attested   Date 6-15-99

Figure 15-9: Keeping Score.

Stroke play is different. It's strictly card-and-pencil stuff. And this time, you are playing against everyone else in the field, not just your playing companion. All you do is count one stroke each time you swing at the ball. If it takes you five strokes to play the first hole, you write 5 on your card for that hole. You don't record your own score, though. The card in your pocket has your playing companion's name on it. You keep his score, and he keeps yours. At the end of the round, he signs his name to your card and gives it to you; you do the same with his card. After you have checked your score for each hole, you also sign your card. Then, if you're in an official tournament, you hand your card to the scorers. If you're playing a casual round, you record your score on the computer.

Take care when checking your card. One rule quirk is that you are responsible for the accuracy of the score recorded under your name for each hole — your companion isn't. Any mistakes are deemed to have been made by you, not him. And you can't change a mistake later, even if you have witnesses. Take the case of Roberto DeVicenzo at the 1968 Masters. Millions of spectators and TV viewers saw him make a birdie three on the 17th hole in the final round. But the man marking his card, Tommy Aaron, mistakenly marked a 4. Checking his score after the round, DeVicenzo didn't notice the error and signed his card. The mistake cost DeVicenzo the chance of victory in a playoff with Bob Goalby. DeVicenzo had to accept a score one higher than he actually shot and lost by that one stroke. Tragic.

DeVicenzo's mistake illustrates what can happen when the score on your card is higher than the one you actually made on the hole. You're simply stuck with that score. If the opposite is the case and the score on the card is lower than it should be, you're disqualified.

One last thing: Don't worry about the addition on your card. You are not responsible for that part. As long as the numbers opposite each hole are correct, you're in the clear.

Penalty Shots

Penalty shots are an unfortunate part of every golfer's life. Sooner or later, you're going to incur a penalty shot or shots. I can't cover all the possible penalty situations in this book, but I'll run you through the most common.

Out-of-bounds

Out-of-bounds is the term used when you hit your ball to a spot outside the confines of the golf course — over a boundary fence, for example. Out-of-bounds areas are marked with white stakes that are about 30 yards apart. If you are outside that line, you're out-of-bounds.

Okay, so it's happened; you've gone out-of-bounds. What are your options? Limited, I'm afraid. First, you are penalized stroke and distance. That means you must drop (or tee up if the shot you hit out-of-bounds was from a tee) another ball as near as possible to the spot you just played from. Say that shot was your first on that hole. Your next shot will, in reality, count as your third on that hole. Count them:

- ✔ The shot you hit
- ✔ The stroke penalty
- ✔ The distance

So you're "playing three" from the same spot.

Airball or missing the point

Airballs happen early in the life of a beginner. You make a mighty swing and miss the ball. The penalty? None, actually. But you must count that swing as a stroke.

If you swing at a ball with intent to hit it, that's a shot regardless of whether you make contact. Airballs can be highly embarrassing, but part of the journey of golf.

Unplayable lie

Inevitably, you're going to hit a ball into a spot from which further progress is impossible. In a bush. Against a wall. Even buried in a bunker.

When the unplayable lie happens (and you are the sole judge of whether you can hit the ball), your situation dictates your options. In general, though, you have three escape routes.

- ✔ You can either pick up the ball and drop it — no nearer the hole — within two club lengths — take your driver and lay it end to end on the ground two times — of the original spot under penalty of one shot.

- ✔ You can pick up the ball, walk back as far as you want, keeping that original point between you and the hole, and then drop the ball. Again, one-stroke penalty.

- ✔ You can return to the point from where you hit the original shot. This option is the last resort because you lose distance, as well as adding the penalty shot. Believe me, there's nothing worse than a long walk burdened with a penalty stroke!

Water hazard

Water hazards are intimidating when you have to hit across one. You hear the dreaded splash before too long. "Watery graves," the old English TV commentator Henry Longhurst used to call these things.

Anyway, whenever you see yellow stakes, you know the pond/creek/lake in question is a water hazard. Should you hit into a water hazard, you may play the ball as it lies (no penalty), or if the ball is unplayable, choose from these three options:

- ✔ Drop another ball within two club lengths of the point where your previous shot crossed the boundary of the hazard.

- ✔ Hit another ball from the spot you just hit from.

- ✔ Take the point that it crossed the water hazard and go back as far as you want, keeping that point between you and the hole.

You have a one-shot penalty in either case.

Lateral water hazard

If you're playing by the seaside, the beach is often termed a lateral water hazard. Red stakes mean lateral. Your options are either to play the ball as it lies (no penalty, but risky), or as follows with a one-stroke penalty:

- ✔ Drop a ball at the point where the ball last crossed the boundary of the hazard two club lengths no nearer the hole.

- ✔ Drop your ball as near as possible to the spot on the opposite margin of the water hazard the same distance from the hole.

- ✔ Hit another ball from the spot you just hit from.

- ✔ Take the point that the ball crossed the water hazard and drop another ball as far back as you want, keeping that point between you and the hole.

When golf is all business

Sure, golf is a game, but sometimes it's also serious business. According to *USA Today*, corporate golf outings have become so popular they're an industry in themselves. One major sports management group alone generated $3.5 million in revenue last year just in fees for organizing corporate outings. That's a lot of head honchos touring the links and a lot of deals getting done. And for every official company event, countless informal foursomes are getting together to schmooze outside the office.

If you play golf, sooner or later a business round is bound to happen to you. Maybe the chance to do a little networking is why you took up golf in the first place. So you need to know some basic rules when you mix business banter with the back nine; it's not all fun and games. Protocol is in this puzzle.

✔ Don't outdo the boss. Remember, golf is business — an extension of the workplace. You wouldn't show up the boss in the boardroom. Don't do it on the fairway either.

✔ Watch the raunchy humor. Sure, you want everyone to have a good time. But unless you know your partners' attitudes and outlooks well, you risk not only offending them but losing their business, too.

✔ Don't try to squeeze profit out of every minute. At the very least, keep up the pretense that you're all golfing for good play and good company — even if they couldn't sink a putt to save their mother's mortgage.

✔ Let your group get settled into its game before dragging it around to business topics. Never talk about business before the 5th hole or before the back nine.

✔ Be prepared to drop the topic or risk losing the business. No matter how seriously businesspeople take their line of work, they may be even more fanatical about their game of golf — especially on that one difficult shot. Let your feel of the individual dictate when to stay off a business conversation.

✔ Watch the wagers. You may choose to accept bets, in the interest of being a good sport, but suggesting them is not wise. If you lose the bet, be sure to do it gracefully — and to pay up pronto. If you win, don't gloat. And don't make an issue of it.

✔ Never, ever cheat or fudge your score in any way, however tempting. What kind of impression does that leave of your business practices?

Hitting the links on a sunny day sure beats working in an office, and it's a great way to get to know the folks in your industry — and sometimes that means some pretty top folks, not just the ones you run into at the water cooler. Believe me, I've been to enough corporate outings to know what a major business schmoozefest is going on around the greens. (Just to give you an idea, my smiling face was at 41 business outings this year. Whew.) The bottom line is, get out on the links and mingle with the boss — it can do your career good. Just remember what you're there for. You're not at qualifying school for the PGA Tour.

The cure of the ball

by Dr. Deborah Graham, sports psychologist

If the professional golfer's reasons for taking up the game of golf reflect those of the general population, then a majority of golfers get their start by tagging along with a mother, father, uncle, neighbor, or friend who was willing to share the experience of this ancient game. The senior tour players are more likely to describe developing a love for golf while caddying for the interesting and colorful characters who frequented their local links.

However you take up the game, your reasons for playing golf evolve with relation to the time, money, and facilities available to you, as well as with your learned and inherent personality.

Those of us who play golf but a few times a year usually do so to have fun, relax with friends, enjoy the outdoors, fulfill social or professional obligations, or just do something different.

Once we are playing a dozen or so times a year, we have usually evolved into playing for other reasons as well, including escaping the "honey-dos" or the demands of the work-a-day world, developing a swing that looks good, or taking on the challenge of hitting the ball as far as we can. At this level of involvement we begin to experience some of the subtle addictive qualities of the game which can then trigger a new set of personal reasons for playing.

Risk-takers and adrenaline junkies begin to discover the gambling aspects of the sport. Perfectionists find themselves drawn to the challenge of a game that defies all efforts to master it. Image-conscious and socially aware individuals begin appreciating the prestige of the proper equipment, name clothing, and the country club environment. The competitive among us discover the continuously exhilarating and nagging challenge of lowering our scoring average. And those in search of purpose often feel they find it in golf.

Golfers who fulfill more than one of these interpersonal needs soon discover their reasons for playing quickly escalate into even more involved dependencies. They are smitten. They are hooked on playing golf. That near or full-on obsession for lowering the scoring average leads to a myriad of other reasons for playing the game. These include finding ways to hit the ball straighter or farther, making more putts and sand saves, and so on. Of course, this necessitates trying new equipment, constantly tinkering with the swing, and conferring with a sports psychologist to learn how to behave and think like a champion golfer.

Once a golfer's reasons for playing the game evolve to this level, a select group of them progress into an ultimate state that is almost surreal. This level of golf seems to transcend players into an almost mystical experience which provides them the ultimate reason for playing this hallowed game.

Those who have not experienced this transformation may find it strange and difficult to understand, but all those who have it feel a kinship with one another and will explain that golf can become almost a religious experience. At this highest level of evolved reasons for playing golf — and not necessarily accompanied by the highest level of skills — this sport provides great perspective and insight. These include a medium for really knowing oneself, for being one with nature, for communing with other golfers, and for gaining a greater understanding of life in general.

Jeff Wallach said it well in his book, *Beyond the Fairway:*

> Thankfully, legions of us know that golf is much, much more than a game. It's become, for some folks, a four-hour religious pilgrimage, a component of a personal vision of the world. We open ourselves to the places golf can take us. We play

(continued)

(continued)

because of the chance — on every shot — for transcendence and redemption. We know that, ultimately, the game can transport us beyond the fairway to where everything converges.

For those who choose to make it so, golf becomes an excellent vehicle or medium for truly getting to know and improve one's confidence, emotional stability, decision-making skills, abilities to concentrate, peace of mind, courage, patience, integrity, and so on. Probably the greatest reason for playing golf is found among this group; as they strive to improve their games, they improve their lives as well.

Chapter 16

Gamesmanship or Good Tactics?

. . . .

In This Chapter

▶ Avoiding hustles . . .

▶ . . . while living it up on the golf course

. . . .

*B*etting is a touchy subject among many golfers. Being the type of game that it is, golf lends itself to gambling. It won't be long before you find yourself playing for money (if you don't mind breaking the law). Oh, at first the money won't be much — if you have any sense, that is. But after a while, the money games can get out of hand if you let them.

Wanna Bet?

GARY SAYS

In my experience, golfers come in two types: those who want a good, even match and those who don't. I recommend that you play with the first group in your early days. Those folks won't take advantage of your inexperience. They'll give you the shots you need to make a good showing in any match you play. The winner will be the one who plays better that day. Nothing wrong with that, of course. If someone is to win, there has to be a loser. And sometimes, that loser will be you.

Unfortunately, the nice people I just described are often hard to find. That second group constitutes the vast majority of gambling golfers. They play golf for one reason: to bet. They don't play for the sunshine. They don't play for the exercise (unless getting in and out of a cart qualifies as exercise). And they surely don't play for relaxation. Most of them need clinical psychologists and straitjackets. They play to gamble with their buddies and beat them into bankruptcy.

The first tee

The winning and losing of bets all starts on the first tee. The arena of negotiation, I call it. It's here that bets are fought over and agreed upon. The key is the number of strokes you will give or receive over the course of a round. All games are won and lost here!

Initially, you're going to be playing with people whose handicaps are lower than your own. So you're going to get strokes from them. No easy task. Say your handicap is 30 and your opponent's is 18. Twelve strokes to you, right? Not if he has his way. He'll argue that his wife just left him. Or that he hasn't played in two weeks because of his workload at the office. Or that old football injury is acting up again. In any case, he'll try to cut your strokes down by at least three. That, he figures, is his edge.

It goes without saying that you either nod sympathetically or spin more tales than he just did. What you do *not* do is give up even a single stroke. Not one.

If you must *give* strokes, never net the strokes so that you play with zero. For example, if your handicap is 12 and your opponent's is 18, netting gives you zero strokes and your opponent six. Take all your strokes because they'll be on the toughest holes.

Never play for more than you can afford to lose. Keep the bets small when you're a new golfer learning the gambling ropes in the big city. It's a great game to play and have fun with, but if you lose enough money that it starts to hurt, the recreational aspects pale somewhat. Be careful and proceed at your own risk.

There's a famous quote about pressure from Lee Trevino, in his early days one of golf's great hustlers. "Pressure," he said, "is $5 on the front nine, $5 on the back, and $5 for the 18 [called a *nassau*] with $2 in your pocket."

Giving putts

On the green is one place where a little tactical planning can pay dividends. It's a fact of golf that no one, from a first-time beginner to Greg Norman, likes short putts, especially when they mean something. For that reason alone, you shouldn't be too generous in conceding short putts to your opponents. Always ask yourself if you would fancy hitting the putt. If the answer is "no" or even "not really," say nothing and watch.

Ten things to say when your partner/opponent hits a bad shot

1. At least you're dressing better.

2. Never up, never in.

3. You'll get better on the back nine.

4. At least we're not playing for that much money.

5. Well, it's a nice day, anyway.

6. I never play well on the weekends, either.

7. Does your spouse play?

8. I have trouble with that shot, too.

9. You should have warmed up more.

10. That's a hard shot with the dew point this low.

That's the hard-nosed approach. If you're playing a friendly round or you're with your boss, be a bit more generous. The demarcation line has long been that anything "inside the leather" was "good." That means any putt closer than the length of the grip on your putter (or in some places, between the grip and the clubhead) was deemed to be a "gimme" or unmissable. Such a policy is still applicable today, although these long putters today have equally long grips — so watch out!

I've looked at the two extremes in conceding — or not conceding — short putts. But there's a middle ground also. The great Walter Hagen was the master of this, or so the story goes. "The Haig" was the best match player of his day. In the 1920s, he won four PGA championships in succession at match play. So he had to know a thing or two about psychology. One of his ploys was to concede a few shortish putts early in the match. That way, two things happened: His opponent got used to being given putts, and perhaps more important, he was deprived of the "practice" of knocking a few in. Then, later in the round, old Walter wasn't so generous. The opponent would suddenly be faced with a knee-knocker, the sort of putt he hadn't hit all day.

I don't really recommend Walter's strategy. You can lose friends in a hurry if they miss that short one on the 17th. And your strategy may not work. Remember, a short putt missed on the 3rd green counts the same as one on the 17th or 18th.

Picking Partners

Again, you can make picking partners as scientific or as easygoing as you like. If you're just playing for fun or for a few dollars, who your partners are doesn't really matter. If you play with the same guys every time, everything will pretty much even out in the end, anyway.

But if things are a little more serious, you need to put some thought into your partners. Here are the rules I try to follow in "money" games:

✔ My partner always has a 1-iron in his bag.

✔ He has more than 37 tags hanging from his bag.

✔ He has used the same putter since he was 5 years old.

✔ He's gone if he tells me about his marital problems on the practice range!

Match Play Tactics

As you've probably guessed by now, match play generally involves a lot more strategy than stroke play. Strict card-and-pencil golf has a simple premise: Score the best you can. Match play is equally simple: Beat the other golfer. But doing so requires more thought. Here are my match play rules:

✔ **Don't go for too much early.** Handing a couple of early holes to your opponent only hurts your confidence and boosts the confidence of the competition.

✔ **Never lose your temper.** Nothing gives your opponent more heart than watching and listening to you lose your cool.

✔ **Pay attention to where your opponent's ball is at all times.** Your opponent's situation dictates your tactics on any given shot. For example, if he is deep in the woods, you may want to be less aggressive.

✔ **Figure that your opponent will hole every putt he looks at.** Then you won't be disappointed if he does make it. Of course, if he misses, you get a boost.

✔ **Watch your opponent.** Watch how fast he walks, for example. If he's slow, go fast; if he's fast, go slow. Anything to break his natural rhythm.

✔ **Try never to hit two bad shots in a row.** Easier said than done, of course!

✓ **Never second-guess yourself.** If you're playing it safe, don't suddenly get aggressive halfway into your downswing. And if you're "going for it," really do it. Even if you miss, you'll feel better. Take it from me, someone who has missed more than once!

✓ **Only concede a hole when the situation is hopeless.** Make your opponent win holes instead of losing them yourself. The more shots he has to hit under pressure, the more likely he is to make a mistake.

Never Give Up

In the 1972 British Open at Muirfield, Lee Trevino and Tony Jacklin were tied standing on the 17th tee in the final round. Distracted by a spectator, Trevino hooked his drive on the par-5 into a deep bunker. Jacklin drove perfectly. After splashing out only a few yards, Lee then hooked his third shot into heavy rough well left and short of the green. Jacklin hit his fairway wood into the perfect spot, about 50 yards from the hole.

How to avoid a hustle

As a relatively new golfer, you're going to be a prime target for hustlers. They'll figure you're neither talented nor savvy enough to beat them. And they'll be right — at least until you've played a while. So avoid them. Here's what to look for:

✓ Does he have a 1-iron in his bag? If so, don't play him. Only good players can hit those things.

✓ Never bet with a stranger.

✓ If you do bet, make it a straightforward nassau (front, back, 18 bet). Don't get bamboozled with lots of side bets.

✓ If he uses a ball that isn't new, say goodbye. Bad players don't have old balls; they lose them too quickly.

✓ Legendary teacher Harvey Penick used to say, "Beware of the golfer with a bad grip." Why? Because he has found a way to make it work.

✓ Another thing about the grip — look at your opponent's left hand. If he has calluses, he's either played or practiced a lot. Adios.

✓ If that left hand is less tan than the right, the same applies. He has spent a lot of time wearing a golf glove.

At that point, Trevino gave up. He quit. He told Jacklin that the championship was all his and did everything but shake his hand right there. Trevino's fourth shot flew right over the green halfway up a grass bank. Jacklin hit a so-so pitch to about 15 feet.

Barely glancing at the shot, Trevino then hit a lazy, give-up chip that rolled right into the cup! Par! Jacklin then three-putted for a six. Trevino won.

I relate this story to you because it is so unusual — quitters never win. Don't be one.

Playing with Your Boss

When playing with your boss (or with anybody), you want to do your best. If you're just starting to play this game, you don't have to worry about beating the boss and feeling bad. He or she has probably played golf a lot longer than you and just wants to get to know you on the course. The golf course is a great place to find out your true personality. The game leaves you psychologically naked in front of your peers.

If your game develops and you become a very good player, you're an asset to your company, and your boss should recognize your potential as a salesperson for the company. Millions of dollars in business deals have been negotiated on the golf course.

Play your best at all times and be helpful to those people who don't play the game as well as you do. You'll reap the benefits from that philosophy for many years to come.

Surviving a Pro-Am

I was sent off to war, a young man still slobbering from the fright. There were going to be people wearing camouflaged plaid, shooting at me, toward whom I had no ill will; would I be man enough to fight back? I was going to learn a lesson about life; the cruel nature of this odyssey was upon me. I was going to play in my first Pro-Am. —Gary McCord, circa 1974, as he embarked without hesitation toward the first tee and certain death

There is a rite of passage on the Tour called a Pro-Am. This is the cornerstone of our being. If you're armed with a sizable amount of cash (the average is about $3,500), you can tee it up with Tiger Woods, Fred Couples, and Greg Norman and tell your friends for the next 300 business lunches how you brought these guys to near fascination with your prowess on the links and your witty banter between shots. In no other sport can a layman go on the playing surface and get this close to the action other than by streaking at a national televised game. The shortcomings of the latter are obvious.

Pro-Ams are played every Wednesday, or on the Senior Tour on Wednesdays and Thursdays. Each team consists of four amateurs and a pro. Corporations pay handsomely for the opportunity to put their names on tournaments and entertain their clients. This setup is unique in sports, and it's the pros' duty to see that the corporate clients have a good time and want to come back for more.

Much has been written about the attitudes of the Tour players in these ubiquitous Wednesday Pro-Ams. The difficulties in concentrating on the day before a tournament while playing with nervous amateurs are many. However, no one seems to offer the quivering victims any advice. I always try to imagine what it would be like for me if I were plucked out of my comfort zone and thrust into the spotlight — say, on the hardwoods with Michael Jordan or in the boardroom with Bill Gates — and told not to make an idiot of myself. The truth is that neither Michael nor Bill would expect me to be any good. I, on the other hand, would still like to give a decent account of myself, or at least limit the damage.

The first thing to remember is that your pro requires one thing from you: that you enjoy yourself. The reason we play for so much money these days is that you do enjoy the game, you do buy the equipment that you don't need, and you do love to watch us on television. So don't be overawed: Chances are you do something for a living that we would be completely useless at doing. A good pro will always do his or her best to put you at ease on the first tee, so when you make your first swing that makes contact with the planet 9 inches behind the ball and induces significant seismographic readings, you can at least have a laugh at it, too.

Here are my "Eight Steps to Pro-Am Heaven" — for pros and amateurs alike. A few do's and don'ts of playing with a pro — a road map through the purgatory of the Pro-Am. I hope that these few guidelines help both you and your pro enjoy the day.

Get a caddie

Having a caddie is the only way to play the game. You can walk free of hindrance and have clubs handed to you clean and dry. If possible, get one of the Tour caddies whose player isn't in the Pro-Am. For $50, you can have someone who is used to being screamed at and blamed for the weather, the rate of inflation, and some of those hard-to-explain skin rashes.

Mind you, the caddie won't be able to club you because you don't know which part of the club the ball is about to bounce off of. However, he or she will be able to regale you with bizarre stories of "looper legends" in their quest for immortality on the fairways of life. These tales are worth the price of admission, and parental guidance is suggested.

Be ready to hit

You need to be ready to hit, even if it isn't your turn. Discuss with your partners the concept of "ready golf" before you tee off. This means forgetting whose honor it is — if you're ready, just go. Pro-Am play is hideously slow at the best of times, and your pro will really appreciate it if you make the effort to keep things going.

Toss the cellular phone

At the very least, turn it off. The surgical removal of a cellular phone from certain regions of the anatomy is painful and, to the best of my knowledge, is not covered under most company health insurance plans.

Get a yardage book

And ask a Tour caddie how to use a yardage book. This will make the pro very happy. Contribute to your pro's mental well-being by being the first "ammy" in the history of his or her Pro-Am career not to ask the question: "How far have I got from here?" There are only a certain number of times in your adult lifetime that you can be asked this question before your spleen bursts. I am a better person without mine.

Pick it up if you're out of the hole

If you're out of the hole, pick it up, ball in pocket. Rest the ammo. Holster the bad boy. And be sure to tell your pro that you have done so. Not only will you contribute to the pace of play, but you will avoid the awkward situation of having the pro wait, expecting you to hit, while you rummage around in your bag looking for the source of that smell that has been emanating from there since you let the kids play with your rain gear.

In this category, only one thing is worse than waiting around for no apparent reason, and that's waiting around for a very bad apparent reason — for example, holing out for a 9, net 8.

Forget about your score

And don't be upset if your pro doesn't know how your team stands. Remember, it's a Wednesday. He probably doesn't even know his own score, and quite honestly, after the 26th Pro-Am of the year, he won't remember what his gender is.

Watch your feet

I know, you're wearing soft spikes and it shouldn't matter, but the tradition of wandering on somebody's line, regardless of what's on the bottom of your soles, is a slow dance with a hot temper. Be very, very mindful of the line of your pro's putt. Look at television coverage of a golf tournament and watch how respectful the pros are of each other's lines. Stepping on another pro's line is close to religious desecration in our sport. I've pulled a groin muscle trying to mark my ball without stepping on the sacred line. But I think that, in my career, I have excelled at acrobatic markings of the ball due to the fact that I was exceptional at the game Twister during my formative years.

Simply ask the pro where his line is, and he'll show you. I usually leave my ball right next to the coin the entire time we're on the green so that my amateur partners will know where my line is and (I hope) avoid contact.

Keep the advice to yourself

Finally, if you're still interested in playing this game with anybody ever again, do not give the pro any advice on how to play the course, even if your family has owned the property since the planet started to warm and you can wander it in the dark without hitting anything. Trust me, he thinks he knows more about it than you do just because he has his name on his bag.

It's a question of knowing what to look for. Even giving the occasional line off the tee can be dangerous because you don't normally play two club-lengths from the back edge of the back tee. I don't know how many times I've heard, "Oops, I could have sworn that you could carry that bunker!"

Part V
Other Golf Stuff

The 5th Wave
By Rich Tennant

"What exactly do the rules say about giving and receiving advice?"

In this part . . .

I've worked as a golf commentator for CBS sports since 1986. In this part, I use my expertise to give you insight into how to watch your favorite pro (if it's not me) play this puzzling game. This part also explores some of the great golfing wonders that the information superhighway has to offer. It covers all my favorite cyber haunts for golf.

Chapter 17

Golf on TV

. . . .

In This Chapter

▶ Televising golf

▶ Checking out the top players

▶ Finding a role model

▶ Understanding the top players' techniques

. . . .

It is a medium that reaches the far corners of humanity; its video displays teach and formulate a way of life. No singular invention has influenced our lives and dictated our roles in society, whether good or bad, as much as television. That is way too much pressure for me; please turn me off.

— Gary McCord's acceptance speech to his audio-visual class at Lincoln Elementary School in 1959 after he was voted "Most Likely to Do the Weather Report Someday"

The year was 1986, and my professional goals and aspirations were making a house call on Dr. Kevorkian. Limited success was now an exaggeration. The Tour was a vast, empty wasteland of setbacks and spent money. I was serving out the rest of my sentence with no chance of parole. Golf sucks.

As I boarded my airplane for Columbus, Ohio, nothing really was on my mind other than the two fat vacuum cleaner salesmen I was going to be sitting between in the coach section. I was in my customary hesitant gaze when I was awoken by harsh criticism coming from the first-class section. It was the CBS crew that does golf, already enjoying the amenities of first class (although in a plastic cup) before takeoff.

Frank Chirkinian, the executive producer and director for CBS at the time, Pat Summerall, Ben Wright (the evil swine): All of them were basking in the knowledge that I was to be forever lost in the coach section wedged between two obese and slightly pungent salesmen who got their wardrobes from the Salvation Army catalogue. They told me that I could come up and use their restroom if I could peel myself from between the two guys. I hoped that the front of the airplane would fall off.

We were all going to Jack Nicklaus's golf tournament called the Memorial in Columbus, Ohio. We had just left Fort Worth, Texas, where I had played and CBS had televised the Colonial Invitational. I had just been elected to the policy board of the PGA Tour — the players elect three members of the Tour, and along with the three officers of the PGA of America and three independent business leaders, we make up the Tour policy board, which basically runs the Tour. It's a very important job for an idiot like me to have, but the players thought that my life wasn't miserable enough, so they staked me to this tree.

I was going to Columbus not to play in Nicklaus's tournament — it was an invitational, and I wasn't high enough on the money list to buy a Big Mac — but to go to policy board meetings for the first three days of the week. They were closed-door meetings in which I usually could catch up on my sleep. The next tournament was in Washington, D.C., for the Kemper, but I wouldn't have to leave until the end of the week.

I was fighting for a position on the armrest of seat 28B, when the flight attendant came by and presented me with a bottle of champagne, compliments of the royal family in first class. These guys really know how to have a good time when the bubbly is free.

I started hesitantly toward the front of the plane to thank my benefactors and get away from the sumo-sized bookends I was seated between. As I scurried to first class, I fell on an idea that could help solve my problem of having nowhere to go after the policy board meetings ended on Wednesday. I couldn't afford to go to Washington early, and I had no money to fly home for the four days in between. I was a golfer caught in the headlights of bankruptcy.

After some quick banter, I told Frank that I had nothing to do from Thursday to Sunday, and because I was on the policy board making decisions about TV contracts, I should watch how a televised event is produced. "Show up Friday for rehearsal at 11 and check into the Stouffer's on Thursday; we'll have a room for you. Now get back to the screaming kids in coach before I have you thrown off the plane for being up here," Frank said. He had the bedside manner of Attila the Hun sporting a bad case of hemorrhoids, but I loved him at that moment.

I showed up promptly at 11, well fed from a gorging on room service and weary-eyed from the menu of movies that I signed to the room. I was a pig, and I enjoyed the wallow.

I opened the door to Frank's office, and he bellowed from the confines of his mobile home for me to go out to the 16th hole. He didn't sound like he wanted to engage in light conversation, so I broke into a slight trot out toward the 16th. I couldn't help but wonder why I wasn't going to sit in the trucks with Frank while he did the telecast to gain some insight into how a telecast is produced, every once in a while getting Frank some snacks or engaging him in casual conversation. Why was I going to the 16th hole?

As I started to walk toward the tee, a voice came serenading down from high atop the tower, beckoning me to come up. It was Verne Lundquist, the veteran announcer, calling. I managed to make my way up the tower and exchanged idle conversation with Verne's spotter. Verne then handed me a headset and told me to grab a chair. I asked what the headset was for, and he said, "Didn't Frank tell you that he wanted to try you as an announcer this week?" As I weighed the decision between doing some spotting with caddies who missed the cut and being on national television, the conversation with myself was, as usual, very short.

"Where do I sit, Verne, and what do I do?" I said.

It looks like this in the tower: A little enclosure is surrounded with clear plastic, much like the front seat of a car, with the windshield surrounding the front and you looking out at the green. Two monitors in front of the announcer show the action taking place and a current leader board. The spotter is next to you, giving you the scores and the clubs the players are hitting. In this case, Carl took up most of the room. Carl, who weighs 385 pounds, looks like he just ate a sumo wrestler. There was not much room left in the front seat of this car.

My seat was outside this cubicle and next to the cameraman. Looking down at the action for the first time was really interesting. Golf looks incredibly easy from way up there. How can they screw up so many shots?!? I was above the tension, up in the clouds. My, how this view changes your perspective of the game.

My first clash with the headphones was like being in on a private conversation with Shirley Maclaine as she channeled; there were voices everywhere. The voice in my left ear was the director, Frank, and the other voices were all the announcers from their towers. Occasionally, I would hear a rogue voice, and I had no idea who it was. I found out later that a guy operating a CB unit in the neighborhood had come through on our headsets. Welcome to network television.

The rehearsal went pretty smoothly. I found out two things: (1) Your conversation must be short. The action jumps all over the place, and you can't get stuck in the middle of a story. (2) Never answer anything Frank says directly. No one can hear Frank. Those are the rules; obey at all costs.

The next day, my first on national television, was going smoothly. Verne and I were clicking like a car counter on a Los Angeles freeway. He would ask a question; I would answer and then get out. I never said, "What did you say, Frank?" I was rolling.

Due to a starter's time that spreads the field, there was a large gap between the group that had just walked off the 16th green and the next group that was approaching the 14th green. I had some free time, so I kicked back in the chair and read some interesting tidbits on the personal lives of the bromide golf pros.

I was awakened from my near-catatonic state by a combination of Frank throwing the action to Verne and Verne asking me what this putt was going to do. I looked down real fast and saw nobody on the 16th green. The next group walking up the 15th fairway. What was going on?

Verne had that Nordic look of desperation as he asked me again, and Frank was starting to annoy me with, "Answer him, you culturally lost golf derelict." I looked down at the green again, and there still wasn't anybody around. Were they seeing ghosts, or was this just a ruse to excite the poor rookie caught lost in thought? After several more verbal harassments from Frank and the look of a desperate sheepdog on the face of Verne, I decided to play along with their game. I said, "Verne, this putt should be fairly fast, because it's going down the hill toward the water." Verne met my response by saying, "Boy, you were right, Gary; that putt cruised by the hole and, if he hit it a little harder, would have gone down in the water."

Wait a minute!

The 16th green at Muirfield Village golf course has no water anywhere near it, except for the drinking fountain on the tee. I made the water stuff up because the boys were trying to get the rookie and I was trying to throw them a curve. I was a wild pitch.

I heard Frank say, "Throw it to 18, Verne." Then Verne looked at me with those screeching Scandinavian eyes and asked if I could respond a little quicker next time. Frank hit his button and began to verbally blast me for my "funereal response," which I took as less than congratulatory.

At this point, I realized that they weren't kidding, and we really were on the air. Oh, no! "Verne," I said, "Could you help me in my moment of conjecture and look down on the 16th green and tell me if you see anybody, or do I have to call a ghostbuster?"

"Of course there's nobody there," said Verne. Now I really was confused. "Verne, if there's nobody there, why did you say the ball rolled 7 feet by the hole when I made up the thing about the water being there in the first place?" I asked, dumbfounded.

"There is water there," Verne said, with a stern look of what-in-the-heck-are-you-talking-about? on his face.

"There's no water on this 16th hole," I said.

"I know that, you idiot, but we were doing the 12th hole!"

"Wait a minute, we're doing the 12th hole also? I was told to go out to the 16th hole with you."

What had happened was that, during rehearsal, we hadn't used a camera for our other hole, the 12th, because the camera was broken. I had no way of knowing that I was supposed to be looking at the 12th hole as well as the 16th, unless I had called the Psychic Friends hotline. Confusing business, huh?

As life weaves its reckless mysteries, the par-3 12th hole has water surrounding the green. The putt had come from the top tier real fast toward the water and had gone 7 feet past the hole. I totally made something up, and it just so happened to be a perfect call in this less-than-perfect business. Welcome to televised golf.

This is my legacy, I am bound by its structure. I cannot deny its existence. It has made me rich. I hope that I can bring you closer to how this medium works so that you can understand our chaos.

The growth in the popularity of golf over the last 40 years has been reflected in the amount of coverage the game receives on television. Christmas week may be the only time of year when you can't watch the pros teeing it up in some exotic locale. Television has embraced golf to the extent that the top players today are as well known as their counterparts in baseball, basketball, and football.

Why Golf's Popularity Has Mushroomed

Golf is a sport that's played all year long, from the first week in January through the second week in December. Golf on the tube has grown proportionately, from a few shows in the 1950s to nonstop golf on TV today. We get that with the Golf Channel, which covers golf 24 hours a day.

The places that TV takes you during the golf year are a vacationer's dream. Every Saturday and Sunday, you can do the couch thing and watch the various tours play from every corner of the globe. The golf is good, but the pictures are stunning. The viewing audience and the PGA Tour start to prepare themselves in the Florida swing for the first major tournament of the year in early April, when Augusta and the Masters Tournament are in full bloom. The Tour settles in to normalcy for a while, and then players start to prepare for the heat and the long rough of the U.S. Open in mid-June. The month of July is for the British Open and its storied past; plenty of plaid and windblown golf balls decorate the landscape. The last of the four majors, the PGA Championship, is played in August. These are the tournaments that all professional golfers gear up to play well in; they are the measure of a player's worth and his quest. And they make for great viewing.

During the first part of the year, many celebrities play in the AT&T Tournament at Pebble Beach and the Bob Hope Chrysler Classic. If viewing the stars is your thing, you can see these would-be golfers hacking away at all their inhibitions during these Pro-Am tournaments.

If Hollywood stars are not your idea of role models, maybe professional golfers can fill the void. You don't see much trash-talking or foul play on the golf course. In fact, golf may be the only game in which the players police themselves. Almost weekly, there's an example of a player on the PGA Tour penalizing himself for some inadvertent rules transgression. Can you imagine a basketball player turning down two points because he had pushed someone out of the way en route to the basket? Probably not!

Golf and Television

Sports and television have become inextricably linked through the years. Remember that television is still a relatively new medium; as recently as 1946, fans were still providing their own images to the dramatic radio broadcast of the 1946 World Series.

Baseball proved to be perfect for the new tube technology that beamed rays of hypnotic light into everyone's home. But golf presented many unique challenges to television coverage. Aside from playing on 150 acres as opposed to being surrounded by fences at a distance of 400 feet from home plate, there was constant, ongoing action with many athletes competing independently at any given moment. No RF frequencies, no microwave signals — what's a broadcaster to do?

Keep it simple — so they did. The first broadcast of any kind of golf event was the renowned Tam O'Shanter Classic from Chicago on Sunday, August 22, 1953. One camera fixed on the 18th hole. Perhaps as an indication of the excitement that golf would eventually bring to the tube, the moment for this particular coverage was opportune. Lew Worsham, a pro, was playing the circuit and had achieved modest success along the way. He approached the 18th not unlike many finishing holes that year, but the difference this time was that this shot would yield an often sought after, but not often produced, result: a hole-in-one. If you're interested, the videotape of that monumental moment is available in video archives.

It was the unbridled charisma of one man that turned the nation's attention to the sport of captains and kings. Arnold Palmer, of the hitch-and-smile, go-for-broke style of unwavering charm, turned the viewing world on its ear and had viewers tuned to their sets to follow his exploits. In 1960, he began the unanticipated task of carrying an industry on his back as golf and television developed together to provide a foundation for the sport that would ultimately reap the rewards of the great sports and television rights fee pot of gold.

How does it work?

It's thought that golf is the most difficult sport to cover. Think about it: The playing field is anything but standard. No precisely measured court or white lines of delineation. The playing field is a park, a wide-open expanse covering acres of competitive challenges. There are no time-outs and no clock. Play begins at ten-minute intervals, and either four or six players embark upon the playing field for their bid at the color red. (For the uninitiated, scores below par are noted on the scoreboard with red numbers.) At any one time, 100 or more individual competitors might be playing on the same course, each of them playing different holes. No orchestrated playing time here. So how does it happen?

First, golf courses have to be technically prepped. That's just a fancy way of saying that you must run cable, and lots of it, in order to broadcast signals from the golf course to the television truck. The small army of engineers and cable-pullers usually invade on the Sunday or Monday preceding broadcast week. Tractor-trailer trucks filled with several million dollars worth of cameras and technical equipment are deployed. The average telecast requires miles of cable, often as many as 19 cameras mobilized in a variety of ways, 6 videotape machines, digital disc recorders, character generators, spotters, and a control room staffed with some of the best producers and directors in the industry.

The staff is divided into what is known as "above and below the line." Those charged with above-the-line duties are the folks who make the production and story line decisions. I'll start at the top:

- **Producer:** This individual is responsible for creating the story line of the event. Remember how different golf is from basketball, football, and most other sports. It may be the only sport in which the participant hits a stationary ball, but often at great distances. All you need are cameras trained on the action. The better producers and directors are able to provide a variety of replays and isolated coverage of the action. It requires them to be intimately conversant with the game itself as well as to know all the key players. Although the story line is dictated by who is performing well during the course of play, the viewer must be mindful that as many as a dozen contestants or more may be newsworthy. The producer's task is to capture the respective shot-making efforts and to weave the drama cohesively as it unfolds.

- **Director:** The director is responsible for placing cameras at strategic spots around the course to capture the best possible angles of coverage. The director communicates with the camera personnel, the audio crew, and the staff of technical people to provide insightful coverage of the action on the course. While the producer may say, "Let's go to Tom Watson next on the ninth green," the director is responsible for readying those cameras and operators and for framing the shots that will most dramatically convey the action to viewers. The director oversees the complex array of audio tracks, graphics, and limitless special effects.

✔ **Associate directors:** One associate director supports the producer and director. Although titles may change from network to network, standard coverage usually involves an "iso" truck in which an associate director records coverage of shots that are central to the story line but not shown live. You might hear an announcer say, "Moments ago . . . ." With the concurrent golf action, it's not surprising that much of the television coverage is taped. It assures the viewer of seeing as many shots as possible in a sensible sequence to show and tell the whole story. Some producers favor using more taped shots than others.

A second associate director is known as the "sundial," or timer. Sundial became an inside joke for one A.D., as his countdowns in and out of commercials were less than accurate. Approximately 12 times in a telecast, the network breaks for at least 2 minutes of commercials or promotional announcements. Someone is responsible for giving a count out of the program action into the commercial time to make the transition appear seamless to the viewer. The same is true coming out of a commercial back to the center of activity the remote truck.

✔ **Talent:** The remaining critical element of the above-the-line team is the talent. The producers and directors provide the blueprint of the telecast, but the talent deliver it. They are the artisans who sell the vision. The National Football League might employ as many as four announcers per broadcast, and baseball maybe three, but the multiple broadcast booths in a golf telecast necessitate a team of announcers in this decidedly individual sport. Networks use up to eight on-air personalities to recite the golf action. Chemistry is key. From Johnny Miller and Roger Maltbie to Mike Tirico and Curtis Strange to the respected talent of Jim Nantz and Ken Venturi, each team possesses a unique personality.

The 18th tower is the focal point where the host and key analyst hold forth. From there, networks differ. Some choose the analyst-per-green format à la CBS, erecting towers adjacent to the final few greens on the course. From these vantage points, the announcers have clear, above-the-gallery views and can call the action of each particular hole or report on a neighboring hole within view of the tower. ABC uses a secondary broadcast studio in which the talent view the monitor and report each shot played. All networks employ on-course personnel. These individuals walk with designated players and report on the action from the ground.

✔ **Technical personnel:** The "below-the-line" folks are comprised of technical people — camera and audio operators, engineers, and technical gurus. Of course, everyone involved in this tightly knit, interlocking puzzle is important, but one key individual brings it all together, being in charge of pressing the buttons that effectively determine which pictures and sounds go on the air. This person is the technical director. The burden of the end product falls to the technical director alone, sitting in the production truck next to the director. If you ever notice a glitch in moving from one shot to another or a graphic appearing and then disappearing hastily, chances are that the technical director made a mistake or received some bad information from the field.

All in all, when you add up all the above-the-line and below-the-line folks, the spotters, the runners, and the craft services personnel (which is a fancy, entertainment-industry way of saying caterers), a network may roll into town with a production crew of more than 100 people. The commitment is significant.

Ever wonder exactly how the pictures get to your TV set at home? Well, there's also a separate satellite truck on site that beams signals from the remote broadcast site off a satellite, to the studio, and eventually to your home.

The deal

Of course, none of this would happen if there weren't a deal or demand to broadcast the more than 1,000 hours of professional golf being played. Golf continues to grow in popularity for a variety of reasons, not the least of which is the support of corporate America. Why? Well, first by golf's very position in the world as a game played by the captains and kings of industry. It's a game of tradition, honor, and integrity. The image of the game presented by the players is essential to the sponsors and magnified in importance by what has become an increasingly cluttered world of athletes whose names are apt to be found on the front page of the newspaper rather than in the back.

The rise in the number of hours of golf being broadcast on television has been monumental. In the last ten years alone, the total number of hours of televised golf has grown nearly 200 percent.

Golf has forged its way to prominence as a major player in television sports today in a rather innovative fashion. It began meekly in an effort to gain exposure on television. Time buys, rights, and production deals are two principal forces dominating network television coverage.

Time buys

A network places an hourly value on its airtime — no different than a supermarket stocking shelves. Each hour of airtime represents a quantifiable asset for the network. In this case, a program buyer negotiates a date and airtime for a program. The program buyer purchases the time from the network, arranges to sell the time to advertisers, and then receives all the revenue produced in the allotted airtime.

Take a look at an example. The McCord Challenge buys two hours of time from GHI Network. McCord pays the network, say $550,000. The network rules allow the producer to sell 18 commercial units within the hour. So, for the $550,000 expended, the McCord group receives 36 commercial units (18×2) to allocate to its list of sponsors or to sell.

The formula is fairly basic, not inexpensive because the packager bears the production cost, and costs average around $500,000 for reasonable golf coverage. With professional talent added, there's more than a million-dollar investment from the outset. That's before the cost of players, a tournament purse, and all the on-site event amenities are covered.

Rights and production

Here's where the network takes a risk. The escalations in sports rights fees over the past several years have resulted in billion-dollar contracts for the NFL and NBA for rights and production deals. Network executives decide that they're willing to pay an upfront fee to the rights holders and provide production in exchange for the opportunity to maximize their investment in the advertising marketplace.

Golf, through its increasing popularity, its broadening appeal, and the valuable image it provides for sponsors — the quality and virtually un-matched demographics delivered — has taken its place among the major sports as a significant provider of sports programming.

The top ten things not to do as a golf announcer

1. Never talk to your director while you're on the air; no one else can hear the director, and people will think that you have an imaginary friend.

2. Don't get the sound guy mad at you; he'll cut you off when you're making a witty comment and keep you on while you're mumbling.

3. Never tell the audience how good a player you used to be.

4. Don't ever say that a shot is impossible.

5. Never talk "down" to the audience.

6. Don't get into long stories; you'll be cut off as the director goes to another hole.

7. Never use cliches; it shows that you're lazy and can't come up with witty banter.

8. Never tell the audience what they see on the TV screen.

9. Never assume that the audience knows anything about the game of golf.

10. Never, ever assume that what you do for a living has any role in the elevation of humankind.

What to Watch for on TV

By all means, take in and enjoy the physical beauty of much of the golf on television. But pay attention to the players, too. You can learn a lot from watching not only their swings but also their whole demeanor on the course. Listen to the language, the jargon, the parlance being used. If you've read this book — or any golf book — I'm sure that you've noticed the complexity of the game's terms. There's a lot of room for confusion. Watching the game on TV helps you get around that problem. This is especially true when a commentator analyzes a player's swing. He or she uses and explains much of the terminology that you need to understand to become part of the golfing world. (See Appendix A for more help with golf terminology.)

Watch the players very carefully. Pay attention to the rhythm of their swings. Pay attention to their mannerisms. The way they waggle the club. The triggers that set their swings in motion. The way they putt. The way they set their feet in the sand before they play from bunkers. The way they stand on uphill and downhill lies. In other words, watch everything. Soak it all in. Immerse yourself in the atmosphere and the ambiance. You'll soon be walking the walk and talking the talk.

That's the big picture. That's what everyone should watch. But what about you specifically?

Find Yourself on TV

Watching Steve Elkington or Patty Sheehan on television is a good idea for everyone. But there's a limit to what most people can learn from most players. Pay particular attention to someone like Steve if you happen to be tall and slim. But if you happen to be shorter and more heavyset, you need to look elsewhere. Make Lee Trevino, Bob Murphy, Craig Stadler, JoAnne Carner, Karrie Webb, or Kelly Rubins your role model. In other words, find someone whose body type approximates your own.

Then watch how that person stands to the ball at address. See how his arms hang. See how much she flexes her knees. Golfers who are taller have much more flex in their knees than their shorter counterparts.

Watch how "your pro" swings the club. Do his arms move away from his body as the club moves back? How much does she turn her shoulders? How good is his balance? Does she have a lot of wrist action in her swing? Or does he use his arms to create width? Watch these people every chance you get. Use their swings and the way they conduct themselves to help your game.

What to Look for in the Top Players

The players who get the most airtime are, of course, the more successful ones. No network is going to waste valuable minutes on someone well out of contention. The audience wants to watch the tournament being won and lost, so those players shooting the lowest scores are the ones you'll see most on TV.

Here's what to look for in some of the more prominent players.

Greg Norman

Controlled aggression. Greg Norman has failed to win as many tournaments as perhaps he should have for two reasons. First, he has been in a position to win more than anybody. Second, he takes risks because he plays to win. That means that he doesn't care about finishing second or third. Winning is everything. If that sounds like your philosophy of life and golf, watch Greg.

John Daly

John Daly is a longer and less controlled version of Greg. Sometimes imagining what John is thinking on the golf course is hard. But John is still one of the biggest draws in the game. Why? Because he hits the ball the farthest. Deep down inside, that's what everyone wants to do.

Laura Davies

The most powerful player the LPGA has ever known. This blaster from Coventry, England, attacks a golf course like Babe Zaharias did before her. I like to watch Laura manage herself around the course. She is so long off the tee that she can take chances other women should not. Laura will be one to watch on the LPGA for years to come.

Lee Janzen

Lee Janzen may be the fiercest competitor in golf. When he gets into contention in a tournament, he tends to win. There aren't many second-place finishes on Lee's résumé. Watch him for his mannerisms, too. He does the same things before every shot. He fidgets. He must have 100 different waggles. But they're all part of his preshot routine. The key for you is that he does the same things *every* time. He rarely gets out of his rhythm.

Fred Couples

Watch Fred Couples for his apparent nonchalance. Watch how he stretches before every shot. (Fred has a bad back. If you do, too, do what he does.) But most of all, watch Fred's swing. See how he slowly and smoothly builds up speed in the clubhead and then lashes at the ball through impact.

Patty Sheehan

This LPGA Hall of Famer is one of the finest players ever to swing a club. And can she swing a club! Television viewers can watch her rhythm and balance. She never seems to overswing the golf club; it's always under control. Patty is not the longest player on the LPGA Tour, but she has an exceptional imagination around the greens, and you can learn from her technique on the short shots.

Nick Price

From 1992 through the end of 1994, there was little doubt who was the best golfer in the world: Nick Price. Watch Nick for his pistonlike action, his quickness, and his "let's get down to business" air. He's a high-strung individual, and that carries over into his golf swing. The key is how Nick makes his character work for him — not against him. There's no rule that says you have to do everything slowly in golf. Find your own rhythm and then stick with it.

Nancy Lopez

Nancy Lopez is arguably still the most popular personality on the LPGA Tour. Watch her for the way she always seems to be having fun. Nancy even seems to enjoy the inevitable setbacks that golf hits you with in every round. She never loses her cool. Neither should you.

Phil Mickelson

Phil is already the best left-handed golfer on the planet. He's a hero to lots of left-handers, so if that's the side of the ball you stand on, he may be your hero, too. And he may be the best putter. His stroke is long and fluid, and the acceleration through impact is easy to spot. In fact, his putting stroke is just like his full swing. That's a good barometer for you. Never mix and match putting strokes and full swings. If you have a short, quick swing, putt that way, too.

Take Your Punishment

You can learn the most from the players on TV by watching how they handle problem situations. Professional players make most of their decisions with their heads — not their hearts. So pay close attention to rules, situations, and the times when a player has to manufacture a weird and wonderful shot to extricate the ball from trouble. And don't forget to watch the much more frequent occasions when the player accepts that a mistake has been made, takes the punishment, and moves on. That's when you know you've been watching a real golfer, one who understands that everyone makes mistakes, and that he or she just made one.

That last point reminds me of a time when I let my heart — or my ego — rule my decision-making process. I was playing in Memphis, I think. Anyway, I had to birdie one of the last three holes during my second round in order to qualify to play on the weekend. After my drive at the 16th, I had 223 yards to the hole, which was cut dangerously close to a large lake. I chose a 4-iron, convinced that I had enough club. I didn't. Splash!

I turned to my caddie and told him to give me another ball. He did. I hit the next shot perfectly. Splash!

"Give me another ball." Splash!

"Give me another ball." Splash!

"Give me another ball." Splash!

By this time, I knew that I clearly was using the wrong club. I knew it. My caddie knew it. The local police knew it. But I wasn't going to give up. This was my manhood we were testing here.

Eventually, my caddie handed me another ball with a 3-iron, one more club. I said, "What's this?" He told me that I had only one ball left. So I took the 3-iron and hit my last ball onto the green. I holed the putt for, I think, a 15.

The moral of the story? Never let your emotions or your ego get in the way of your decision-making.

Me at the Masters

The entire CBS production crew, including Frank Chirkinian (my producer at the time) and I, were dining at the Tournament Players Championship two weeks prior to the Masters. The conversation turned quickly to who would be assigned to which holes during the telecast in Augusta. Everyone had his assignments except for me. I was left holding air.

I had been working with CBS on a part-time basis for only a few months, but the announcing crew was excited that I would be going to Augusta. When Frank excluded me from the fracas, anarchy prevailed. Pat Summerall led the charge for my induction into the mix, and the others followed, but to no avail. It was late in the day on the Saturday telecast when Frank, between commercial breaks, announced to everyone that I was going to the hallowed grounds of Augusta National after all.

I was told to be at Augusta by Tuesday for a meeting with Hord Hardin, the tournament director. Frank was waiting patiently for me when I arrived. We proceeded to Hardin's office; I felt like I was going to the principal's office. There was a look of concern on Frank's face as we went into the catacombs of the clubhouse at Augusta.

Jim Nantz joined us as we walked down the narrow corridor toward the door at the end of the hall. I was dressed rather spectacularly in white Calvin Klein jeans and a bulky DKNY sweater ablaze in yellow, the whole outfit topped with a Panama straw hat. I was a walking ridicule to tradition.

As we approached the darkened door at the end of the hall, it creaked open as if willed by a higher power. A shadowy figure appeared backlit against a ray of sun filtered through the lone window. Hord Hardin greeted us like Lurch of *The Addams Family*. Frank and Jim sat in the corner, and I proceeded to take residence in the big couch in front of Hardin's desk. I was the plot.

After introductions and small talk about my work on television, Hardin proceeded to make a passionate speech about the flavor of this tournament. "We must maintain tradition; it is the cornerstone of the tournament," he said with conviction. The speech was beautiful and actually kept my attention, which is hard to do. But I couldn't keep from looking around and seeing the dimly lit pictures of Bobby Jones and the 13th hole that filled the room. It dawned on me that this was Augusta National, home of the Masters, and that this was a big deal. At moments like these, when I'm truly moved, I do stupid things. I think I do them because it relieves tension. I waited until Hardin had made his closing remarks, and then abruptly stood up and asked him if he thought the clown outfit I had planned to wear on Saturday was out of the question. Frank immediately put his head in his hands, and Jim started to whistle.

Hardin looked at Frank, who was not about to look up, and then addressed me. "Probably not a good idea," he said. "Darn, I'm gonna lose the deposit," I said with my Panama hat pulled down over my eyes. It was a retort that would have made Bill Murray proud.

As Hardin closed the aging oak door of his office behind us, Frank reached up, grabbed the back of my neck, and applied a pressure hold that would have choked a Burmese python. "Don't you ever just shut up and listen, you moron?" he asked. I couldn't respond because of the restriction of air in my esophagus, but Jim was faintly heard to say, "Maybe this is a bad idea bringing him here." Frank affirmed the notion with more pressure on my neck.

And, as they say, the rest is history. Which is what my very colorful commentary has become with the Masters tournament officials — history!

Chapter 18

Golf Online

· ·

· ·

*Y*ou'd be amazed at the wonderful things you can see without leaving your lounge chair. You can travel to exotic locales, buy *...For Dummies* books, sell stocks, and, yes, go golfing! It's time to surf the Net.

Some Stuff You Need to Know

Navigating the Internet requires three things:

✔ An account with an Internet service provider (ISP), such as MindSpring, or an online service, such as AOL

✔ Communications hardware, which ranges from a traditional phone-line modem to a blazing-fast cable modem or a Digital Subscriber Line (DSL)

✔ A Web browser, such as Internet Explorer or Netscape Navigator

But today I'm not interested in all the technobabble and cybergyrations it takes to get online. That's a topic for a nerdier day. If you're really interested, refer to *The Internet For Dummies,* by John Levine, Carol Baroudi, and Margy Levine Young (IDG Books Worldwide, Inc.). In the meantime, get out your hat with the propeller.

I'm going to explore some of the great golfing wonders that the information superhighway has to offer. As you can see in Figure 18-1, *Yahoo!* is a great place to start. This online index contains golf-related sights on the World Wide Web. For your convenience, I've broken down Yahoo! into three main categories:

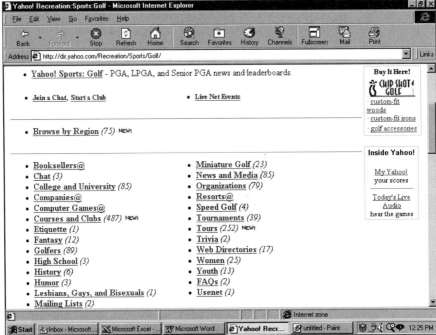

Figure 18-1:
Yahoo!
Golfing in
cyberspace.

✔ Cool cyber golf hangouts

✔ Cyber courses

✔ Virtual pro shops

I introduce you to some of my favorite golf hangouts on the information superhighway. I explore everything that cyberspace has to offer, from articles to tips to "Extreme Golf." I also journey through the land of virtual golf courses. Believe it or not, you can "see" thousands of golf courses from around the world without leaving the comfort of your own chair. Finally, I take a quick look at some of the cool golf products you can buy at various virtual pro shops.

Cool Cyber Golf Hangouts

The World Wide Web offers thousands of golf-related sites. If you surf the Net aimlessly, you'll drown in the cyber whitewash. Here's a quick look at some of my favorite cyber golf hangouts. Together, these sites offer 99 percent of what you need on the information superhighway. You can thank me later.

GOLFonline — www.golfonline.com

If you're familiar with the iGOLF Web site, you'll be glad to know that it did not drop off the face of the cyberplanet. iGOLF merely merged with GOLFonline to produce an even cooler hangout on the Web. Many of the features you loved on iGOLF are still there — check out the former home page of iGOLF (`www.igolf.com`) for a quick rundown of new locations for old favorites.

GOLFonline is an example of an interactive magazine. This online phenomenon combines the interactive nature of networking with the informational content of a golf magazine (see Figure 18-2). GOLFonline includes original, up-to-date editorial information from well-known golf writers and personalities, including David Feherty (fellow CBS golf commentator), Thomas Bonk *(The Los Angeles Times),* and Curtis Strange (*GOLF Magazine* playing editor). GOLFonline is all about insight and interactivity on subjects ranging from tournaments and travel to equipment and instruction, all presented by using the best text and multimedia capabilities available. It's one of the best resources I've seen at the intersection of two of society's most popular bodies: golfers and online users.

Figure 18-2: The GOLFonline home page.

CBS Sportsline's GolfWeb — www.golfweb.com

GolfWeb is the Internet's premier golfing Web site. A subsidiary of SportsLineUSA and accessible through a direct link from CBS Sportsline (www.cbssportsline.com), GolfWeb provides complete Web coverage for golf fans everywhere. It offers something for everyone with an interest in golf — from the latest professional tournament scores to extensive course information to an online pro shop.

As you can see in Figure 18-3, GolfWeb is organized into several different sections for quick and easy access to information. A few of the major sections are What's New, Golf Action (all the latest results and statistics from golf tours around the world), Course Guide (a complete interactive course database), ProShop, Library (where I hope you'll see this book someday), and Classifieds (where people can advertise and buy golf equipment). GolfWeb is probably one of the most professional and well-maintained cyber golf sites on the information superhighway.

Figure 18-3:
The GolfWeb home page.

ESPN — espn.go.com/golf

What list of golf-related Web sites would be complete without something from our friends at ESPN? Check out schedules, statistics, and player rankings for the PGA, LPGA, Senior PGA, Nike Tour, and European tours, along with the day's top golf headlines. And if that's not enough to keep you occupied, additional features, including cool contests and weekly columns, make this golf site one of the hottest on the Web. (See Figure 18-4.)

CNN/Sports Illustrated — www.cnnsi.com/golf

Get inside golf with combined coverage from two of the media's heaviest hitters. CNN and *Sports Illustrated* bring you the top news stories, tournament schedules, leader boards, statistics, and player information, all updated daily. Beyond being a great sports news site, CNN/SI makes its editorial staff and even pro golfers available to address your questions and comments. You can e-mail one of the daily columnists, find your Q&A posted on the site, and even have your swing-technique questions answered by a tour professional on a CNN television program. There's plenty to see on this informative site (see Figure 18-5).

Figure 18-4: ESPN's golf site.

Figure 18-5:
CNN and
*Sports
Illustrated*
come
together to
bring you
great golf
coverage.

The Golf Channel Online — www.thegolfchannel.com

From the only television network devoted to golf 24 hours a day comes this well-organized, interactive Web site (see Figure 18-6). Check live leader boards, get domestic and international tour information, find the latest stats, and read up-to-date news features from Golf Channel columnists. The site also features the only interactive instructional show of its kind, where each week a PGA teaching professional gives you live help with your game. You can also e-mail your questions and opinions to the staff during some of their live television shows to get instant professional advice. With these great free features, there's almost no need to pay for lessons!

PGA of America — www.pga.com

Millions of cybersurfers can't be wrong. With "the world's best real-time golf event scoring system," www.pga.com is the place to be during the big tours (if you can't be in the gallery or on the fairway, that is). The official site of the Professional Golfer's Association of America features the latest golf headlines and industry news, as well as current tour schedules and standings. Plan a golf vacation, enter to win cool golf stuff, or check out additional PGA-recommended golf links.

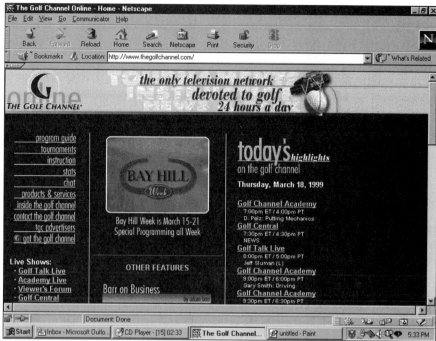

Figure 18-6:
The Golf
Channel
online.

One feature of this site that sets it apart from the others is the Cool Kids page
(see Figure 18-7). There, you can find tips not only for kid golfers, but also for
parents and junior golf leaders. You can also locate a PGA instructor near you
and get a few free pointers while your little darlings learn from the pros.

Golf.com

One of the best golf sites on the World Wide Web is www.golf.com, the
cyber launching pad for NBC Sports' Golf tour site, Total Sports, and Golf
Digest online (see Figure 18-8). There's a great mix of information on this
site, which features excellent coverage of golf travel destinations, tour
commentary, and the latest equipment, as well as audio files from cybercast
interviews. You can also find classifieds, a pro shop, and tips specifically for
women and kids.

But probably the most impressive online resources are tournament coverage and player profiles. At the click of a button, you can find out more than
you ever wanted to know about any professional tour and the players who
populate it. You can get weekly updates and detailed player profiles. You can
even get inside the heads of some of today's golfing legends, including Jack
Nicklaus, Arnold Palmer, and Greg Norman.

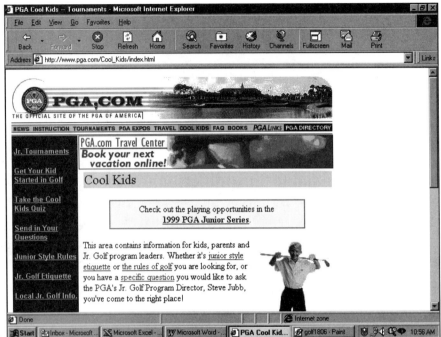

Figure 18-7:
The Cool
Kids page
on the
PGA site.

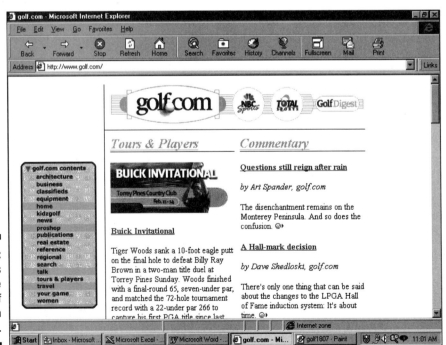

Figure 18-8:
Golf.com is
one of the
best golf
sites on
the Web.

Golf Digest — www.golfdigest.com

Golf Digest, one of the premier golf magazines on the shelves and on the Web, is chock full of great commentary, interesting stories, and professional instruction. You can also find an equipment hotline, get information about *Golf Digest's* golf schools, and browse through back issues of the magazine. (See Figure 18-9.)

World Golf — www.worldgolf.com

Anytime I feel like exploring the "world" of golf, I tootle on over to World Golf. This site is an online international golf and travel guide. It includes numerous hot links that enable you to bounce easily from one area of the golfing world to another. You can make reservations at St. Andrews in Scotland and then view pictures of desert courses in Palm Springs. World Golf is easy to maneuver and provides a variety of departments, as shown in Figure 18-10.

If you've had a bad day at the golf course, check out the collection of golf jokes and laugh at the misfortunes of others playing this sometimes-cruel sport. Or take a moment to check out tips from the pros, ask them a question or two in the Q&A area, or just soak up the history of the game.

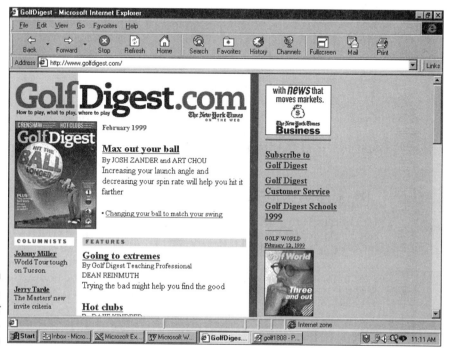

Figure 18-9:
Golf Digest
online.

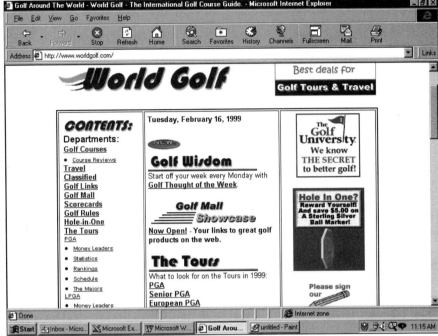

One of my favorite sections on this site is "Links Around the World" (which you get to by clicking Golf Links on the left side of the page). You never know when you might need to know about a golf course in the Czech Republic!

The Virtual Golfer — www.golfball.com

A hole should always give one the impression that it owes its existence to its own intrinsic merits, to its individuality and character, and not as too often happens, to the fact that it had to be there because forsooth there was no other place to put it. —Darden G. Smith, *The World of Golf* (1898)

Been looking all over for that cigar holder and divot tool all in one? Search no more! For all your golfing needs, `www.golfball.com` is the place to start! (see Figure 18-11). Like most other sites, there's coverage of the tours, an online magazine, tips for improving your game at the practice tee, and directories of hot golf travel destinations. But there's also an interactive golf clubhouse where cyber golfers can hang out and exchange their thoughts on the game, not to mention a pro shop where you really can buy that cigar holder! Check out this site; the Virtual Golfer is a cool place to hang out.

Figure 18-11:
The Virtual
Golfer home
page.

Cyber Courses

Are you having fun yet? Sure you are. As you can see, a whole new virtual world is out there, just waiting to be discovered. Don't be shy. Now it's time for cyber courses.

If you don't have enough time or credit cards to play all the great courses in the world, don't fret. The information superhighway can take you to them for free. Various sites on the World Wide Web include descriptions, layouts, and scorecards for thousands of golf courses around the world. From the comfort of your own desk chair, you can explore championship layouts from Alabama to Zimbabwe.

For example, Figure 18-12 shows the home page for golf's oldest and greatest course: The Old Course at St Andrews, Scotland (www.standrews.org.uk). From this site, you can view historical information about the course, make hotel and tee time reservations, and even play a virtual round. Similar pages cover other famous golf courses and resorts, including Pebble Beach (www.pebble-beach.com), PGA West (www.pgawest.com), and Pinehurst No. 2 (www.pinehurstresort.com).

Thousands of Web sites spout information about golf courses. I can't possibly name them all, so here are a few of my favorites to give you a taste of what's out there.

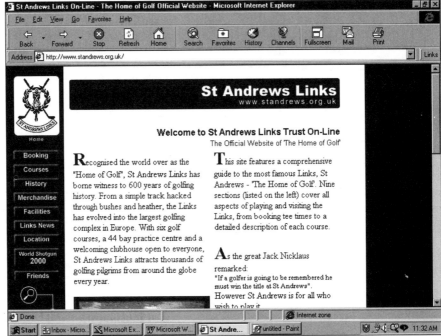

Figure 18-12:
The Web
site for the
Old Course
at St.
Andrews,
Scotland.

features.yahoo.com/golfcourses

This handy site provides extensive lists of U.S. golf courses categorized by state and then by city. You can read a review of a course, get the weather report, green fees, and course data, and even hook into a Web directory that provides local news, entertainment, and shopping information about the destination of your choice.

www.globalgolf.com

If you always wanted to tee it up in Thailand, slice in Spain, or putt in Portugal, this site can make your dreams come true. Explore courses from ten countries with in-depth descriptions, pictures, maps, and course cards. You can also book tee times, find accommodations, access tour operators, visit an online pro shop, and even learn a bit of history about each area, all on one Web site. (See Figure 18-13.)

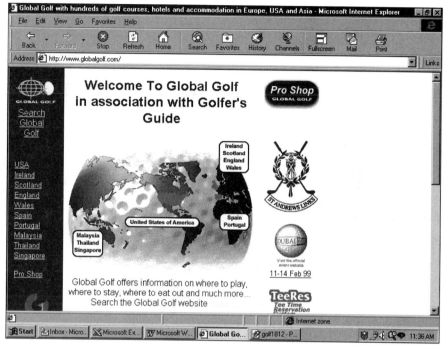

Figure 18-13:
Global Golf
lets you
tour
courses
in ten
countries.

www.golfuniverse.com

Golf Universe boasts the world's largest golf course database, and with 24,000 course listings, it very well may be. But never fear: You can search by course name, keyword (city, region, and so on), or world map, so it's easy to find what you need, even if you don't quite know what you're looking for. Information listed for each course varies; some descriptions tell only the address, phone number, and number of holes, and others give yardage, par, cart fees, user reviews, and so on.

Beyond its course listings, Golf Universe (shown in Figure 18-14) features golf tips, classified ads, news, rules, online golf games, and its very own chat room. You're bound to find something useful on this site!

www.teeitup.com

Getting tee times just got a lot easier. As you can see in Figure 18-15, the information superhighway has an online golf reservation system called Fore! Reservations, Inc. This global reservation system provides you with direct access to thousands of courses at the click of a button. Simply choose a region from the world map, and a list of available courses appears. Double-click the course you're interested in, and — voilà! — you're there. I can almost smell the fresh-cut grass.

Figure 18-14:
Golf
Universe.com
includes
a handy
course
database.

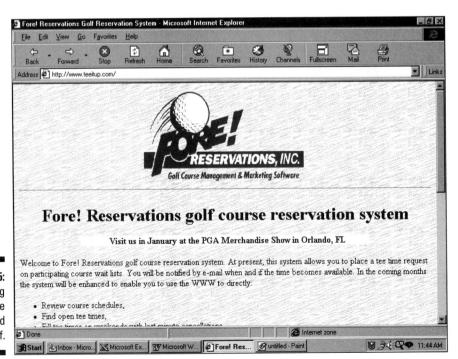

Figure 18-15:
Reserving
your place
in the world
of golf.

Play Golf Now — www.playgolfnow.com

For an annual fee of $59.95, membership to Play Golf Now (see Figure 18-16) gives you 50 percent off ball fees at participating ranges and significant discounts at 2,000 golf facilities, 120 world-renowned golf resorts, and 2,100 hotels, inns, and resorts around the world. Membership also gets you discounts from car rental companies, discounts at the United States School of Golf, and a monthly newsletter. The Web site features a golf course and driving range locator, a hotel and resort directory, and golf news. The company plans to expand its online content and product offerings to make the site bigger and better, so keep checking in with these folks. What are you waiting for? Play Golf Now!

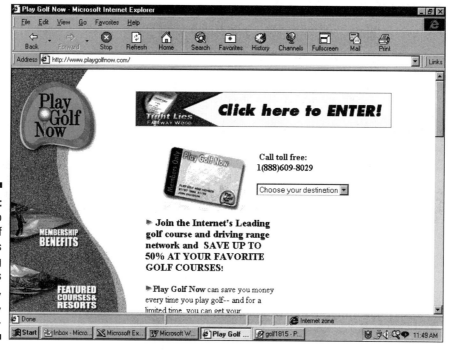

Figure 18-16:
Membership in Play Golf Now gets you big discounts at ranges, courses, and resorts.

Virtual Pro Shops

I couldn't let you get away from my tour of the information superhighway without trying to sell you something. In addition to golfing hangouts and virtual courses, cyberspace offers a plethora of great pro shops selling golf-related products. Every major manufacturer (and even some unusual minor ones) has a presence on the World Wide Web, and many of the cyber hangouts listed earlier in this chapter offer links to their own pro shops (Golf.com, GOLFonline, and GolfWeb, to name a few). The sites mentioned in this section specialize in bringing you discounted prices on brand-name products.

www.golfdiscount.com

For more than 20 years, GolfDiscount.com has helped golfers around the world purchase equipment at incredibly low prices. It even has an entire page dedicated to loyal customer feedback! With great prices on top brands like Callaway, PING, Top-Flite, and Mizuno and an online golf expert for recommendations, questions, or prices, GolfDiscount.com is hard to beat. The site also includes links to the Web sites of every manufacturer it carries.

www.mammothgolf.com

Calling itself the golf superstore to the world, Mammoth Golf offers a great selection of brand names at competitive prices. The site features equipment and accessories for men, women, seniors, and juniors and offers a 5 to 10 percent discount on select items with payment of an annual $19.95 membership fee. Mammoth Golf also has a club repair and reshafting service with guaranteed two-week delivery.

www.nevadabobs.com

With stores located in 37 states and 18 countries, Nevada Bob's is the world's largest specialty retailer of golf equipment. The site offers leading golf equipment brands plus products designed by major vendors exclusively for Nevada Bob's. Shop online, use the toll-free customer service number, or try the store locator — chances are there's a Nevada Bob's store near you!

www.chipshot.com

At chipshot.com, you can find not only great low prices on brand-name equipment but also advice and gift ideas specifically tailored for beginners, juniors, men, and women. PGA professional Grant Barnes offers a new tip each day, and every two weeks he and Tad Hanich post a different lesson. Buy your clubs and improve your game, all on this one-stop-shopping site!

www.golfbids.com

For an alternative to virtual pro shops, try golfbids.com, where live golf auctions are in progress at this very moment. Bid the highest, and your selected product will be shipped to you within 14 days. The site also features up-to-the-minute golf news (provided by FOX Sports), travel packages, and an online pro shop. Do I hear a bargain calling?

Planet Golf — www.planetgolf.com

A few years ago, Planet Golf was founded on the notion that golfers don't have to wear "golf" clothing. The site sells hip links apparel and sportswear for frustrated golf dudes and dudettes surfing the Web. Heck, it sure beats knickers.

Just for Fun

You can *play* golf on your computer, too. Electronic golf simulators have gotten so good that they're almost as much fun as the real thing — and you can play Pebble Beach all by yourself in 45 minutes for free. This is sounding better and better all the time. Many great golf simulators are available, but I've narrowed them down to the top three (just for you, because I care):

- ✔ *Microsoft Golf* from Microsoft and Access Software
- ✔ *Links386* from Access Software
- ✔ *PGA Tour '99* from EA Sports

As you can see in Figure 18-17, the realism is remarkable. In this example, I'm playing the picturesque 7th hole at Pebble Beach. Can't you just smell the salt water? Can't you just feel the breeze in your hair? Some of these golf simulators are so good that you'll never get any work done. But that's okay — after all, that's what golf is for!

Congratulations! You survived this rollercoaster ride through the wacky world of cyber golf. Whew, that was a lot of nerdy information all in one day — does your head hurt? If so, take off your propeller. It's okay; I'm done for now.

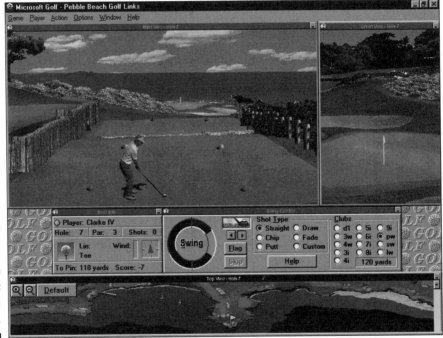

Figure 18-17:
Enjoying a round of CyberGOLF at Pebble Beach.

Part VI
The Part of Tens

The 5th Wave   By Rich Tennant

@RICHTENNANT

I'm watching The Jerry Springer Golf Tournament. The leader just shoved his opponent's face in a sand trap for cheating on the last hole, and the 3rd place player's caddie is about to reveal to him that he's secretly been caddying behind his back for the 4th place player.

In this part . . .

This is my favorite section of the book. I give you ten timeless tips so that you can avoid the common faults I see repeated on golf courses all over the world. I tell you about some of my favorite golf courses, some of my favorite public golf courses, and who I think are the best male and female players of all time. I even give you my ten top golf disaster stories.

This "Part of Tens" section was my therapy. I needed to write this stuff to keep my sanity. I hope you enjoy this section and remember: In golf, we all speak the same language — utterances of the insane!

Chapter 19
Ten Timeless Golf Tips

*H*aving been around golf for a while, I've noticed certain bad habits that my friends constantly repeat on the golf course. Just knowing not to repeat these habits will help the average player live a long and peaceful life on the links.

I've racked my feeble brain and jotted down ten tips so that you won't repeat these common faults that I see repeated on golf courses all over the world.

Take Enough Club to Get to Your Target

I am constantly playing with amateurs who consistently come up short for their approach shots to the green. For whatever reason, they always choose a club that — even if they were to hit the most solid shot they've ever hit — would get their shot only to the front of the green. Take a club that you can swing at 80 percent and still get to the hole. Conserve your energy; you have a long life ahead of you!

If You Can Putt the Ball, Do It

Don't always use a lofted club around the greens. I've got a friend at home called "flop-shot Fred" who is always playing high sand wedge shots around the green, regardless of what the shot calls for. I think his idol is Phil Mickelson, who can hit these shots straight up in the air. Leave this kind of shot to guys like Phil who can handle them. My best advice is to use a club that can hit this shot with the lowest trajectory possible. If you can putt the ball, do it.

Keep Your Head Fairly Steady

You're going to move your head a little during the swing, especially with the longer clubs. But try not to move your head in excess. Moving your head too much leads to all sorts of serious swing flaws that make this game very difficult to play. Have someone watch you to see whether you move your head, or watch yourself in the mirror while you take practice swings.

Keep Your Sense of Humor

If everything else fails, you can keep your sense of humor and still survive, or at least die laughing.

Bet Only What You Can Afford to Lose

You can cause some serious problems among friends by betting for more money than you have. Never bet on your golf game what you can't afford to lose. My theory was to bet everything in my pocket except for $10, and that was to pay for the gas home.

Keep the Ball Low in the Wind

When the wind starts to kick up, I see golfers play their normal shots and fail to hit the ball lower to allow for the conditions. Play the ball back in your stance, put your hands ahead of the ball, and keep them ahead when you make contact. Keep the ball as low as you can, and you can manage your game much more efficiently. You probably won't lose as many golf balls, either.

Take Some Golf Lessons

If you really want to have fun playing this game, start off with a few lessons to get you on the right track and, of course, read this book in its entirety. It's amazing what you can do with a clear concept in your mind of how to make a golf swing.

Do Not Give Lessons to Your Spouse

Giving golf lessons to your spouse can be a federal offense. Don't do it! Doing so can only lead to disaster. Invest some money in lessons. Get good instruction and reap the benefits (peace of mind).

Always Tee It Up at the Tee Boxes

Whenever it's legal (in the teeing area), tee the ball up. This game is more fun when the ball's in the air.

Never Blame Yourself for a Bad Shot

Give yourself a break. This game is hard enough without blaming everything on yourself. Find creative ways to blame something else. I like to blame my bad shots on the magnetic force field from alien spacecraft. Let your mind go and see how crazy your excuses can be. Save your sanity!

Chapter 20

Gary's Ten Favorite Courses

● ●

In This Chapter

▶ Pebble Beach

▶ Pine Valley

▶ Cypress Point

▶ Shinnecock Hills

▶ Pinehurst No. 2

▶ Royal Melbourne

▶ Harbour Town Links

▶ San Francisco Golf Club

▶ Long Cove Golf Club

▶ San Luis Rey Downs

● ●

The longer you play golf, the more golf courses you visit. Some courses are along the ocean, and others are in the desert. Many courses have trees that frame your every shot. Other golf courses are devoid of trees, but the horizon is ongoing.

Some golf courses are fastened onto flat land, and others are borne onto the hills and valleys of rural America. Limitless features attach themselves to each golf course. You'll notice vast differences that make each golf course a separate journey. One of the reasons this game is so much fun is that the playing field is always changing.

Many golf architects have put their fingerprints on the map of American golf courses. These architects incorporate different design philosophies, which keep the look of every golf course different. Robert Trent Jones incorporates large, undulating greens with enormous bunkers guarding the landing areas. Pete Dye uses railroad ties to reinforce the greens, giving his courses the "Dye" look. Jack Nicklaus uses wildly undulating greens and expansive fairways as his trademark. You can see a variety of golf courses in your golfing life.

I based my choices of the all-time great golf courses on their challenge and beauty. One of the courses, Royal Melbourne, I haven't even played. Greg Norman told me that this course is in his top three, so who am I to argue? San Luis Rey Downs was my stomping ground when I was an adolescent and in discovery. My friends play at this course.

These courses are my favorites. Most of the courses listed are private, and an act of Congress would not get you through the gates. (I list my favorite public courses in Chapter 21.) The great thing about being a professional on tour is that after a well-placed phone call, you can usually get access to these courses. Four of the golf courses on my list have public access: Pinehurst No. 2, Pebble Beach, Harbour Town, and San Luis Rey Downs. The rest, the Pope would have a tough time getting on — unless, of course, he promised them a ride in the Popemobile.

Pebble Beach — Monterey, California

Pebble Beach is an extraordinary place to do anything. Golf has made Pebble Beach popular, and the land has made it legendary. Robert Louis Stevenson called this stretch of land "the greatest meeting of land and sea in the world." Pebble Beach is truly one of the most beautiful spots on earth, and it's blessed with two of my favorite courses in the world, Pebble Beach and Cypress Point.

Pebble Beach Golf Course is one I've been playing since age 15. We used to play the California state amateur on these storied links. We would get ten guys and rent a motel room. We based the sleeping arrangements on how well we played that day. Low round would get his pick of the two beds. High round would get the other bed — we figured he needed some sleep with all the swinging he did that day. Everybody else grabbed some floor. Those were the fun days, when golf was a twinkle in your eye, and innocence made the game appear easy.

Pine Valley — Clementon, New Jersey

Pine Valley is the greatest course without an ocean view. If you have a week to hang with your friends and play golf, Pine Valley is the place. The grounds are spectacular. Cottages house the overnight guests, a great dining room is full of old golf memorabilia, and the walls are saturated with tall tales of Pine Valley's golf history.

The course is one of the great designs in the world. You measure a course by how many holes you can remember after playing one round on it. This golf course is etched in your mind, every hole, every tree, and every bunker. I'm in total fascination when I walk through Pine Valley's corridor of perfectly maintained grass. This course is a place that breathes with exuberance.

Cypress Point — Monterey, California

Cypress Point is a golf course of such beauty and solitude, you think that it has holy qualities. From the quaint pro shop to the confining locker room and dusty rooms that perch atop the clubhouse, Cypress Point is the place for your final round.

This golf course winds from the pines into the sand dunes. Deer are everywhere, often dodging your errant tee shots. The turbulent Pacific can be seen on a few holes going out and then again on most of the back nine, including the famous 16th. This hole has to be seen to be believed.

I'll never forget Cypress Point, which was the site of my first tournament in 1974. I birdied seven holes in a row (holes 7 through 13) and posted an opening round of 65. My career tapered off after my initial explosion.

Shinnecock Hills — Southampton, Long Island, New York

America's premier links golf course, Shinnecock Hills is an American treasure. At this course, you play the game as it was designed to be played — along the ground when the wind blows.

From the porch of America's oldest clubhouse, out to the Atlantic Ocean, Shinnecock Hills is an American-bred beauty. Wind and golf course are meshed into your being as you stroll through this artwork.

Pinehurst No. 2 — Pinehurst, North Carolina

Pinehurst No. 2 is a masterpiece of design and host to the 1999 U.S. Open. Hidden in the pines of Pinehurst, this golf course combines every facet of the game. Pinehurst has some of the best-designed greens in the world.

This entire complex at Pinehurst takes you back half a century with its rustic, southern motif. Golf courses are everywhere, and golf is the central theme of the town.

We used to play a tour event at Pinehurst No. 2 every year, and we would get into a golf frenzy weeks before our arrival. Pinehurst No. 2 is a great golf course to be revered and enjoyed.

Royal Melbourne — Melbourne, Australia

My information about Royal Melbourne comes from the Aussies I know on tour. Greg Norman and Steve Elkington rave about the greens, which are supposed to be some of the fastest in the world. The tournament course is made up of 18 holes out of the 36 they have on site. Large eucalyptus trees stand sentinel over this site.

Harbour Town Links — Hilton Head Island, South Carolina

An intensely beautiful and intriguing golf course, Harbour Town is set in the old oaks and then flirts with the Calibouge Sound for the finishing holes. Harbour Town is great spot to vacation and enjoy world-class golf.

We play the Heritage Classic, which was first played in 1969, over this golf course. Harbour Town meanders through the pines and is extremely tight for driving your golf ball. This course has some of the smallest greens on tour, which drives the pros mad trying to figure out which club to hit to these elusive surfaces.

My memories of this golf course are many. One of the strangest was back in the '80s when Bill Mallon — who was on the tour then; he is now a doctor — and I were the first guys off the tee on Sunday's round in the tournament. We weren't playing that well so we decided we'd try to see how fast we could play the round. I was the last to putt on the 18th and holed a 6-footer for 75, which tied Bill, in the time of 1 hour, 37 minutes, and 15 seconds. We finished the 18th hole when the group behind us was walking down the 9th fairway — and they say we play slow on the PGA Tour!

San Francisco Golf Club — San Francisco, California

San Francisco Golf Club is one of the great golf courses that no one has heard about. Perched on a hill overlooking the storied Olympic Club, this golf course is right out of San Francisco's past. The clubhouse is ancient, and when you walk into the locker room, musty is a word that comes to mind. The lockers have that old wire mesh on the front of them that reminds you of the grill on a 1947 Oldsmobile.

The golf course winds throughout the hills and valleys and confronts many stately old trees that have seen San Francisco's past. A monument by the par-3 seventh marks the last legal duel in California's history. That par-3 is a tough shot!

I remember one Sunday that two of us were going to be fortunate enough to play this great track. We showed up on a gorgeous day at 10:30 a.m. The pro shop was closed, and nobody was around. We finally found caddies and inquired where everybody was this time of day. "The 49ers are in town, and this is a ghost town." We played and never saw a single soul the whole day.

Long Cove Golf Club — Hilton Head Island, South Carolina

Long Cove Golf Club is a great course that I get to play when we go to Hilton Head Island to broadcast the Heritage Classic for CBS. A wonderful blend of water and trees that soothe and scare you at the same time, this golf course will kick your rear end if you're not playing well — but it does so in a dignified manner.

There's something so relaxing about this place that I slow down when I pass through the gates. Plenty of large yachts and alligators keep your interest as you wander through this Pete Dye masterpiece.

If you're ever lucky enough to be invited to this frolic in the forest, cast your eyes toward the water off the 17th tee. If you squint hard enough, you may be able to see the iron that I threw in the lake — it's sitting on the bottom along with my golf ball. I never could hit the green with that 1-iron. Let it rest.

San Luis Rey Downs — Bonsall, California

San Luis Rey Downs is not the prettiest golf course in the world. It's not the best maintained, either. But it is the place where I sharpened my clubs and my wit for the PGA Tour. San Luis Rey Downs was full of scoundrels who would make any kind of bet, as long as they had the edge. Jimmy the Greek would have loved this place.

San Luis Rey Downs sits in a river bottom that fills up whenever California has one of its infrequent wet spells. The bar is a melting pot of horse owners, trainers, and jockeys from the thoroughbred training facility located across the street. Mix them with public-fee golfers, and you get a rodeo of fun.

This course is the place where I plagiarized most of my weird TV lines. Everybody had a nickname, and a few golfers had served time. San Luis Rey Downs was a place where my friends were, and I enjoyed every minute of their company. After you play this game enough, you learn that you can play the best-looking, most immaculately conditioned golf course in the world, but if you don't enjoy the company, the course's condition matters not. I enjoy San Luis Rey Downs.

Chapter 21
Gary's Ten Favorite Public Courses

. . . .

In This Chapter
▶ Alvamar Golf Course

▶ Bethpage State Park Golf Course

▶ Blackwolf Run (River Course)

▶ Cog Hill No. 4

▶ Grayhawk Golf Club (Talon and Raptor)

▶ The Homestead (Cascades Course)

▶ Pinon Hills Golf Course

▶ Torrey Pines Golf Course

▶ TPC at Sawgrass

▶ Whispering Springs

. . . .

Alvamar Golf Course — Lawrence, Kansas

I won the Kansas Open at Alvamar Golf Course when I was a mere lad, and I remember this course as one of the finest conditioned golf courses I had ever seen in my life. The course is set on rolling hills, and my putter was on fire. I really like places where I have won because they are few and far between.

Go to Kansas and look up this course. My name should be on something at the course; tell the employees that I sent you. I don't believe you'll regret your trek.

Bethpage State Park Golf Course — Long Island, New York

Bethpage State Park Golf Course is the best state park golf course in the United States. The course is a treat to play — it's a real challenge, and the greens fees won't bust your credit line. Rumblings always say that this place could hold a golf event of major proportions. Only time and a little money will tell.

This municipal layout has a wonderful design that catches the attention of well-seasoned players and offers novices a place to grow and learn the game.

Blackwolf Run (River Course) — Kohler, Wisconsin

I got to do a corporate outing at Blackwolf Run in 1995. At first, I wondered where in the world was Kohler, Wisconsin, and what kind of golf course would be out there in the sticks. Well, let me tell you this outing was one of the greatest experiences I've had playing golf. This Pete Dye gem is located on one of the finest pieces of property I've ever seen and hosted the 1998 U.S. Women's Open. A ridge runs throughout the course, and holes are located high on the ridge and down in the valley. A river runs through much of the course and from the back tees you can hear it growl.

I remember going to the back tee on No. 1 when the starter asked whether I was sure that I wanted to play from those tees. "I have my name on my bag," I said. He told me that my bag lacked all the clubs I would need to finish the round. He was just about right — I broke the course record by one shot. I shot a 70. Now that's a hard course.

The next time I get near that area, one hour north of Milwaukee, I'm going to grab my sticks and head to Kohler to enjoy this fine facility again.

Cog Hill No. 4 — Lemont, Illinois

Cog Hill is one of the great golf complexes in the United States. The Western Open is played at this course. The tour pros flock to this place with nothing but nice things to say, which is a rarity on the PGA Tour nowadays.

Cog Hill has a great layout and can host a major event without doing much to the course. If you want to really find out how your game is, show up and go to the back trees. Bring along some provisions — you're going to be a while. They don't call it Dub's Dread for nothing.

Grayhawk Golf Club (Talon and Raptor) — Scottsdale, Arizona

This brand new facility opened in 1995. Located up in the higher desert of north Scottsdale, this beautiful public facility has it all: a great clubhouse, two championship golf courses, a great practice facility, and me. That's right: Peter Kostis and I have a golf school at Grayhawk Golf Course. Phil Mickelson and Howard Twitty also represent the facility on tour. You can see why I'm a little prejudiced about our place.

The service at this place has to be seen to be believed. You'll be treated like you just won the Masters. The golf course is also superb. Phoenix and the McDowell Mountains make for a spectacular setting.

If you ever get out to Phoenix, come up the hill and join us at Grayhawk for fun in the sun. You never know, Phil Mickelson might be around, and we can get him to buy us a beer!

The Homestead (Cascades Course) — Hot Springs, Virginia

The Homestead is one of the most peaceful settings you will ever behold. This old golf facility — the first course was built in 1892 — has a certain civility about it. Grandeur is everywhere, and the course is fantastic. Settle in and enjoy the lifestyle.

I recommend seeing this beauty in October or early November for the unbelievable scenery. Take a few friends with you and spend at least three or four days at this facility.

Pinon Hills Golf Course — Farmington, New Mexico

Finding Farmington, New Mexico, takes some doing, but once there, you'll see the outstanding Pinon Hills Golf Course laid out in the high mesas of New Mexico. The views from anywhere on the course are spectacular.

This course is probably the best bargain on earth. The last report we got of the greens fee was $13 on the weekend, and you can walk anytime. Getting those rates is almost impossible today. So grab a friend and get up to Farmington; they're waiting for you, and you don't need a lot of pesos to have fun.

Torrey Pines Golf Course — San Diego, California

Torrey Pines Golf Course is the site of the San Diego Open. A great public golf course, Torrey is well maintained and offers a challenge for the golfer. Torrey has many long and demanding holes that are tougher than the winds kicked up by the Pacific Ocean.

You can see the ocean throughout the course, and you get a really good look as you walk along the cliff on No. 4. Hang gliders and ultralights fill the sky. During the right time of the year, you can see whales migrating to Mexico. You have to do a lot to concentrate on the golf at Torrey.

The city of San Diego has a real gem in Torrey Pines Golf Course. Pick the right time of the year, and you can enjoy the golf and sunshine.

Tournament Players Course (TPC) at Sawgrass — Ponte Vedra, Florida

Our flagship TPC (Tournament Players Course) golf course is a beauty. Pete Dye conjured up this course from his cauldron. Carved out of the trees and swamps in north Florida (near Jacksonville), this course plays host to one of the biggest tournaments of the year on the PGA Tour — The Players Championship. This event has the best field of any tournament we play on tour, and the golf course provides a wonderful challenge.

I remember that when I first saw this place, I couldn't believe the difficulty of the golf course. I went home to San Luis Rey Downs and told the boys about the fright that possessed me on every hole. Through the years, the staff has made many refinements to the course, and in 1995, Greg Norman shot 24 under par to clobber the field. So the course can be had, and if you get a chance to play it, you will be had, too. TPC is a marvelous facility. You can watch for yourself when the best players in the world are at the course at the end of March every year.

Whispering Springs —
Fond du Lac, Wisconsin

Believe it or not, Wisconsin offers up some pretty spectacular and challenging golf courses. One in particular is the 18-hole course at Whispering Springs. This is one the most beautiful courses in the Midwest and a good deal at less than $30 per person. You can choose to walk the course for some great exercise and fresh air, or for a few bucks more take the golf cart route.

Once the spring hits the Midwest and the ground begins to thaw, golfers come out of the woodwork to enjoy the great outdoors, the lush greenery, and the (mostly) agreeable temperatures. However, for those die-hard golfers who can't wait for warmer temperatures, Whispering Springs offers early-season rates from the time it opens — with Mother Nature's blessing — through the middle of May, as well as late-season rates until just after Labor Day.

Public golf goes big time

Good news: The largest area of growth in golf over the past few years has been in public, not private, courses. Lots of those courses come to you courtesy of your state, county, or city government — proof that your tax dollars are hard at work. Actually, golf courses are usually a big source of revenue, which is part of the reason governments are building more of them.

The courses are also better built. Forget the image you had of worn and tattered municipal links. Chances are, a quality public course offering bargain rates is within an easy drive from your home. Fees are low, and most facilities offer a range of amenities from clubhouses to carts (not that you'd want to use a cart, would you?).

Public golf isn't just for homebodies, either. If you're interested in traveling the U.S., you can plan a fun, inexpensive vacation by touring the courses at the country's best open-to-everyone facilities. One good example is the Robert Trent Jones Trail in Alabama. Built by — guess who — Robert Trent Jones, that grandmaster of greens design, this string of courses offers the same brilliant planning and layout features of Jones's most famous sites.

The courses run the length of the state and among them offer classic 54-hole spreads as well as a selection of par-3 courses for individuals looking for the chance to develop their skills on a course that offers real character. Each course is different and reflects the distinctive topography of its location. And each course charges between $29 and $49. How's that for a deal too good for a cash-conscious golf traveler to pass up?

Great-value public courses throughout the country offer charm and challenge to spare — and I'm not just talking about my favorite courses. Maybe you'll discover one or two favorites of your own.

To find out more about public courses across America and in your own hometown, check out Chapter 18. You'll find Web sites with descriptions, details, directions, and more.

Chapter 22

Gary's Top Ten All-Time Favorite Male Players

*T*hose individuals who play the game of golf at a different volume are meant to be heard. The golf course turns into their canvas as they display a certain panache in going about their work. To watch people of this caliber is to gaze upon the brightest of stars. They play the game as it was meant to be played. I have played with some of them and have heard stories about the others. They all wrote their own scripts and have set themselves apart from the norm. They got game.

Seve Ballesteros

This Spaniard has a flair for playing golf that is contagious to watch. He pounces on the course like a fighter who has his opponent on the ropes. His mastery of the short game and the imagination that it entails is a sight to behold. He plays the game with pride and intensity and has carried the European Ryder Cup team on his back on many occasions.

Walter Hagen

"Sir Walter" won the PGA Championship five times, the British Open on four occasions, and the U.S. Open twice. While doing so, he redefined the role of the professional golfer in society. Before Hagen, the golf pro was low on the social food chain. He was never allowed in the front door of the clubhouse and was certainly never seen socializing with members.

Hagen changed all that with his golf game and his flamboyant personality. The public took him to their hearts. He would arrive in limousines, park next to the clubhouse he was barred from entering, and then have his chauffeur serve lunch in the back of the car. Not just any lunch. Full compliments of wine and silver settings were the norm.

Hagen played golf with kings and queens, dukes and duchesses. On one famous occasion, he asked King Edward VIII to tend the flag for him. "Hey, Eddie, get the stick, will you?"

Hagen elevated himself to full celebrity, and the golfing world never looked the same again. Sir Walter really could play the game, and he was the first to make his living doing only that.

Ben Hogan

Hogan was a man driven by the search for perfection. Once a wild-hitting young pro, Hogan dismantled his swing. He wanted to stop hooking the ball and rely on strong *fades* (shots that curve slightly to the right) to ensure that his game would hold up under pressure. His resolve and command in his approach to the game remains unmatched. He showed what total dedication can achieve.

When we have a good ball-striking day on the PGA Tour, we commonly say, "I hit it like Hogan." He set the standard for hitting the golf ball. There have been many great proponents of this game, but when you ask someone to name the golfer who could really play, the answer, more often than not, is "Hogan."

Fairway Louie

I went to school with this wise sage. He took seven years to get out of Riverside City College, a two-year college, but he eventually got it right. He got his master's from some faraway college and is now managing an avocado orchard in the hills of Bonsall, California. He lives in a mobile home and wears a lot of flannel, but he's still my friend. He took me to my first rock concert, showed me how to cheat on tests, and came to my first wedding. I've known Fairway a long time.

He is the on-again, off-again player's president of a course where I grew up. That's the only way he can play for nothing. He advised me to quit the tour many years ago — a wiser man I do not know. We see each other rarely nowadays, and I miss his dialogue. He is a voice of reason in these days of madness.

Jack Nicklaus

He simply was the one I grew up watching as he won and won and won.

Mac O'Grady

A few paragraphs will not do our relationship justice. Mac showed me how to really understand this game. He knows more about the golf swing than anyone I have ever met. He is a man of many complexities and much conjecture. He has a passion for the game and for life. My own existence has been immeasurably enhanced by his friendship.

Arnold Palmer

No one man has been more responsible for making golf the huge business success that it is today than Arnold Palmer. He came to the tour swinging hard at every shot, never laying up, and always (it seemed) getting his golf ball out of trouble when it appeared that he was doomed to fail. He was flamboyant and charismatic and had a swagger that galleries flocked to see. And he happened along in the early days of golf on television. The nation had a new hero.

Arnie was responsible for all the attention that golf got in those early cathode-ray moments. He held our banner and set us on a new course for marketing. Golf — or any sport, for that matter — could not have had a better spokesman. He is, and always will be, the king.

Sam Snead

Sam started playing golf by carving up an old stick to resemble a club and then whacking away at rocks at the West Virginia farm where he grew up. What came of that youthful folly was the most natural-looking golf swing man has ever devised. Sam's swing is still the standard today.

Samuel Jackson Snead won 81 tournaments on the PGA Tour (he'll tell you that he won more). His flair for telling jokes and kicking the tops of door-jambs around the world's clubhouses is legendary. I had the opportunity to play and practice with Sam in his last years on tour. I will never forget those moments.

Titanic Thompson

Golf has a way of attracting gamblers of all kinds. There's none more legendary than Titanic Thompson. I have encountered very few of my peers who have not heard of or played a round of golf with this famous oddsmaker. As I understand it, Titanic would make bets that he had no way of losing, no matter how ridiculous they seemed. He roamed with the rich and famous during the middle of this century and supplied us with stories we tell deep into the night. He lived by his wits and imagination and added to the lore of golf.

Lee Trevino

In 1967, a 27-year-old Mexican-American came out of nowhere to finish fifth in the U.S. Open. He didn't go back to El Paso, where he lived, but stayed to play a few more tournaments. He won enough money to stay on tour. "How long has this been going on?" he asked in jest.

He has been on and around the tour ever since. Our lives have been richer for Lee Trevino's presence. A nonstop conversationalist, Lee talked his way through 27 tour victories, stopped off at NBC for a while to do some announcing, and then went on to the Senior PGA Tour, where he still competes.

The man has a flair for words and shot-making that has no equal. He takes this sometimes staid game played on the tour and makes it fun. I hope we see another one like him in the future; he is a pleasure to watch and listen to.

Chapter 23

Gary's Top Ten All-Time Favorite Female Players

*W*omen have embraced the sport of golf in growing numbers. In fact, 20 percent of the population playing golf today are women, who play an average of 16 rounds of golf a year.

The dominance of some of these fine athletes has secured women's golf in the scheme of sports. Babe Zaharias is considered by some to be the greatest athlete, male or female, who ever lived. Kathy Whitworth has won more golf tournaments than *anybody* who has ever picked up a golf club. These women have shown the world that they can play this game, and they have done it with dignity and élan.

Pat Bradley

One of the great competitors, Pat entered the LPGA Hall of Fame in 1992. She was the fourth player in LPGA history to reach the $1 million mark, but became the first player in LPGA history to surpass the $2, $3, and $4 million milestones in 1986, 1990, and 1991, respectively.

JoAnne Carner

This outgoing Hall of Famer is one of the reasons the LPGA has drawn so many people to watch its tournaments. "Big Mama," as she is called, is one of the greatest personalities the women's tour has ever known. She has won 42 events and was the leading money winner three separate times. The LPGA Tour is enriched by her presence as its ambassador.

Laura Davies

Laura has the ability to dominate the women's tour for years to come. Her enormous power can reduce courses to mere pitch-and-putt competition. She has an engaging way about her and is fun to watch as she destroys golf courses. She has won 17 times through 1998, including four majors, and is a sure bet to win more as her career continues.

Betsy King

Betsy was inducted into the LPGA Hall of Fame in 1995. A ferocious competitor, Betsy didn't win for the first seven years on the Tour. But from 1984 through 1989, she won 20 golf tournaments, establishing her as the dominant force in golf. In 1998, she became the first player in LPGA history to pass the $6 million mark in career earnings. She stalks the golf course and never gives up trying. Watch and learn from her tenacity.

Nancy Lopez

Nancy constantly has a smile on her face and plays the game with a youthful zest. She is one of the great putters in our sport and is an outstanding representative of the LPGA. She has won 48 times as of this writing and remains very active on the Tour. She adds life to everyone around her.

Meg Mallon

Meg started playing on the LPGA Tour in 1987. She flirts with the golf course as she plays it, always trying something new to see if it will help her perform better. Viewers can watch as she has fun playing the game; that's why I like to watch Meg. Her most productive year was in 1991, when she won two major titles. She has nine wins in total, including a 1998 victory in which she won with an impressive four rounds in the 60s.

Annika Sorenstam

This highly disciplined individual is one of the hardest workers on the LPGA Tour. From Stockholm, Sweden, she has won three events, including the 1995 and 1996 U.S. Women's Opens. This star is a perfectionist whose work ethic is highly regarded by her peers. She is the first woman to have an annual scoring average under 70. She has as bright a future as anyone the Tour has produced in many years.

Kathy Whitworth

Of all the people who have played this game, men and women, Kathy Whitworth has won more times than anybody. In her glorious career, she won 88 times, including six major championships. She dominated the Tour from 1965 to 1973, finishing first on the money list eight times and second one other year. She was named player of the year seven times.

Mickey Wright

In the late 1950s and early 1960s, Mickey Wright was responsible for raising women's professional golf to a new level and placing it in the public eye. I was fortunate enough to get to see her play an exhibition match a few years ago. I had heard so much about her golf swing and was not disappointed. She may have the best swing of anybody who has ever played this game. She's probably the greatest player the LPGA has ever known. She won 82 times.

Babe Zaharias

Perhaps the greatest athlete of all time, she won two gold medals and one silver medal for track and field in the 1932 Olympics. Earlier that year, she won eight of ten events in the AAU's National Women's track and field championship and won the meet as a one-woman team for Employer's Casualty. She then decided to take up golf. In a very brief tenure on the LPGA — eight years — she won 31 events and ten major titles. This woman was a legend beyond the sport of golf, but she died from cancer at the early age of 45.

Chapter 24

The (More Than) Ten Most Horrendous Golf Disasters

In golf, there's no place to hide. And that's the honor of it. The quarterback who's having a disgraceful day can retire to the bench. The batter who fears Randy Johnson can fake an injury. But the golfer who's brave enough to reach the lead has an extra kind of courage; he knows that, having gotten to center stage, there's no limit to how much he can disgrace himself.

—Thomas Boswell

Golf has to be the easiest sport in which to snatch defeat from the jaws of victory. The game can be positively diabolical — the worst always seems to happen, and complacency is severely punished. Ultimately, it's not whether the wheels come off, but when. Why do we delight in these debacles? I think there's a strong element of *schadenfreude,* a sort of perverse consolation, when the greats occasionally suffer the humiliation and heartbreak that we regular mortals deal with every day. And that's the key, I think: Awful as they are, these meltdowns happen to the best players on the planet.

A word on terminology: I prefer *disaster* to *collapse.* A collapse is your fault, but a disaster is something beyond your control, like a flood or an earthquake. Also, there's a fine line between "choking" and being the victim of a disaster. Choking is somehow culpable: Miss a 3-footer to win a major, and it's your fault. In any case, it's devastating when disasters happen, and nobody is immune — not even the best players in the world at the top of their game.

Greg Norman, 1996 Masters

The greatest disaster in golf history happened to the reigning number-one player in the world. With more than 70 tournament victories worldwide, Greg Norman is certainly the best player never to have won a green jacket (the symbol of a Masters victory), although he's come close twice: In 1986, he bogied the 18th to lose by a stroke to Jack Nicklaus, and the following year he lost in a playoff when Larry Mize chipped in from 50 yards. But his opening three rounds at Augusta in 1996, including a record-tying 63 the first day, gave him a seemingly invincible six-shot lead. (No one with such a lead going into the final round had ever lost before.)

But on Sunday, he couldn't do anything right. He bogied the 9th, 10th, and 11th. He hit into the water on both 12 and 16 for double-bogey 5s. All told, he missed 10 of 18 greens on his way to a 6-over-par 78. He lost to Nick Faldo's 5-under 67 by 5 shots, an incredible 11-shot turnaround.

Norman somehow managed to smile during the excruciating post-round press conference. "God, I'd love to be up there putting that green jacket on, but it's not the end of the world," he told reporters. "I'm disappointed, I'm sad about it. I'm going to regret it, because I know I let it slip away. It's not the end of my life." He exhibited such dignity in the face of crushing disappointment that he received thousands of cards and letters praising him for his sportsmanship. He later described the outpouring of support as a transforming experience, claiming that he took more from the loss than he would have gained from a win.

Gil Morgan, 1992 U.S. Open at Pebble Beach

After opening rounds of 66 and 69, the 45-year-old former optometrist had a seven-shot lead when the wind started to gust off the Pacific. He double-bogied the 8th, bogied the 9th, double-bogied the 10th, bogied the 11th and 12th, and double-bogied the 14th. Though he managed to birdie 16 and 18, his lead was reduced to one shot. He shot 81 on Sunday for a tie for 13th. He never came as close to winning a regular tour major. "I kind of fell out of the sky," he said later. "It felt like my parachute had a hole in it."

Mark Calcavecchia, 1991 Ryder Cup at Kiawah Island

Calcavecchia was four up with four holes to play in his singles match against Colin Montgomerie. He lost the 15th and 16th, and then, at the par-3 17th, after Montgomerie hit his tee shot into the water and all he had to do was put his ball somewhere on dry land, Calcavecchia topped his tee ball into the water. He then missed a 2-foot putt, which would still have given him the win. All told, he made two triples and two bogies to lose the final four holes and halve (tie) the match, which would have clinched a victory for the United States. Fortunately for Calcavecchia's subsequent mental health, the United States won the Ryder Cup anyway.

Patty Sheehan, 1990 U.S. Women's Open at Atlanta Athletic Club

With the last two rounds being played on Sunday, Sheehan took a nine-shot lead into the final 27 holes but lost to Betsy King by one stroke. Most collapses are mental, but in Sheehan's case, the breakdown was physical. "I had no fuel on board when I went out [Sunday morning]," she said. "I started losing it. I was dehydrated. My body couldn't work. I couldn't think properly and I had no strength."

Sheehan redeemed herself with victories in the 1993 and 1994 U.S. Opens. "It doesn't hurt anymore," she said. "Thank God I was able to win and get rid of all the demons."

Scott Hoch, 1989 Masters

You're never safe — certainly not when you're nervous, and apparently not even when you're calm: On the 10th green of a playoff with Nick Faldo, Hoch missed a 2-footer to win the Masters, and lost the playoff on the following hole.

Sometime later, Hoch expounded on the nightmare: "I was so at ease. I just knew the way things had transpired all week, especially that day, that the tournament was mine. I took it for granted. Standing over that putt, I didn't feel a thing. Nothing. It was like I was out there during a practice round. Why, I don't know. And I've never felt like that since. That's why, when the putt missed, it was more like, wait a minute — destiny doesn't happen like this. . . . I wasn't thinking. My mind was doing things it shouldn't have been. It should've been strictly on that putt, nothing else. Then it was like, 'Who am I going to go on with, Bryant Gumbel or the other guy tomorrow morning?' That kind of stuff. Then it was the biggest surprise in the world to me when it didn't go in. I'd been saying to myself, 'This is what it all comes down to — all the hardship and heartache — all comes to this moment. Finally.' Then it crashed down on me."

Jeff Sluman, 1987 Tournament Players Championship at Sawgrass

Sluman and Sandy Lyle were in a sudden-death playoff, with Sluman facing a 5-footer on the 17th to win. Just as he was about to strike the putt, a spectator dove into the lake surrounding the island green, causing the gallery to break into cheers and catcalls. Sluman stepped back to compose himself and then stepped up . . . and missed the cup completely. Sluman bogied the next hole to lose the playoff.

T. C. Chen, 1985 U.S. Open at Oakland Hills

After shooting 65-69-69, Taiwan's Tze-Chung Chen carried a two-stroke lead into the final round and increased it to four by the time he reached the par-4 fifth hole. After a good drive, he pushed a 4-iron into the trees and then hit his third shot into the thick greenside rough. He took a sand wedge for the short chip, but the ball popped straight up and the clubhead somehow hit it again in midair, sending it sideways and costing him a penalty stroke. Unnerved by the double hit, he chipped onto the putting surface and then two-putted for a quadruple-bogey 8. He bogied the next three holes, losing the title to Andy North by a single stroke and earning the ignominious nickname "Two Chips" Chen.

Hale Irwin, 1983 British Open at Royal Birkdale

On Saturday, in contention for the lead during the third round, Irwin whiffed a 2-inch tap-in on the par-3 14th. On Sunday, he lost the championship to Tom Watson by one stroke. "I guess I lifted my head," he said afterward, "because my club just bounced over the ball."

Jerry Pate, 1982 World Series of Golf at Firestone

The 1976 U.S. Open champion reached the fringe of the par-5 second hole in two and had a 50-footer for eagle. His approach putt rolled 5 feet past the hole, and his comebacker for birdie was also too strong, ending up 3 feet away. Annoyed at himself, Pate carelessly hit the short par putt, and it lipped out. Fuming, he then made a careless backhand stab at the bogey tap-in. Not only did the ball miss the cup, but it also hit his foot for a two-stroke penalty. Lying 8, he managed to hole out for a quadruple-bogey 9. "That was the stupidest hole I ever played," he said afterward. "It just goes to show you that in golf, it's never over until the ball is in the hole."

Tommy Nakajima, 1978 Masters

The Japanese professional tried to cut the dogleg of the par-5 13th, but his drive caught a tree and his ball ended up in Rae's Creek. He took a penalty drop and played a 5-iron down the fairway, leaving himself 100 yards to the green. When his wedge found the creek in front of the green, he tried to hit it out rather than take a drop, but the ball popped straight up and landed on his foot for a two-stroke penalty. Then, when he handed the muddy club to his caddie, it slipped from his grasp and fell into the water for another two-stroke penalty for "grounding" a club in a hazard. Lying 9, he hit his next shot over the green and then chipped back on and two-putted for a 13, tying the record for the highest one-hole score in the history of the Masters.

Asked about it later, Nakajima replied, "I don't like to recall unpleasant occurrences."

Billy Casper, 1968 Bob Hope Desert Classic

Casper was two shots off the lead in the final round when he came to the par-3 4th hole. Just as he reached the top of his backswing, a spectator slipped on the rocky hill above him, causing a landslide that startled Casper into a cold shank. The resulting double-bogey 5 dashed his chance to win the tournament.

Roberto DeVicenzo, 1968 Masters

Widely regarded as one of the nicest guys in professional golf, the 45-year-old Argentinian began the final round two shots behind the leader and shot a sizzling 65. His playing partner and marker, Tommy Aaron, mistakenly gave him a par 4 on the 17th instead of a birdie 3, and DeVicenzo hastily signed the incorrect card and submitted it to the official scorer. Because the rules state that a scorecard may not be changed after it has been turned in, DeVicenzo was effectively penalized one stroke. Bob Goalby finished tied with DeVicenzo's actual 72-hole score, but because of the error, Goalby won the Masters by one shot.

This incident, a "rules disaster," was perhaps even more tragic than a standard on-course collapse — claiming not one but three victims: DeVicenzo; Aaron, who would donate a vital organ if it could undo his blunder; and Goalby, whose victory is forever tarnished as resting on a technicality. For his part, DeVicenzo accepted his fate with good humor. At the awards ceremony, he said, "What a stupid I am!"

Marty Fleckman, 1967 U.S. Open at Baltusrol

Twenty-three-year-old Marty Fleckman shot 67-73-69 in a bid to become the first amateur to win the U.S. Open since Johnny Goodman (in 1933), but he ballooned to an 80 in the final round and finished 18th. Asked by reporters what happened, Fleckman replied, "I finally got back on my game."

Arnold Palmer, 1966 U.S. Open at the Olympic Club

With a seven-stroke lead over Billy Casper and only nine holes left to play, Palmer, in typical style, went for the U.S. Open record instead of playing it safe. But he scored five over par on holes 10 through 17 and barely managed to par 18 for a tie with Casper, who shot 32 on the back nine. Palmer lost the Monday playoff with a 73 to Casper's 69. He never won another major.

After the obligatory post-tournament press conference, an official asked Palmer if he wanted to leave by a back door to avoid the crowd waiting outside. He declined. "The way I played," he said, "I deserve whatever they do to me." He was pleasantly surprised to find that "Arnie's Army" was even more adoring than they would have been if he'd won.

Arnold Palmer, 1961 Los Angeles Open at Rancho Park

Palmer needed a par 5 on the 18th for a 69 in the second round. After a good drive, instead of laying up with an iron for the tight second shot, he went for a birdie and pushed a 3-wood out-of-bounds onto the adjacent driving range. He paused briefly to regroup and then hit another 3-wood. O.B. right again. He gathered himself again and hit another 3-wood. This time, he hooked it onto Patricia Avenue. Stubborn if not downright foolhardy, Palmer hit the 3-wood yet again, and again hooked it out-of-bounds. On the fifth try, after four straight penalties, he finally put his 3-wood on the green and went on to make a 12. A long, sad story. Arnie's description was more succinct. Asked by a reporter how he managed to make a 12, he replied, "I missed my putt for an 11."

Billy Joe Patton, 1954 Masters

The affable young amateur from South Carolina found himself in the lead on Sunday after a 32 on the front nine, which included a hole-in-one on the 6th. When he reached the par-5 13th, he was told that his closest competitor, Ben Hogan, had just made a double bogey on 11. All Patton had to do was play it safe to become the first amateur to win the Masters. But no. Instead of laying up to avoid Rae's Creek, he went for the green, and his ball found the water. He removed his shoes and socks and waded into the stream, but reconsidered and decided to take a drop for a one-stroke penalty. Still barefoot, he pitched onto the green and two-putted for a bogey 6. Patton then parred in for a 290, one shot behind Hogan and Sam Snead (who defeated Hogan in a playoff).

In retrospect, Patton claimed that he wouldn't have played it any differently. "I was elated to play as well as I did," he said. "I'm almost delighted I lost, in fact. Otherwise, I might have turned pro."

Byron Nelson, 1946 U.S. Open at Canterbury

After his caddie accidentally kicked his ball, costing him a penalty stroke, Nelson ended up tied with Lloyd Mangrum and Vic Ghezzi. He then lost to Mangrum in a 36-hole playoff.

Sam Snead, 1939 U.S. Open at Spring Mill

Snead, who has won more PGA events than anyone in history, is undoubtedly the best player never to have won a U.S. Open. He came close several times: He lost by one stroke in 1937; he lost in a playoff in 1947; and at the Spring Mill course at Philadelphia Country Club in 1939, prior to the advent of electronic leader boards, he mistakenly believed that he needed a birdie on the par-5 final hole to win and went for the green in two. He hit his second shot into a bunker and eventually made a triple-bogey 8 to lose by two strokes, when a par would have won.

Ray Ainsley, 1938 U.S. Open at Cherry Hills

Ainsley, a club pro from Ojai, California, hit his approach on the par-4 16th into a stream fronting the green. Rather than take a penalty, he decided to play the ball from the water. As the ball drifted with the current, he slashed at it repeatedly, stubbornly refusing to take a drop. He finally carded a 19, which is still the U.S. Open record for the highest score on a single hole.

From the self-inflicted department

- **Bobby Cruickshank, 1934 U.S. Open at Merion:** On the 11th hole during the final round, Cruickshank's second shot over a stream skipped off the water and ran onto the green. Jubilant, he threw his club in the air in celebration. He was knocked unconscious when it came down on his head.

- **Al Capone, 1928:** The Chicago gangster loved to play golf, although he never shot under 100. But one day in 1928, at the Burnham Woods course near Chicago, he managed to shoot himself — when the loaded revolver he kept in his bag went off accidentally and wounded him in the foot.

- **Mary, Queen of Scots, 1587:** The most irrevocable golf disaster in history involved Mary, Queen of Scots, who angered Parliament by playing golf a few days after her husband's death. Her apparent lack of widowly grief was used against her at her trial for plotting the murder of Queen Elizabeth I, and Mary was beheaded.

Roland Hancock, 1928 U.S. Open at Olympia Fields

Hancock, an unknown 21-year-old club pro from Wilmington, North Carolina, reached the final two holes with a seemingly insurmountable lead. As he approached the 17th tee, one of the spectators shouted, "Make way for the next U.S. Open champion!" Hancock promptly double-bogied the 17th and 18th, missing a playoff by a single stroke.

Part VII
Appendixes

In this part . . .

Golfers have a language all their own. Appendix A lists phrases, terms, and slang you need to add to your vocabulary. Appendix B lists some of the more popular golf organizations, as well as selected golf schools.

Appendix A
Golfspeak

● ●

*F*ive minutes spent listening to the conversation in any clubhouse in the world will be enough for you to figure out that golf has a language all its own. Here are phrases, terms, and slang to help make sense of it all. Besides, if you're going to be a real golfer, you need to sound like one.

These terms are written with right-handed golfers in mind. Lefties will have to think in reverse!

A

ace: A hole-in-one. Buy a round of drinks for the house.

address: The positioning of your body in relation to the ball just before starting your swing. And your last conscious thought before the chaos begins.

airball: Your swing missed the ball! Blame it on an alien's spacecraft radar.

albatross: British term for *double eagle,* or three under par on one hole. I've only had one.

amateur: Someone who plays for fun — not money. Playing golf for fun?

angle of approach: The degree at which the clubhead moves either downward or upward into the ball. A severe test of agility.

approach: Your shot to the green made from anywhere except the tee. Sounds dangerous; really isn't.

apron: The grass around the edge of a green, longer than the grass on the green but shorter than the grass on the fairway. Or what I wear to barbecue in.

attend: To hold and remove the flagstick as a partner putts, usually from some distance.

away: Term used to describe the ball farthest from the hole and, thus, next to be played.

B

back door: Rear of hole.

back lip: The edge of a *bunker* (a hazard filled with sand) that's farthest from the green.

back nine: The second half of your round of golf; the first half is the front nine holes.

backspin: When the ball hits the green and spins back toward the player. *Galleries,* or spectators, love backspins.

backswing: The part of the swing from the point where the clubhead moves away from the ball to the point where it starts back down again. I hope that your backswing is smooth and in balance.

baffie: Old name for a 5-wood.

bail out (hang 'em high): You hit the shot, for example, well to the right to avoid trouble on the left.

balata: Sap from a tropical tree, used to make covers for balls.

ball at rest: The ball isn't moving. A study in still life.

ball marker: Small, round object, such as a coin, used to indicate the ball's position on the green.

ball retriever: Long pole with a scoop on the end used to collect balls from water hazards and other undesirable spots. If the grip on your ball retriever is worn out, get some lessons immediately.

ball washer: Found on many tees; a device for cleaning balls.

banana ball: Shot that curves hugely from left to right (see *slice*).

bandit: See *hustler*. Avoid bandits at all costs.

baseball grip: To hold the club with all ten fingers on the grip.

best ball: Game for four players; two teams of two. The low score on each side counts as the team score on each hole.

birdie: Score of one under par on a hole.

bisque: Handicap stroke given by one player to another. Receiver may choose which hole it is applied to.

bite (vampire, bicuspid, overbite): A spin that makes the ball tend to stop rather than roll when it lands.

blade: Not pretty. The leading edge of the club, rather than the clubface, strikes the ball, resulting in a low shot that tends to travel way too far (see *thin* or *skull*). Also a kind of putter or iron.

blast: Aggressive shot from a bunker that displaces a lot of sand.

blind shot: You can't see the spot where you want the ball to land.

block (H&R Block, Dan Blocker): Shot that flies straight but to the right of the target (see *push*).

bogey: Score of one stroke over par on a hole.

borrow: The amount of curve you must allow for a putt on a sloping green. Or what you need to do if you play a hustler.

boundary: Edge, of course; it confines the space/time continuum. Usually marked by white stakes.

brassie: Old name for a 2-wood.

break: See *borrow*.

British Open: National championship run by Royal and Ancient Golf Club of St. Andrews — known in Britain as "the Open" because it was the first one.

bulge: The curve across the face of a wooden club.

bunker: Hazard filled with sand; can be referred to as a *sand trap*.

buried ball/lie: Part of the ball below the surface of the sand in a bunker.

C

caddie: The person carrying your clubs during your round of golf. The person you fire when you play badly.

caddie-master: Person in charge of caddies.

Calamity Jane: The great Bobby Jones's putter.

carry: The distance between a ball's takeoff and landing.

cart: Motorized vehicle used to transport lazy golfers around the course.

casual water: Water other than a water hazard on the course from which you can lift your ball without penalty.

center-shafted: Putter in which the shaft is joined to the center of the head.

character builder: Short, meaningful putt; can't possibly build character.

charting the course: To pace each hole so that you always know how far you are from the hole.

chili-dip (Hormel, lay the sod over it, pooper scooper): A mishit chip shot, the clubhead hitting the ground well before it hits the ball.

chip: Very short, low-flying shot to the green.

chip-in: A holed chip.

choke: To play poorly because of self-imposed pressure.

choke down: To hold the club lower on the grip.

chunk: See *chili-dip*.

cleat: Spike on the sole of a golf shoe.

cleek: Old term for a variety of clubs.

closed face: Clubface pointed to the left of your ultimate target at address or impact. Or clubface pointed skyward at the top of the backswing. Can lead to a shot that goes to the left of the target.

closed stance: Player sets up with the right foot pulled back, away from the ball.

clubhouse: Main building at a golf club.

club length: Distance from the end of the grip to the bottom of the clubhead.

collar: See *apron*.

come-backer: The putt after the preceding effort finished beyond the hole. Usually gets harder to make the older you get.

compression: The flattening of the ball against the clubface. The faster you swing and the more precisely you hit the ball in the middle of the clubface, the more fun you have.

concede: To give an opponent a putt, hole, or match.

core: The center of a golf ball.

course rating: The difficulty of a course, measured with some silly formula by the USGA.

cross-handed: Grip with the left hand below the right.

cross wind: Breeze blowing from right to left or from left to right.

cup: Container in the hole that holds the flagstick in place.

cuppy lie: When the ball is in a cup-like depression.

cut: Score that eliminates a percentage of the field (or players) from a tournament. Usually made after 36 holes of a 72-hole event. I've missed a few in my time.

cut shot: Shot that curves from left to right.

D

dance floor: Slang for green.

dawn patrol: The players who tee off early in the day.

dead (body bags, cadaver, on the slab, perdition, jail, tag on his toe, wearing stripes, no pulse — you get the idea): No possible way out of the shot!

deep: High clubface from top to bottom.

deuce: A score of two on a given hole.

dimple: Depression on the cover of a golf ball.

divot: Turf displaced by the clubhead during a swing.

dogleg: Hole on which the fairway curves one way or the other.

dormant: Grass on the course is alive but not actively growing. Also my hair.

dormie: The player who's winning the match in match play — for example, five up with only five holes left, or four up with four left.

double bogey: Score of two over par on a hole.

double eagle: Score of three under par on a hole. Forget it, you'll probably never get one. See also *albatross*.

down: Losing.

downhill lie: When your right foot is higher than your left when you address the ball (for right-handed players).

downswing: The part of the swing where the clubhead is moving down, toward the ball.

DQ'd: Disqualified.

drain: To sink a putt.

draw: Shot that curves from right to left.

drive: Shot from teeing ground other than par-3 holes.

drive for show, putt for dough: Old saying implying that putting is more important than driving.

driving range: Place where you can go to hit practice balls.

drive the green: When your drive finishes on the putting surface. Can happen on short par-4, or when the brakes go out on your cart.

drop: Procedure by which you put the ball back into play after it's been deemed unplayable.

dub: Bad shot or player.

duck hook (shrimp, mallard, quacker): Shot curving severely from right to left.

duffer: Bad player.

dying putt: A putt that barely reaches the hole.

E

eagle: Score of two under par for a hole.

embedded ball: Portion of the ball is below ground.

erosion: Loss of land through water and wind damage — most common on the coasts.

etiquette: Code of conduct.

explode: To play a ball from a bunker moving a large amount of sand. Or what you do if the ball doesn't get out of the bunker.

extra holes: Played when a match finishes even (is tied).

F

face: The front of a club or bunker.

fade: Shot that curves gently from left to right.

fairway: The prepared surface running from tee to green.

fairway wood: Any wooden club that's not your driver. Nowadays, you say *fairway metal* because you don't see many wooden clubs anymore.

fat: To strike the ground before the ball.

feather: To put a delicate fade on a shot — don't try it yet!

first cut: Strip of rough at the edge of a fairway.

first off: Golfers beginning their round before everyone else.

flag: Piece of cloth attached to the top of a flagstick.

flagstick: The stick with the flag on top, which indicates the location of the cup.

flange: Projecting piece of clubhead behind the sole (bottom).

flat: Swing that is less upright than normal, and more around the body than up and down.

flub: To hit the ball only a few feet.

flex: The amount of bend in a shaft.

flier: Shot, usually hit from the rough, that travels way too far past the target.

fly the green: To hit a shot that lands beyond the putting surface.

follow-through: The part of the swing after the ball has been struck.

foozle: To make a complete mess of a shot.

Fore!: What to shout when your ball is headed toward another player.

forged irons: Clubs made one by one, without molds.

forward press: Targetward shift of the hands, and perhaps a right knee, just prior to takeaway.

foursome: Depends where you are. In the States, a group of four playing together. In Britain, a match between two teams of two, each hitting one ball alternately.

free drop: Drop for which no penalty stroke is incurred, generally within one club length of where the ball was.

fried egg: When your ball is semiburied in the sand.

fringe: See *apron*.

frog hair: Slang for *apron, fringe,* or *collar*.

front nine: The first half of your round of golf; the second half is the back nine holes.

full swing: Longest swing you make.

G

gallery: Spectators at a tournament.

gimme: A short putt that your opponent doesn't ask you to hit, assuming that you can't possibly miss the shot.

G.I.R: Slang for *greens in regulation* — greens hit in regulation number of strokes.

glove: Usually worn on the left hand by right-handed players. Helps maintain grip.

Golden Bear: Jack Nicklaus.

golf widow(er): Your significant other after he or she finds out how much you want to play!

go to school: Watching your partner's putt and learning from it the line and pace that your putt should have.

good-good: Reciprocal concession of short putts. (See *gimme*.)

grain: Tendency of grass leaves to lie horizontally toward the sun.

Grand Slam: The four major championships: Masters, U.S. Open, British Open, and PGA Championship.

graphite: Lightweight material used to make shafts and clubheads.

Great White Shark: Greg Norman.

green: The shortest-cut grass where you do your putting.

greenies: Bet won by player whose first shot finishes closest to the hole on a par-3.

green jacket: Prize awarded to the winner of the Masters Tournament in Augusta, Georgia.

greens fee: The cost to play a round of golf.

greenside: Close to the green.

greensome: Game in which both players on a team drive off. The better of the two is chosen; then they alternate shots from there.

grip: Piece of rubber/leather on the end of a club. Or your hold on the club.

groove: *Scoring* along the clubface.

gross score: Actual score shot before a handicap is deducted.

ground the club: The process of placing the clubhead behind the ball at address, generally touching the bottom of the grass.

ground under repair: Area on the course being worked on by the groundskeeper, generally marked by white lines, from which you may drop your ball without penalty.

gutta percha: Material used to manufacture golf balls in the 19th century.

H

hacker: Poor player.

half: Tied hole.

half shot: Improvised shot with ordinarily too much club for the distance.

halve: To tie a hole.

ham and egging: When you and partner play well on alternate holes, forming an effective team.

handicap: For example, one whose handicap is 16 is expected to shoot 88 on a par 72 course, or 16 strokes over par.

hanging lie: Your ball is on a slope, lying either above or below your feet.

hardpan: Very firm turf.

hazard: Can be either sand or water. Don't ground your club in hazards — it's against the rules!

head cover: Protection for the clubhead, usually used on woods.

heel: End of the clubhead closest to the shaft.

hickory: Wood from which shafts used to be made.

high side: Area above the hole on a sloping green.

hole: Your ultimate 4¼-inch-wide target.

hole-high: Level with the hole.

hole-in-one: See *ace*.

hole out: Complete play on hole.

home green: The green on the 18th hole.

honor: When you score lowest on a given hole, thus earning the right to tee up first on the next tee.

hood: Tilting the toe end of the club toward the hole. Lessens the loft on a club, and generally produces a right-to-left shot.

hook: Shot that curves severely from right to left.

horseshoe: When ball goes around the edge of the cup and "comes back" toward you. Painful!

hosel: Curved area where the clubhead connects with the shaft.

hustler: A golfer who plays for a living. Plays better than he claims to be. Usually leaves your wallet lighter.

I

impact: Moment when the club strikes the ball.

impediment: Loose debris that you can remove from around your ball as long as the ball doesn't move.

Impregnable Quadrilateral: The Grand Slam.

improve your lie: To move the ball to make a shot easier. This is illegal unless local rules dictate otherwise.

in play: Within the confines of the course (not out-of-bounds).

into out: Swing path whereby the clubhead moves across the ball-target line from left to right.

in your pocket: After you've picked up the ball! (Generally after you finish a hole without holing out.)

insert: Plate in the face of wooden clubs.

inside out: Clubhead moves through the impact area on a line to the right of the target. Most tour players do this. (See also *outside in*.)

inside: Area on your side of a line drawn from the ball to the target.

intended line: The path on which you imagine the ball flying from club to target.

interlocking: Type of grip where the little finger of the right hand is entwined with the index finger of the left.

investment cast: Clubs made from a mold.

J

jail: Slang for when you and your ball are in very deep trouble.

jigger: Old term for a 4-iron. Also a great little pub to the right of the 17th fairway at St. Andrews.

jungle: Slang for heavy *rough,* or an unprepared area of long grass.

K

kick: Another term for bounce.

kill: To hit a long shot.

L

ladies day: Time when course is reserved for those of the female persuasion.

lag: A long putt hit with the intent of leaving the ball close to the cup.

laid off: When the club points to the left of the target at the top of the backswing.

lateral hazard: Water hazard marked by red stakes and usually parallel to the fairway.

lay-up: Conservatively played shot to avoid possible trouble.

leader board: Place where lowest scores in tournament are posted. I don't stay on the leader board too long. In fact, when the scorers are putting up the "d" in McCord, they're usually taking down the "M." Sometimes I wish my name was Calcavecchia.

leak: Ball drifting to the right during flight.

lie: Where your ball is on the ground. Also, the angle at which the club shaft extends from the head.

lift: What you do before you *drop.*

line: The path of a shot to the hole.

line up: To stand behind a shot to take aim.

links: A seaside course. Don't expect trees.

lip: Edge of a cup or bunker.

lip-out (cellophane bridge): Ball touches the edge of the cup but doesn't drop in.

local knowledge: What the members know and you don't.

local rules: Set of rules determined by the members, rules committee, or course professional.

loft: The degree at which a clubface looks upward.

long game: Shots hit with long irons and woods. Also could be John Daly's game.

loop: Slang for "to caddy." Or a round of golf. Or a change in the path of the clubhead during the swing.

low-handicapper: Good player.

low side: Area below the hole on a sloping green.

LPGA: Ladies Professional Golf Association.

M

make: Hole a shot.

makeable: Shot with a good chance of being holed.

mallet: Putter with a wide head.

mark: To indicate the position of the ball with a small, round, flat object, such as a coin, usually on the green.

marker: Small, round object, such as a coin, placed behind the ball to indicate its position when you lift it. Or the person keeping score.

marshal: Person controlling the crowd at a tournament.

mashie: Old term for a 5-iron.

mashie-niblick: Old term for a 7-iron.

Masters: First major tournament of each calendar year. Always played over the Augusta National course in Georgia. The one tournament I can't go to.

match of cards: Comparing your scorecard to your opponent's to see who won.

match play: Game played between two sides. The side that wins the most holes wins the match.

matched set: Clubs designed to look and feel the same.

medal play: Game played between any number of players. The player with the lowest score wins (can also be called *stroke play*).

metal wood: Wooden club made of metal.

mid-iron: Old term for a 2-iron.

miniature course: Putting course.

misclub: To use the wrong club for the distance.

misread: To take the wrong line on a putt.

miss the cut: To take too many strokes for the first 36 holes of 72-hole event and be eliminated. I did this once or twice.

mixed foursome: Two men, two women.

model swing: Perfect motion.

mulligan: Second attempt at a shot, usually played on the first tee. This is illegal.

municipal course: A course owned by the local government and thus open to the public. Generally has lower greens fees than a privately owned public course.

N

nassau: Bet in which a round of 18 holes is divided into three — front nine, back nine, and full 18.

net score: Score for a hole or round after handicap strokes are deducted.

never up, never in: Annoying saying coined for a putt that finishes short of the hole.

niblick: Old term for a 9-iron.

nine: Half of a course.

19th hole: The clubhouse bar.

O

O.B. (Oscar Bravo, set it free): Out-of-bounds.

off-center hit: Less than a solid strike.

offset: Club with the head set farther behind the shaft than normal.

one-putt: To take only a single putt on a green.

one up: Being one hole ahead in the match score.

open face: Clubface aligned to the right of the target at address, or to the right of its path at impact. Can lead to a shot going to the right of the target.

open stance: Player sets up with the left foot pulled back, away from the ball.

open up the hole: When your tee shot leaves the best possible angle for the next shot to the green.

out-of-bounds: Area outside the boundaries of the course, usually marked with white posts. When a ball finishes "O.B.," the player must return to the original spot and play another ball under penalty of one stroke. He or she thus loses *stroke and distance.*

outside: Area on the far side of the ball.

outside in: Swing path followed by the clubhead into the ball from outside the ball-target line. (See *inside out.*)

over the green: Ball hit too far.

overclub: To use a club that will hit the ball too far.

overlapping: A type of grip where the little finger of the right hand lies over the index finger of the left hand.

P

pairings: Groups of two players.

par: The score a good player would expect to make on a hole or round.

partner: A player on your side.

penal: Difficult.

persimmon: A wood from which many wooden clubs are made.

PGA: Professional Golfers' Association.

Piccolo grip: A very loose hold on the club, especially at the top of the backswing.

pigeon: An opponent you should beat easily.

pin: The pole placed in the hole.

pin-high: See *hole high*.

pin-placement: The location of the hole on the green.

pitch: A short, high approach shot. Doesn't *run* much on landing.

pitch and putt: A short course. Or getting down in two strokes from off the green.

pitch-and-run: Varies from a pitch in that it flies lower and *runs* more.

pitching-niblick: Old term for an 8-iron.

pivot: The body turn during the swing.

plane: The arc of the swing.

playoff: Two or more players play extra holes to break a tie.

play through: What you do when the group in front of you invites you to pass.

plugged lie: When the ball finishes half-buried in the turf or a bunker.

plumb-bob: Lining up a putt with one eye closed and the putter held vertically in front of the face.

pop-up: High, short shot.

pot bunker: Small, steeply faced bunker.

practice green: Place for working on your putting.

preferred lies: Temporary rule that allows you to move the ball to a more favorable position because of wet conditions.

press: You've lost your match, but you want your money back. This new bet takes place over any remaining holes.

private club: A club open to members and their guests only.

Pro-Am: A competition in which professional partners team with amateurs.

professional: A golfer who plays or teaches for his or her livelihood.

pro shop: A place where you sign up to start play and can buy balls, clubs, and so on.

provisional ball: You think your ball may be lost. To save time, you play another from the same spot before searching for the first ball. If the first ball is lost, the second ball is *in play.*

public course: A golf course open to all.

pull: A straight shot that flies to the left of the target.

punch: A shot hit lower with the ball back in the stance and a shorter-than-normal follow-through.

push: A straight shot that flies to the right of the target.

putter: A straight-faced club generally used on the greens.

Q

quail high (stealth, skull, rat-high): Low.

qualifying school: A place where aspiring professional golfers try to qualify for the PGA and LPGA Tours. A punishing week of pressure golf. The ultimate grind.

quitting: Not hitting through a shot with conviction.

R

rabbit: A beginning player.

rake: Device used to smooth the sand after you leave a bunker.

range: Practice area.

range ball: Generally a low-quality ball used on a driving range.

rap: To hit a putt firmly.

read the green: To assess the path on which a putt must travel to the hole.

regular: A shaft with normal flex.

regulation: Par figures.

release: The point in the downswing where the wrists uncock.

relief: Where you drop a ball that was in a hazard or affected by an obstruction.

reverse overlap: Putting grip in which the little finger of the right hand overlaps the index finger of the left hand.

rhythm: The tempo of your swing.

rifle a shot: To hit the ball hard, straight, and far.

rim the cup: See *lip out*.

ringer score: Your best-ever score at each hole on the course.

Road Hole: The 17th hole at St. Andrews — the hardest hole in the world.

roll: On wooden clubs, the curve on the clubface from the top to the bottom of the face.

rough: Unprepared area of long grass on either side of the fairway.

round: Eighteen holes of golf.

Royal & Ancient Golf Club: The organization that runs the British Open.

rub of the green: Luck.

run: The roll on the ball after landing.

run up: A type of shot to play when the ground is firm. You bounce the ball onto the green and let it roll to the hole.

S

sandbagger: A golfer who lies about his or her ability/handicap to gain an advantage.

sand trap: A bunker.

sandy: Making par after being in a bunker.

scorecard: Where the length, par, and rating of each hole is recorded. Also, your score.

scoring: The grooves on the clubface.

scramble: To play erratic golf but still score well. Or a game where a team of, say, four all tee off and then pick the best shot. All then play their balls from that spot; continues with each set of shots.

scratch play: No handicaps used in this type of game.

scratch player: One with a 0 handicap.

second cut: Second level of *rough,* higher than first cut. Some courses have three cuts of rough.

semiprivate: A course with members that is also open to the public.

semirough: Grass in the rough that is not too long, not too short.

setup: See *address.*

shaft: The part of the club that joins the grip to the head.

shag: To retrieve practice balls.

shag bag: To carry practice balls.

shallow: Narrow clubface. Or a flattish angle of attack into the ball.

shank: Shot struck from the club's hosel; flies far to the right of the intended target.

shooting the lights out: To play very well.

short cut: Cut of grass on the fairway or green.

short game: Shots played on and around the green.

shut: Clubface aligned left at address or impact; looking skyward at the top of the backswing. Results in a shot that goes to the left of the target.

sidehill lie: Ball either above or below your feet.

sidesaddle: Putting style where a player faces the hole while making the stroke.

sink: To make a putt.

sit down (full flaps, pull a hamstring, develop a limp): A polite request for the ball to stop.

skins: Betting game where the lowest score on a hole wins the pot. If the hole is tied, the money carries over to the next hole.

skull (hit it in the forehead): See *blade* or *thin.*

sky: Ball flies off the top of the clubface — very high and short.

sleeve of balls: Box of three golf balls.

slice: Shot that curves sharply from left to right.

smile: Cut in a ball caused by a mishit.

smother: To hit the ball with a closed clubface, resulting in a horrible, low, hooky shot.

snake: Long putt.

snap hook: Severe hook.

socket: See *shank*.

sole: Bottom of the clubhead.

sole plate: Piece of metal attached to the bottom of a wooden club.

spade-mashie: Old term for a 6-iron.

spike mark: Mark on the green made by a golf shoe.

spin-out: Legs moving too fast in relation to the upper body on the downswing.

spoon: Old term for a 3-wood.

spot putting: Aiming for a point on the green over which the ball must run if it is to go in the hole.

square: Score of a match is even. Or the clubface and stance are aligned perfectly with the target.

square face: Clubface looking directly at the hole at address/impact.

square grooves: USGA banned them from clubfaces.

St. Andrews: Located in Fife, Scotland, the home of golf.

stableford: Method of scoring by using points rather than strokes.

stance: Position of the feet before the swing.

starter: Person running the order of play (who plays when) from the first tee.

starting time: When you tee off at the first tee.

stick: The pin in the hole.

stiff: A shaft with reduced flex. Or very close to the hole.

stimpmeter: Device used to measure the speed of greens.

stroke: Movement of club with the intent to hit the ball.

stroke hole: Hole at which one either gives or receives a shot, according to the handicap of your playing.

stymie: Ball obstructing your route to the hole — now obsolete.

sudden-death: Form of playoff whereby the first player to win a hole wins the match.

superintendent: Person responsible for the upkeep of the course.

surlyn: Material from which most balls are made.

swale: Depression or dip in terrain.

sway: To move excessively to the right on the backswing without turning the body.

sweet spot: Perfect point on the clubface with which to strike the ball.

swing plane: Angle at which the club shaft travels around the body during a swing.

swing weight: Measure of a club's weight to its length.

T

takeaway: Early part of the backswing.

tap-in: Very short putt.

tee: Wooden peg on which the ball is set for the first shot on a hole. Also, the area from which that initial shot is hit.

teeing ground: Area in which you must tee your ball, between the tee markers and neither in front of them nor more than two club lengths behind them.

tee it up: To start play.

tempo: The rhythm of your swing.

temporary green: Used in winter to save the permanent green.

Texas wedge: Putter when used from off the green.

that'll play: A kind reference to mediocre shot.

thin: To hit the ball around its equator — don't expect much height.

three-putt: Undesired number of strokes on a green.

through the green: The whole course except hazards, tees, and greens.

Tiger tee: Slang for the back tee.

tight: Narrow fairway.

tight lie: The ball on bare ground or very short grass.

timing: The pace and sequence of movement in your swing.

titanium: Metal used in lightweight shafts and in golf balls.

top: Ball is struck on or above the equator. See *thin*.

torque: Twisting of the shaft at impact.

tour: Series of tournaments for professionals.

tradesman's entrance: Ball goes in the hole from the rear of the cup.

trajectory: Flight of the ball.

trap: See *bunker*.

triple bogey: Three over par on one hole. Not good.

turn: To make your way to the back nine holes. Or the rotation of the upper body during the backswing and forward swing.

twitch: See *yips*.

U

uncock: See *release*.

underclub: To take at least one club less than needed for distance.

unplayable lie: You can't hit the ball. One stroke penalty is your reward.

up: Ahead in the match. Or the person next to play. Or reaching the hole with a putt.

up and down: To get the ball into the hole in two strokes from somewhere off the green.

upright: To swing with a steep vertical plane.

USGA: United States Golf Association. The ruling body for golf in the United States.

U.S. Open: National men's golf championship of America.

U.S. Women's Open: National women's golf championship of America.

V

Vardon grip: See *overlapping*.

W

waggle: Movement of the clubhead prior to the swing.

water hazard: Body of water that costs you a shot to leave.

wedge: Lofted club (iron) used for pitching.

whiff: See *airball*.

whipping: The string around the shaft/head of a wooden club.

whippy: A shaft more flexible than normal.

windcheater: Low drive.

winter rules: See *preferred lies*.

wood: Material that long clubs used to be made of.

wormburner: Low mishit.

Y

yips: When a golfer misses short putts because of bad nerves, which reduces the afflicted unfortunate to jerky little snatches at the ball, the putterhead seemingly possessing a mind all its own.

Appendix B
Golf Organizations

*T*his appendix lists selected golf associations and golf schools. Some states are more golf oriented than others, but you can find golf schools all over the country — and all over the world. To find the golf school nearest you, check under "Golf Instruction" in the Yellow Pages or search the World Wide Web.

Some of the addresses listed are the headquarters for a chain of schools. Many chain golf schools have seasonal instruction in the northern states; call their headquarters to find out which schools have programs near you.

Associations

American Junior
Golf Association
2415 Steeplechase Ln.
Roswell, GA 30076
770-998-4653
www.ajga.org

American Society of
Golf Course Architects
221 N. LaSalle St., #3500
Chicago, IL 60601
312-372-7090
www.golfdesign.org

Ladies Professional
Golf Association
100 International Golf Dr.
Daytona Beach, FL 32124-1092
904-274-6200
www.lpga.com

Minority Golf Association of America, Inc.
P.O. Box 1081
Westhampton Beach, NY 11978-7081
516-288-8255
www.mgaa.com

National Association of
Left-Handed Golfers
3249 Hazelwood Dr. SW
Atlanta, GA 30311
800-844-6254
www.dca.net/golf

National Golf Foundation
1150 S. U.S. Highway 1, Suite 401
Jupiter, FL 33477
888-NGF-2500
561-744-6006

Professional Clubmakers Society
70 Persimmon Ridge Dr.
Louisville, KY 40245
800-548-6094
www.proclubmakers.org

Professional Golfers'
Association of America
100 Avenue of the Champions,
Box 109601
Palm Beach Gardens, FL 33410-9601
561-624-8400
www.pgaonline.com

Royal Canadian Golf Association
1333 Dorval Dr.
Oakville, Ontario L6J 4Z3
Canada
905-849-9700
www.rcga.org
www.pgaonline.com

United States Golf Association
P.O. Box 708
1 Liberty Corner Rd.
Far Hills, NJ 07931
908-234-2300
www.usga.org

Golf Schools

The Academy of Golf
1000 Avenue of the Champions
Palm Beach Gardens, FL 33418
800-832-6235

Aviara Golf Academy
7447 Batiquitos Dr.
Carlsbad, CA 92009
800-433-7468
760-438-4539
www.kipputt.com

Barton Creek Golf Advantage School
Barton Creek Resort
8212 Barton Club Dr.
Austin, TX 78735
800-336-6157

Ben Sutton Golf School
P.O. Box 9199
Canton, OH 44711
800-225-6923
www.golfschool.com

Bill Skelley School of Golf
1847 East John Sims Pkwy.
Niceville, FL 32578
800-541-7707

Boyne Super 5 Golf Week
Boyne Mountain Resort
600 Highland Dr.
Harbor Springs, MI 49740
800-GO-BOYNE

Dave Pelz Scoring Game School
1310 R.R. 620 South, Suite B-1
Austin, TX 78734
800-824-8899
www.pelzgolf.com

David Leadbetter Golf Academy
9100 Chiltern Dr.
Orlando, FL 32827
407-857-8276
800-424-3542
www.leadbetter.com

Doral Golf Learning Center
4440 NW 87th Ave
Miami, FL 33178
800-72-DORAL

Floating Green Golf School
Coeur d'Alene Resort
115 S. 2nd St.
Coeur d'Alene, ID 83814
800-688-5253
208-765-4000

Galvano International Golf Academy
P.O. Box 626
Lake Delton, WI 53940
800-234-6121
608-254-6361

Golf Advantage Schools
The Homestead
P.O. Box 2000
Rt. 220 North
Hot Springs, VA 24445
800-336-5771
703-839-5500

Golf Digest Schools
5520 Park Ave., Box 395
Trumbull, CT 06611
800-243-6121
203-373-7130
www.golfdigest.com

Hank Haney Golf Ranch
4101 Custer Rd.
McKinney, TX 75070
972-542-8800

John Jacobs' Golf Schools
7825 East Redfield Rd.
Scottsdale, AZ 85260
888-853-3739
www.jacobsgolf.com

Kapalua Golf Club
300 Kapalua Dr.
Lahaina, HI 96761
808-669-8044

The Kingsmill Golf School
The Kingsmill Resort and
Conference Center
1010 Kingsmill Rd.
Williamsburg, VA 23185
800-832-5665
804-253-170

Kostis/McCord Learning Center
8620 E. Thompson Peak Pkwy.
Scottsdale, AZ 85255
602-502-2656
602-502-1600
kmlc@grayhawk.com

Legends Golf Academy
P.O. Box 2038
Myrtle Beach, SC 29578-2038
800-530-1874
www.golfthelegends
.com/academy.htm

Nicklaus/Flick Golf School
11780 U.S. Highway One
North Palm Beach, FL 33408
800-642-5528
www.jnigc.com/flick99/
faults_schedule.html

Phil Ritson-Mel Sole Golf School
P.O. Box 2580
Pawleys Island, SC 29585
800-624-4653
www.ritson-sole.com

Pinehurst Golf Advantage Schools
P.O. Box 4000
Pinehurst, NC 28374
910-295-8128

Seven Springs Golf School
Seven Springs Mountain Resort
Helens Rd.
Champion, PA 15622
800-452-2223, ext. 4

Stratton Golf School
Stratton Mountain Resort
R.R. 1, Box 145
Stratton Mountain, VT 05155
800-843-6867
802-297-2200
www.stratton.com

Sugarloaf Golf Club & School
The Sugarloaf Inn
Route 27, Box 5000
Carrabassett Valley, ME 04947
800-THE-LOAF

U.S. Schools of Golf
718 1/2 Promenade
Richmond, IN 47374
800-354-7415
www.ussog.com

Wintergreen Golf Academy
Wintergreen Resort
P.O. Box 706
Wintergreen, VA 22958
800-325-2200
804-325-2200

Component Companies

Dynacraft Golf Products, Inc.
P.O. Box 4550
71 Maholm St.
Newark, OH 43058
800-423-2968
614-344-1191
www.dynacraftgolf.com

Golfsmith
11000 N. 1H-35
Austin, TX 78753
800-815-3873
512-837-4810
www.golfsmith.com

GolfWorks Division
Ralph Maltby Enterprises
P.O. Box 3008
4820 Jacksontown Rd.
Newark, OH 43023
800-848-8358
740-328-4193
www.golfworks.com

Hornung's Pro Golf Sales, Inc.
815 Morris St.
Fond du Lac, WI 54935
414-922-2640

Kenneth Gording Co.
1209 Distributors Row
Harahan, LA 70123
800-727-2704
504-734-1433

Wittek Golf Supply Co.
3650 N. Avondale Ave.
Chicago, IL 60618
800-869-1800
773-463-2636
www.wittekgolf.com

Index

overclubbing, 376
overlapping, 376
oversized irons, 34

• *p* •

pace/speed of swing, 119
pairings, 376
Palmer, Arnold, 24, 25, 156,
199–200, 268, 300, 349, 361
par
defined, 12, 376
regulation yardages
defining, 12
Park, Willie, 19
partners, 89–90, 286, 377
Pate, Jerry, 359
Paterson, Adam, 17
Patton, Billy Joe, 361–362
Pebble Beach
course, 336
Web site, 321
penal, 377
penalty shots, 277–279
pencils, 43
Penick, Harvey, 78, 80, 287
performance enhancement.
See also physical fitness
integrated, 47
persimmon wood, 377
personality types among
golfers, 126–127, 281–282
PGA (Professional Golfers'
Association), 24, 377, 384
PGA Championship/Tour, 22,
24, 299
PGA of America Web site,
316–317
PGA Tour '99 (golf simulator
game), 327
PGA West Web site, 321
physical fitness program
areas to address, 48
club behind spine, 51–55
customization to the
individual, 50
golf-specificity, 49–50
importance of, 45, 46, 215
prone torso lift, 59–60
recumbent abdominal and
shoulder blade
squeeze, 58
recumbent chest and spine
stretch, 55–58
seated hip rotation, 65–67
seated trunk rotation, 62–64
single leg balance drill, 61–62
standing balance sway, 60

supine hip rotation stretch,
67–68
supine trunk rotation
stretch, 64–65
themes of release,
reeducate, and
rebuild, 49
warmups and stretches,
242–244
women gaining power on
swing, 96
piccolo grip, 377
picking up balls, 89
pigeons, 377
pin placement, 377
Pine Valley course, 336–337
Pinehurst No. 2 course
described, 337–338
Web site, 321
pin-high, 377
Pinon Hills Golf Course,
343–344
pins, 377
pitch and putt, 377
pitch mark repairers, 43, 270
pitch outs (shanks), 229
pitch-and-putt courses, 377
pitch-and-run shots,
173–174, 377
pitching. *See* chipping and
pitching
pitching-niblick, 377
pivoting, 377
Planet Golf Web site, 327
play clubs, 18
Play Golf Now Web site, 325
Player, Gary, 24, 47, 134
playing lessons, 76
playing through, 377
playoffs, 377
plugged lie, 377
plumb-bobbing, 150–152, 377
pooper scooper chip
shots, 369
pop-ups, 377
posture, importance to good
golf, 48, 50
pot bunkers, 377
practice
Gary's preferred routine, 85
importance of, 176, 177, 182,
188, 257
pre-round, 244–246
sample schedule for, 258
practice greens, 377
preferred lies, 377
pressing, 377
Price, Nick, 134, 307
private clubs, 76, 85–87, 377

pro shops, 326–327, 377
Pro-Am tournaments
described, 288–289, 377
survival hints, 289–291
producers of TV golf
coverage, 301
product endorsements by
champions, 20
ProDynamics, 46
Professional Clubmakers
Society, 384
professional golfers. *See also*
individuals by name
defined, 377
disasters, 355–363
Gary's all-time female
favorites, 351–353
Gary's all-time male
favorites, 347–350
as "looper legends," 290
taking their punishment,
308, 361
tips for playing with, in
Pro-Am tournaments,
289–291
what to look for, 306–307
Professional Golfers'
Association. *See* PGA
provisional balls, 377
public courses, 84–85,
341–345, 377
pulls, 230–231, 377
punches, 377
pushes, 230, 378
putters. *See also* clubs
center-shafted, 35, 146,
147, 369
described, 378
long, 35, 140–141, 158
mallets, 375
putting cleeks, 18, 369
recommended to carry, 36
technology's future, 40
as Texas wedges, 381
types of, 35, 146–147
which to use, 146–147
putting. *See also* optics in
putting; short game
advantages over lofted
shots, 332
aiming and optics, 158–168
aiming for 14-18 inches past
cup, 147
"being the ball," 156
come-backers, 369
correctives for poor aim,
227–228
gimme, 285, 372
going to school, 372
good-good, 372

KOSTIS
McCORD
L E A R N I N G   C E N T E R

Let the Kostis/McCord Learning Center get your game back on solid ground. With a unique system designed by renowned PGA professionals and CBS golf commentators Peter Kostis and Gary McCord, our skilled instructors will improve your game and, more importantly, make learning fun. No matter what your needs, the Kostis/McCord Learning Center has a program just for you.

• 3-DAY GOLF SCHOOL •

The 3-Day Golf School is designed for players of all skill levels and combines on-course playing lessons (cart and green fee included) and video analysis with traditional lesson-tee instruction.

• HALF-DAY WORKSHOP •

If your game just needs a little touching up, a Half-Day Workshop at the Kostis/McCord Learning Center is for you.

• ONE-DAY SCHOOL •

Spend an entire day with the Kostis/McCord Learning Center and receive three hours of instruction, lunch, and a 9-hole playing lesson.

• PRIVATE INSTRUCTION •

We'll create a custom program for you and monitor your progress every step of the way.
Call toll free for details! (877) 259-2505 or contact us online at www.KostisMcCordLearning.com.

Mail-in Coupon

10% off 3-Day School for readers of Golf For Dummies, 2nd Edition!!!

NAME: _____

ADDRESS: _____

CITY, STATE, ZIP: _____

HOME PHONE: _____

WORK PHONE: _____

Offer expires December 31, 2001

MAIL TO:
THE KOSTIS/MCCORD LEARNING CENTER
GRAYHAWK GOLF CLUB
8620 E. THOMPSON PEAK PARKWAY
SCOTTSDALE, AZ 85255

Stay on Top of Your Game

Check out Taylormadegolf.com where you will find:

- Tour news and updates from Gary McCord
- Question & Answer sessions with Taylor Made Golf Pros
- Online contests and giveaways for free golf merchandise
- Special sites for kids and women
- The latest in golf products and technology
- Taylor Made Golf Demo Days schedule

Playing games is really fun... The Dummies Way™!

Pressman®
©1998 Pressman Toy Corporation, New York, NY 10010

Crosswords For Dummies™ Game

You don't have to know how to spell to have a great time. Place a word strip on the board so that it overlaps another word or creates a new one. Special squares add to the fun. The first player to use up all their word strips wins!
For 2 to 4 players.

Trivia For Dummies™ Game

You're guaranteed to have an answer every time! Each player gets 10 cards that contain the answer to every question. Act quickly and be the first player to throw down the correct answer and move closer to the finish line!
For 3 or 4 players.

Charades For Dummies™ Game

Act out one-word charades: when other players guess them, they move ahead. The special cards keep the game full of surprises. The first player around the board wins.
For 3 or 4 players.

----For Dummies and The Dummies Way are trademarks of IDG Books Worldwide, Inc.

BUY ANY ...For Dummies™ GAME AND RECEIVE $3 REBATE

Not responsible for late, lost, undelivered or illegible requests. Reproduction, purchase, sale or trade of this certificate, proof of purchase or cash register receipt is prohibited. Requests from groups, clubs or organizations will not be honored or acknowledged. Sponsor reserves right to verify identification. Rebates will not be mailed to P.O. boxes; only street or rural route addresses are acceptable. Fraudulent submission could result in federal prosecution under mail fraud statutes. Materials submitted become property of sponsor and will not be returned. Offer good only in the continental U.S., Alaska and Hawaii. Void where prohibited.

To receive your $3 rebate check by mail you must buy any "... For Dummies Game" between June 1, 1998 and June 30, 1999. **Mail this form with the UPC code from the purchased game and the original store cash register receipt to:**
Dummies Game Rebate, P.O. Box 1013, Grand Rapids, MN. 55745-1013.

Valid only in the US. This offer may not be combined with any other coupon or offer, and may be withdrawn without notice. Requests must be postmarked by 7/15/99. Allow 4 to 6 weeks to process your request. *Please print.*

Name: _____ Age: _____ Sex: M / F

Address: _____

City: _____ State: _____ Zip: _____

Was game received as a gift?   Yes _____   No _____

Who will play with the game? (check one)

Friends _____   Parent _____   All Family/Children _____   Other _____

IDG BOOKS WORLDWIDE
BOOK REGISTRATION

We want to hear from you!

Register This Book and Win!

Visit **http://my2cents.dummies.com** to register this book and tell us how you liked it!

✔ Get entered in our monthly prize giveaway.

✔ Give us feedback about this book — tell us what you like best, what you like least, or maybe what you'd like to ask the author and us to change!

✔ Let us know any other *...For Dummies*® topics that interest you.

Your feedback helps us determine what books to publish, tells us what coverage to add as we revise our books, and lets us know whether we're meeting your needs as a *...For Dummies* reader. You're our most valuable resource, and what you have to say is important to us!

Not on the Web yet? It's easy to get started with *Dummies 101*®: *The Internet For Windows*® *98* or *The Internet For Dummies*®, 5th Edition, at local retailers everywhere.

Or let us know what you think by sending us a letter at the following address:

...For Dummies Book Registration
Dummies Press
7260 Shadeland Station, Suite 100
Indianapolis, IN 46256-3917
Fax 317-596-5498

™

BESTSELLING
BOOK SERIES